Intellectual Disability

For Jamie

Intellectual Disability

Ethics, Dehumanization, and a New Moral Community

Heather E. Keith
Green Mountain College

and

Kenneth D. Keith
University of San Diego

WILEY-BLACKWELL
A John Wiley & Sons, Inc., Publication

This edition first published 2013

Wiley-Blackwell is an imprint of John Wiley & Sons, formed by the merger of Wiley's global Scientific, Technical and Medical business with Blackwell Publishing.

Registered Office
John Wiley & Sons Ltd, The Atrium, Southern Gate, Chichester, West Sussex, PO19 8SQ, UK

Editorial Offices
350 Main Street, Malden, MA 02148-5020, USA
9600 Garsington Road, Oxford, OX4 2DQ, UK
The Atrium, Southern Gate, Chichester, West Sussex, PO19 8SQ, UK

For details of our global editorial offices, for customer services, and for information about how to apply for permission to reuse the copyright material in this book please see our website at www.wiley.com/wiley-blackwell.

Library of Congress Cataloging-in-Publication Data applied for

Hardback ISBN: 978-0-470-67432-1

A catalogue record for this book is available from the British Library.

Cover design by Simon Levy Associates.

Set in 10.5/13pt Minion by Aptara Inc., New Delhi, India
Printed and bound in Singapore by Markono Print Media Pte Ltd

1 2013

Contents

Acknowledgements

For introducing me to the humane possibilities of philosophy, I would like to thank Thomas Alexander, Larry Hickman, Eugenie Gatens-Robinson, Charlene Haddock Seigfried, the late Michael Eldridge, Mark Johnson, and other members of the Society for the Advancement of American Philosophy. Thanks to Todd Lekan and Micah Hester for conversations, responses, and enlightening work about philosophy and disability, and to Mag. Cathrin Dorner, of the Schloss Hartheim memorial and education center in Alkoven, Austria, for helping me to understand the complex roots of dehumanization. The philosophy department at Dartmouth College was gracious in hosting me as a visiting scholar during the early stages of this research. I am a better teacher and researcher thanks to my students and colleagues at Green Mountain College, and I especially appreciate the help of library staff members and my enthusiastic undergraduate research assistant, Pragatee Dhakal.

I also thank Ken Keith for introducing me, inside and outside of a classroom, to the diverse nature of humanity and the importance of respect and care for all people, and for continuing to be an important influence on my professional life. And I thank Connie Keith for instilling a desire to be my best self. Steven Fesmire will always have my gratitude for his seemingly undying interest in my intellectual life (as well as our family life), his imaginative work in philosophy, and his patience.

H.E.K.
Poultney, VT

First and foremost, my life has been enriched, since the time I was a child, by the friendship and good company of congenial people, too numerous to name, with intellectual disability. I will, however, single out Nancy Ward, whose unabashed honesty deserves unabashed admiration. I will never forget the courage and integrity of the late Shirley Dean, Sara Kramer, and Mark Rapley, who gave their lives to the welfare of people with intellectual disability. Bob Schalock has been a valued friend, collaborator, and sounding board for more than four decades, and for that I will always be grateful. Larry Hinman provided encouragement, good ideas, and congenial conversation, all helping to shape our perspective. I also owe thanks to David Braddock and the Coleman Institute for Cognitive Disabilities at the University of Colorado for access to a wealth of archival material, and to the University of San Diego for support of research leading to this project. Our editor, Matt Bennett, encouraged this project, and we thank him for that. And, as always, Connie Keith continues to make my work and my life better in ways she will never know.

K.D.K.
Omaha, NE

Prologue
Why Study Disability?

Any student of history, culture, or science might wonder whether it is anachronistic to study something that may seem to be a shrinking concern. With medical technology, industrialization, state of the art tools for genetic testing, and wider availability of education, we might forecast that disability is, or soon will be, a thing of the past. However, it is these very social goods that require us to continue to investigate what it means to be disabled in our time. For example, one benefit of modern medicine is a longer lifespan, but with an increasingly elderly population come physical and intellectual impairments such as dementia (Halpern, 2008). Susan Wendell (2008) noted that "unless we die young, we are all disabled eventually" (p. 828).

Some educational tools, such as literacy and technology, are increasingly a cause of lower social functioning for individuals who cannot read or manage complicated tasks. In medieval times, an inability to read was not disabling, nor was surfing the Web an essential skill 50 years ago. Today, however, reading and technology use are essential to most kinds of employment and many facets of citizenship, creating disabilities where none may have existed before. New methods of genetic testing during pregnancy beg many ethical questions about what choices parents have regarding the potential for raising children with intellectual challenges. And physical impairment due to wars, such as those in Afghanistan and Iraq, also heightens the importance of studying the effects of disability on quality of life and functioning in society. Though we will primarily discuss intellectual disability in this book, our theoretical frameworks will be interdisciplinary and will also incorporate some work from the broader and appropriately growing field of disability studies. Our aim will be twofold: to present a pluralist, social constructivist view of intellectual disability and its history; and to develop a contextual, pragmatist moral response to complex ethical questions surrounding disability that are increasingly relevant to us all.

Why an Interdisciplinary Approach?

Many authors have written books on intellectual disability. From clinical textbooks to education manuals to historical analyses, there is a wide range of research on disability from both individual and social perspectives. However, most of this work represents fairly specialized approaches within the disciplines of psychology, psychiatry, sociology, or education. Philosophers (appropriately) have very recently begun to consider intellectual disability within fields such as applied ethics and political theory.

Previous work has provided valuable empirical data and theoretical and philosophical perspectives that have illuminated many of the important issues affecting the lives of people with intellectual disability. An interdisciplinary approach, we believe, can extend our understanding and contribute in important ways to scientific and philosophic study and to the development of humane practice and policy. Working together and using research from a variety of disciplines, we suggest that the partnership of psychology and philosophy (which are, of course, only recently distinct fields) provides an interesting and useful approach that values both scientific and ethical analysis. Though we appreciate that specialization is essential to the deep study of any field, issue, or practice, we also believe that bringing specialized work back to a more human level is needed to create positive change in the world. In the introduction to his final work, *The Conquest of Mental Retardation*, the late social theorist Burton Blatt (1987) argued that specialization without a wider context causes isolation, allowing the public, as well as specialists, to believe that "only a specialist can understand anything about a mentally retarded person" (p. 8), which may lead others in society to assume they have nothing to do with disability. Specialization, then, "causes far greater and more widespread problems than the very 'difference' that sets the isolation mechanisms in motion" (p. 8). Blatt believed that making the study of intellectual disability a more natural part of the continuum of human relationships was needed, in addition to more skilled clinical services, in order to improve quality of life. We hope that this volume contributes to a social consciousness and theoretical foundation that integrates rather than isolates.

Three concepts in particular impel us toward an interdisciplinary approach with foundations in psychology and philosophy (both of which are integrally tied to education). First, an approach from multiple disciplines prevents reductionism. Reductionistic approaches are characterized by relying on only one perspective to explain the vast diversity of human experience. For example, some theorists use Freud's work to reduce all, or most, human motivation and behavior to a fairly specific description of the mind. Likewise, some geneticists exclude the influences of cultural experience when claiming that human behavior can be reduced to genetic makeup. In studying ethics, some philosophers limit themselves to one theorist or one theoretical approach, such as deontology (the idea that morality is a matter of intention) or utilitarianism (the idea that morality is a matter of consequences) to address a vast universe of moral questions. Although these varied approaches may be useful to understanding particular aspects of psychology, morality, or education, and you will see some of them explored in depth in this volume, we hope with our approach to create a pluralistic, nonreductionistic understanding of intellectual disability. Studying disability from multiple perspectives makes it less likely that we will have just one or a very few theoretical tools with which to respond to the complexity of human experience.

This perspective has important consequences for the field of disability studies. For example, many theorists and practitioners debate the very concept of "disability" as either something internal to the individual ("impairment") or external and social, such as a person being made "disabled" by lack of accessibility to buildings or to education. Activists have long argued that a strictly "medical" model of disability (focused on genetics and biology) ignores social structures as they contribute to the inability of individuals to thrive (e.g., Silvers, Waserman, & Mahowald, 1998). On the other hand, Shakespeare and Watson (2001) criticized some aspects of the "social" model of disability, prevalent in British activist movements, which emphasizes social structures that create disability (as opposed to physical impairment as disabling) in individuals, a model which they believe leaves out our embodied nature. Although we will often use a social constructivist approach in our theoretical work here, reducing disability almost entirely to society opens otherwise interesting ideas to a claim of *reductio ad absurdum* (argument from the absurd), a fallacy which might assume that human embodiment makes little difference to one's ability to function in the world. This claim is obviously problematic. One's genetic structure, biology, and physical nature all combine with one's family, culture, and society to determine one's experience of the world. We hope to explore more pluralistic approaches that avoid a simple choice between the dueling medical and social models, allow for social criticism while also considering the possible contributions of medicine, biology, and education, and appropriately consider the vast and varied influences on our experience of the world.

Second, an interdisciplinary approach between philosophy and psychology ensures a foundation in empirical data. Although theories, stories, and personal perspectives are essential to the study of any aspect of human experience (e.g., Coles, 1989), and will be important in an account of the social construction of disability, the kind of story that we can tell with a foundation in research and data will be more useful in its relevance and persuasiveness. Without empirical evidence, we cannot be sure that even our best theories adequately touch human life. This is especially true in the study of intellectual disability. While our approach will explore theoretical ideas such as social construction and ethics, it will be grounded also in the empirical study of individual ability and quality of life, social policy, history, and culture.

Finally, we suggest that theories, stories, and personal perspectives are essential partners to even the most specialized research. Born out of the desire to know more about our world, philosophy is often characterized by the method of one of its first Western proponents. The Socratic method of asking questions and cultivating virtues of inquiry is the starting place of the most rigorous scientific study. Blatt (1987) noted the importance of social theory to science, which he says "follows rather than leads to the dominant beliefs of an age" (p. 10); and "the data of the clinical field are inextricably bound to the values and beliefs of society as a whole" (p. 7). No course of study, including science, is done in a vacuum. Knowing this in advance, and allowing for the creative interaction of philosophy, history, and culture, will make the empirical study of humanity, as Blatt suggested, a more reasonable and responsible endeavor. Otherwise, we might commit what psychologist and philosopher William James (1950/1890) called the "psychologist's fallacy," which occurs when we falsely impose our preconceived concepts onto human experience, rather than using critical thinking in our research to explore new possibilities and practices in trying to understand the experiences of others. We will see unfortunate examples of this fallacy in our exploration of the history of intelligence testing. On the other hand, the scientific method, in starting with hypotheses and then trying to falsify them, *is* the Socratic method.

Socrates, as recorded by Plato (1981/c. 399 BCE), in his philosophical pursuit of wisdom, also knew that the admission of *not* knowing was as important to research as claims of knowledge. About the politicians of his time, who eschewed both theoretical and empirical foundations to their claims of wisdom (they were more interested in prestige and power), he said that his wisdom was greater because he knew that he did not know everything. Intellectual humility is an essential part of any study of human behavior, nature, and experience. We know that we do not know, but we also know that we are willing to learn diverse and empirically and theoretically rich ideas. Eva Kittay (2010), in her writing on cognitive disability, has argued that we need more "epistemic modesty," because arrogance about what we think we know impedes our ability to develop responsible theories and practices.

The work of American philosopher, psychologist, and champion of progressive education John Dewey is a prime example of a partnership among disciplines aspiring to solve the problems of his time with both empirical and theoretical study. In the spirit of Dewey (1985/1917), we believe that education, as a social process, emerges out of our best-informed beliefs about human nature and growth. As such, themes in education regarding intellectual disability are integrated throughout the chapters, and not consigned to just one chapter or section.

About philosophy, Dewey (1985/1917) wrote that it "recovers itself when it ceases to be a device for dealing with the problems of philosophers and becomes a method, cultivated by philosophers, for dealing with the problems of men" (p. 46). We hope that what we are embarking on here becomes useful for dealing with the problems of humanity, as well as pointing the way toward progressive practices and policies that will make for a brighter future, not only for people with intellectual disability, but for a society that is also impaired as a result of its own construction of disability.

Models of Disability Studies

The 1990 Americans with Disabilities Act is important not only for its groundbreaking legal protection for individuals in their access to social goods such as political involvement, education, medicine, and the logistics of ordinary life. It also underscores, at least in our best practices, that disability is not merely a matter of individual health or impairment; rather, one's ability to function well in society and have a good quality of life is also a matter of concern for government and other institutions—of society itself. This is something of a change from earlier views of disability based on traits native to the individual. In the case of intellectual disability, the idea that intelligence was a gift from genetics, unchangeable, and therefore easily measured by intelligence testing, allowed doctors, caretakers, and families to assume that patients' impairments could or could not be fixed, an idea which we will explore in depth in Chapter Two. This medical model was contested, especially in the UK, in the 1970s and 1980s by the "social" model of disability, whose proponents assert that the root of disability is not in individuals, but in society itself. In a sense, it is society that disables people through inaccessibility, exclusion in education, and other forms of oppression based on perceived difference. As Blatt (1987) suggested, this model concludes that it is society that is disabled.

Our aim here is influenced by the social model, though we take something of a modified social constructivist view. We fully accept that disability is in part created by social norms and practices, but we also allow that any one model can be reductionistic and limiting. Though the social constructivist model that influences much of our approach obviously involves the study of culture, history, and institutions, we understand that "the social" is itself constructed of individuals in relationships and that sometimes it makes sense to discuss disability (or impairment) on a more individual level. On the other hand, while we concur that individual abilities or impairments are important factors in determining how to help people function more effectively, we will argue that sometimes disabilities are made worse, or even caused, by society's inability to adjust to the complexity of human existence and to create environments where diverse people can thrive. Our attempt to balance the individual and the social will be integral to our development, throughout the volume, of a view of moral community that is flexible, relational, and evolving in accord with our best theories and practices.

Our interdisciplinary, relational approach is philosophically pragmatic, in the fashion of Dewey. While we have a critical view of much historical and some contemporary work in psychology and philosophy, we will also mine this work for rich wisdom about the humane treatment of others and intellectual humility in our own approach. Dewey's (1988/1922) method was to develop a pluralistic moral theory, eschewing reduction to just one set of principles or values (many of which exclude people with intellectual disability, as we will discuss in Chapter Four), while using the best social science research of his time toward democratic politics and education. As we will see in several recent movements in ethics, Dewey believed that the complexity of human nature required that we explore how we ought to behave based on how we do behave. Thus, our best moral theory should emerge from our best practices. Here, we aim to merge good research in psychology with great moral theories, applying both to issues of practice and policy affecting people with intellectual disability and our social environment.

Thus, in this volume, you will find language that highlights a variety of disciplinary, theoretical, and practical approaches. We will discuss disability and impairment, as well as social institutions and individual health and well-being. We will also use a variety of terms for intellectual disability, reflecting and depending on historical eras and conceptions of individuals. Thus, the appearance of such labels as *people with disabilities*, *mentally retarded*, *mental deficiency*, *feeble-minded*, *idiot*, *imbecile*, and *moron* reflects and conveys the language and understanding of the culture and the authors of various times and places. Though there is some contemporary debate (Shakespeare, 2010) about language regarding individuals ("people with disabilities") versus some proponents of the social model's use of "disabled people," we tend to be in accord with the "people first" ideals of recent social movements and their focus on what all humans have in common, first, rather than what divides us. Therefore, we will frequently use "people with disabilities" or "individuals with disabilities," but also acknowledge that at times it is important to emphasize the "disabled" characteristic of individuals, especially in unpacking social causes of disability. Our goal is thus to investigate the threshold of individual and society, through psychology, moral theory, and educational philosophy, with the aim of creating a better understanding of how our historical and contemporary institutions and thinking have shaped our views of disability, and how those views can be enhanced to be more humane and constructive.

The Roots of Dehumanization

The first four chapters of the book illustrate the nature and scope of dehumanization and its origins in Western culture. We explore how societies have historically viewed intellectual disability, labels, and their effects, and more contemporary understanding of the construct of disability. We examine the ways the culture has viewed the social and treatment needs of individuals with intellectual disability, and the sometimes shameful role of institutions as reflections of social values. Philosophy has also played its role in dehumanization, sometimes, for example, defining as subhuman those whose ability to use language or reason does not meet the threshold philosophers have used to define what it means to be human. And of course traditional conceptions of intelligence and the intelligence testing movement in psychology have played a significant role in the marginalization of people with disabilities and, for a time, relegating them to the dark shadows of eugenics.

Out of the Darkness

The middle section of the volume discusses philosophical and cultural approaches to selfhood with the aim of developing a conception of the moral person that is helpful to ethical theories which embrace diversity and serve more than just a population graced with traditional, testable intelligence. We put forth more expansive and pluralistic moral and political theories from perspectives such as pragmatist ethics, and explore the possibility that such theories are strengthened by, and are fluid enough to grow with, our understanding of an increasingly intellectually diverse population. With these inclusive approaches in mind, we will also explore the intersection of disability with theories of race, gender, popular culture, and cross-cultural experience and philosophy.

Disability Ethics for a New Age

Finally, we will apply our theoretical work to issues such as multidimensional quality of life, genetic testing, our increasingly technological society, and new images of intellectual disability. In the spirit of scholars like Blatt and Dewey, our great theories and best research agendas are worthwhile only if they touch real lives and change society for the better. It is our hope that a new age will bring not only greater complications from technology, genetics, and social norms, but also greater resources in our struggle to rehumanize us all.

Part I

The Roots of Dehumanization

1

Intellectual Disability
History and Evolution of Definitions

Our friend Clyde was a man with, according to his case records, moderate mental retardation. Although he worked in a sheltered employment center, Clyde slipped away from work to smoke cigarettes as frequently as possible, despite his doctor's warnings about their danger to his health. In his free time Clyde liked to visit with relatives who lived nearby, and to ride horses. One of his greatest pleasures was to eat dinner and drink coffee at a truck stop café, where he could imagine himself traveling the open road in a cross-country truck. Clyde was one of those people who can spot an old friend in the crowd nearly anywhere they go; and if he didn't see an old friend, it didn't take Clyde long to make a new one. He always lived near the boundaries of socially acceptable behavior, often taxing the ingenuity and the patience of his family, friends, and caretakers. Yet, despite life's challenges, including myriad health problems and frequent conflict with program staff, friends, neighbors, and others, Clyde never thought of himself as a person with mental retardation. He was just a man trying to get along, to live as well as he could in the circumstances of his own life.

We talk today about people with *intellectual disability*, at least in part as a departure from former labels that individuals and their advocates came to see as demeaning or dehumanizing (Parmenter, 2011). This reflects a fairly recent change; for example, until 2006 the American Association on Developmental and Intellectual Disabilities (AAIDD) was known as the American Association on Mental Retardation (AAMR), and before that the American Association on Mental Deficiency. That same organization came into existence in 1876 as the Association of Medical Officers of

Intellectual Disability: Ethics, Dehumanization, and a New Moral Community, First Edition.
Heather E. Keith and Kenneth D. Keith.

American Institutions for Idiotic and Feeble-minded Persons. As Berkson (2006) observed, the terminology describing what we now call developmental disabilities or intellectual disabilities has typically changed once or twice in each generation. Times change, and so does language—in ways that can be critical to people who are categorized and labeled. So, we might ask, what does it mean to talk about people with intellectual disability, how have we arrived at the words we use to describe them, and how do these words affect our thinking?

Thinking in Categories

The penchant for organizing things (including people) into groups is a natural, universal human tendency. Even when the differences between and among people or objects are subtle or gradual, we tend to draw lines and place them into groups (Macmillan, 1987). Although some categories (e.g., colors, emotional expressions, or geometric shapes) may be universal, the ways people group many other things vary, depending on context or culture. Categories may include *objects* that possess common characteristics or attributes—the kind of groups that we call concepts; or categories may be used to group *people*, based on perceived common characteristics—the kind of groups that we call stereotypes. Thus the objects constituting a concept like "chair" have features such as: furniture; has a seat, legs and a back; and useful for people to sit upon (e.g., Matsumoto & Juang, 2008). These characteristics of chairs are the common attributes that define the concept. Similarly, we may group people and form stereotypes according to our perceptions of their salient attributes (e.g., race, sex, abilities, religion, intelligence, nationality).

Categorization results in a tendency to consider each member of the category as equivalent to other members, and different from nonmembers (Rosch, 1978); and stereotypes, according to Allport (1954), are characterized by oversimplified generalizations about the people who belong to the category and may play a role in justification and rationalization of behavior directed toward people who are members of the stereotyped group. Further, categories may be based on taxonomic classification (defined by similar attributes of members of the class) or thematic classification (defined by relations among class members; Markman & Hutchinson, 1984). The latter distinction is key to understanding the foundations of categorization in differing cultural contexts, which, as we will see, is a critical issue for people with intellectual disability.

People with different cultural experience have different grouping styles and they pay attention to different things in their perceptions of groups (Ji, Nisbett, & Zhang, 2004). In Western cultures (such as the US), individuals are likely to group according to perceived specific attributes of group members (taxonomic classification), whereas people of Eastern cultures may be more likely to group members of a class according to their relationships to one another (thematic classification). Chiu (1972), for example, in a study of American and Chinese children, found that the Americans grouped according to such common characteristics as size, while the Chinese grouped according to relationships, such as parent and child. Easterners (e.g., Asians) are also more inclined than people of Western cultures to use external referents and context in their perceptions (Choi, Dalai, Kim-Prieto, & Park, 2003; Chua, Boland, & Nisbett, 2005; Miyamoto, Nisbett, & Masuda, 2006). The latter tendency (external vs. internal referents) also plays a role in how people perceive others in their environmental context, how they judge the behavior of others, and how they think of themselves.

Perceiving People in Context

Do we think of people with intellectual disability in terms of a single defining feature (e.g., intelligence or physical aspects) or do we think of them as they exist as people in relation to family, community, or other aspects of their environmental context? Research on human perception may shed some light on this question. For example, Norenzayan, Smith, Kim, and Nisbett (2002) studied the perceptual patterns of European Americans, Asian Americans, Koreans, and Chinese people whom they asked to identify common characteristics among groups of 20 visual stimuli. European Americans were more likely to make unidimensional judgments (similarity based on a single common characteristic) than were the Asian Americans and East Asians, who made more complex judgments based on patterns of similarity. Kitayama, Duffy, Kawamura, and Larsen (2003) used a different test (a line-drawing task) to evaluate the tendencies of American and Japanese students to attend to specific or whole aspects of a stimulus, and drew a similar conclusion: Americans more often made judgments based on absolute characteristics of the stimulus, and Japanese students were more likely to focus on the relational characteristics of the task.

These findings are interesting, but do they apply to people? Masuda, Gonzalez, Kwan, and Nisbett (2008) provided at least a partial answer in a study involving Caucasian American, African American, Chinese, Japanese,

Taiwanese, and Korean participants. The researchers provided instructions in use of the focus and zoom controls on a digital camera, and asked people to take portrait photographs of a model. The Americans made portraits that were more object-oriented and individual-focused, with significantly larger depictions of the face of the model; on the other hand, the Asians' portraits were more context-inclusive, showing the person in relation to the larger contextual background. In previous research Masuda and Nisbett (2001) compared Japanese and American perception and memory using video clips of a complex scene involving objects and background. The Japanese participants were much more likely to be influenced by the background, and they were able to provide much more contextual information than were the Americans. Taken together, these studies suggest that perceptual judgments are intimately related to both immediate context and cultural backdrop—facts that may constitute an important foundation for our judgments of people.

These studies, consistent with many others, suggest that the US, like numerous other Western countries, is a low-context culture, and others, including East Asian and some South American cultures, are high-context. In high-context cultures people tend to be more deeply involved with each other (Hall, 1976), with strong bonds among family members, community, friends, and the general society (Kim, Pan, & Park, 1998). In a low-context culture, people are more highly individualized, relatively less involved with others, and more likely to withdraw or move away from others when things are not going well (Kim et al., 1998). In other words, in the low-context setting the focus is on the individual; in the high-context culture, the focus is on connection to the group. This individual-oriented vs. other-oriented distinction is also apparent in views of the self. People of Western, individualistic cultures view the person as an independent, separate entity; in non-Western collectivistic cultures the self is seen as inseparable from, and interdependent with, important others—family, friends, co-workers (Markus & Kitayama, 1991). We will see this distinction, and its consequences for moral relationships, again in later chapters.

Why People Act as They Do

Perceptions of people and their characteristics are related to the attributions individuals make for the behavior of others. If we think in high-context, interdependent ways, we are likely to emphasize the relation of people to their environment, and the power of the situation, to account for their behavior. On the other hand, if we think in a low-context, independent way, we will be more prone to see the behavior of others as a product of their individual dispositional characteristics—the kinds of characteristics that lend themselves to formation of stereotypes.

The tendency to disproportionately attribute others' behaviors to characteristics of the person (dispositional attributions), even in the face of obvious situational constraints, is pervasive in Western cultures and is known as the fundamental attribution error (also called the correspondence bias; Jones & Harris, 1967; Ross, 1977). However, people of interdependent Eastern cultures are less likely to make the fundamental attribution error, and are instead more inclined to use situational (contextual) attributions to account for the behavior of others (Gilbert & Malone, 1995; Miller, 1984). For example, Americans may describe people whom they know as "irresponsible" or "proud," while Hindus are more likely to use situational explanations such as social roles or duties (Miller, 1984).

Some evidence suggests that caregivers are more likely to make dispositional attributions for challenging behavior of people with intellectual disability if the disability is mild (as opposed to severe; Tynan & Allen, 2002), and caregivers who perceive individuals to be in control of their own challenging behavior may experience negative emotions toward those individuals (Wanless & Jahoda, 2002). Weisz (1981) found that university students were more likely to attribute failure or low expectancy for success to "insufficient ability" in children identified as "mentally retarded" than in an unlabeled child. And interestingly, Palmer (1979) reported that classroom teachers' attributions for the *success* of "normal achieving," "educationally handicapped," and "educable mentally retarded" children were not affected by background information about the students; however, the teachers' attributions for student *failure* did show the influence of background information. Information about the students, Palmer suggested, may have led teachers to expect that handicapped and intellectually disabled students would experience academic difficulties.

It should not be surprising therefore, that in American culture individuals may form stereotyped views of groups of people based on perception of salient characteristics of the person, independent of relationships or context. In nineteenth-century America, for example, a common stereotype of the Irish characterized them as obese, violent, and wasteful (Heine, 2012). People with intellectual disability have similarly experienced stereotyping, and the list of labels they have worn is lengthy (e.g., childlike, defective, incompetent, dumb, immature; Beirne-Smith, Patton, & Ittenbach, 1994). When people are labeled, others of course view them differently (Farina, 1982), and the effects of the labels can be powerfully stigmatizing (e.g., Page, 1977), taking on a life of their own (Rosenhan, 1973). What are the labels, popular and professional, that have described individuals with intellectual disability? We recognize, of course, that "individuals with intellectual disability" is also a label that we are choosing to use in this discussion.

Labeling Individuals with Disability

The history of the field of intellectual disability has long included reports of the ancient Greeks' practice of "allowing the mentally deficient to perish, or, as was done in Sparta, of directly exposing them to death—peril" (Barr, 1904, p. 24). However, although the Greeks may have chosen not to rear some infants with physical anomalies (and the evidence for this practice is not as clear as some may presume; Edwards, 1996), we cannot assume that people of the early Greek era would have recognized intellectual disability in the modern sense, especially in infancy (Goodey, 2011). Nevertheless, such scholars as Aristotle and Hippocrates recognized such conditions as epilepsy, and probably mental deficiency (e.g., Whitney, 1949). The vocabulary used by the Greeks to describe the types of infants exposed to death was vague and imprecise (Edwards, 1996), and they thus left no clear labels for intellectual disability. In the Roman era, Latin had several words that have been translated as "mental disability" or "cognitive disability," and the Roman physician Galen apparently associated what would later be known as "idiocy" with big ears (Evans, 1945). By the end of the second century CE the Mishnah (a gathering of Jewish oral law) used the Hebrew word *shoteh* to mean "imbecile," although it has also been translated as "mentally defective" or "mentally deficient" (Berkson, 2006). The practice of labeling people with intellectual disability had been established.

The construct of intellectual disability diverged from the generic idea of mental illness sometime prior to the thirteenth century (Neugebauer, 1996; Stainton, 2001a), although centuries later both "idiots" and "lunatics" still lived in the same asylums (Race, 2002). Thirteenth-century British legal doctrine distinguished between "idiots" and "lunatics" (the former unable to inherit property due to supposed mental deficiency; Clarke, 1975; Rushton, 1988). By the seventeenth century, case reports in Wales sometimes referred to those considered mentally deficient with such labels as "idiot," "fool," "not *compos mentis*" [not of sound mind], and "innocent" (Rushton, 1988, p. 37). Itard (1962/1801), in his account of the storied "wild boy" of Aveyron, discovered at the end of the eighteenth century, referred to the child as a "savage."

"Idiocy" was recognized in both the law and the religion of Puritan colonial New England (Wickham, 2001), and the colonists also used other terms—"incapashous, simplish, and natural fool" (p. 148)—to refer to idiocy. The term "idiot" was well entrenched from the middle (Howe, 1851) to the end of the nineteenth century (e.g., Bateman, 1897). "Cretin," sometimes used synonymously with "idiot," probably dates from the eighteenth century, and was also a French word for Christian—perhaps as a reminder that those with disabilities are nevertheless Christian or human. The British Parliament, in the Mental Deficiency Act of 1913, wrote the term "idiots," along with "imbeciles," "feebleminded persons," and "moral defectives," into law (Race, 2002). At about the same time Tredgold (1914) proposed use of the term "amentia" (*a*, without; *mens*, mind; p. 1) to denote those whose minds had never attained normal development, and American psychologist Henry H. Goddard (1912, 1927) added "moron" to the litany of words used to describe those considered "dull." The term "retarded" seems to have first occurred in the work of Ayres (1909), who used it to denote children who failed to progress in school, and who simply meant it to refer to intellectual slowness.

Sometimes labels have been idiosyncratic, developed by administrators or professionals to suit their own unique circumstances or time. Blatt and Kaplan (1966), for example, reported a curious misunderstanding that occurred when they could not comprehend an assistant superintendent's discussion of "materials" and "items." Eventually they realized that, in this particular facility, people with disabilities were "materials" and staff members were "items." These state administrators used labels to dehumanize not only patients, but paid professionals as well. What, we might ask, are the effects of these labels, for those who are labeled and for those who apply the labels?

Although the term "mental retardation" was in common use in the US for a half century or more (Wolfensberger, 2002), in the early twenty-first century the AAIDD changed the term to "intellectual disability" (Schalock et al., 2007). According to Schalock et al., the construct of disability involves limitations of individual functioning that are a disadvantage to the person and that occur in a social context, and intellectual disability exists within the broader notion of disability. These authors describe an evolution of understanding of disability that recognizes the social construction of disorders, the blurred distinction between social and biological causes of disability, and the multidimensional nature of human functioning. This approach reflects a changing perception of disability from a person-centered trait ("deficit") to a social-ecological concept reflecting the interaction between person and environment, the role of individualized supports to enhance individual adjustment to environment, and efforts to develop "disability identity" based on such attributes as well-being, pride, and self-worth (Schalock et al., 2007). Current use of the term intellectual disability denotes a changing recognition of the locus of the disability; earlier terms (e.g., mental retardation, mental deficiency) saw the disability as a defect lying within the individual, whereas the current conception suggests that intellectual disability is a state of functioning reflected in the relation between individual and context (Wehmeyer et al., 2008). This recent development reflects a potentially significant departure from labeling as it has existed for most of the history of concern with intellectual disability, and has been incorporated into the most recent procedures for definition and classification (Schalock et al., 2010).

Effects of Labels

Sticks and stones, according to the old saw, may break my bones, but words can never hurt me. Or can they? Consistent with the processes by which humans label all kinds of concepts and people, labels applied to such groups as "retardates" connote generalizations about the people to whom we apply the labels (Goffman, 1963). And labeling has typically suggested deviance (e.g., Becker, 1963; Memert, 1951) and stigma (Edgerton, 1993). People with intellectual disability identities acquire the label because others see them as differing from a culturally defined standard of "normal" intellect (Manion & Bersani, 1987). Investigators have often viewed people with intellectual disability as objects of study, sometimes overlooking the fact that these "objects" are humans with all the feelings, thoughts, opinions, and complexities of experience that characterize any humans (Castles, 1996).

Effects on Individuals with Intellectual Disability

The field of mental retardation, Blatt (1985) argued, has too long perseverated on the "educability" issue, with assignment of labels driving expectancies about the abilities of individuals. Although the categories to which we assign people may be important, they are nevertheless, Blatt asserted, inventions—individuals are retarded because someone (e.g., an agency or organization) said so. The result, according to one person receiving such a label, may be devastating:

> The problem is getting labeled as being something. After that you're not really as a person. It's like a sty in your eye—it's noticeable. Like that teacher and the way she looked at me. In the fifth grade—in the fifth grade my classmates thought I was different, and my teacher knew I was different (Bogdan & Taylor, 1976, p. 48).

In a review of literature on the social identity of people with intellectual disability, Beart, Hardy, and Buchan (2005) concluded that the label "intellectual disabilities" is powerful and dominant, over-riding such other identities as gender (Burns, 2000). This is also a label that is likely to stay with the person for a lifetime (Harris, 1995), and that may be accompanied by awareness of the stigma connected to it (Rapley, Kiernan, & Antaki, 1998), although there is some evidence (e.g., Beart, Hardy, & Buchan, 2004) that self-views may be to some extent malleable in response to such activities as self-advocacy. Some writers have assumed that people with intellectual disability are unaware of the effects of their own labels, but interviews with these people have suggested otherwise (e.g., Lea, 1988).

Wolfensberger (2002), writing about what he called the "language wars" centered on the words used to describe those with intellectual disability, identified 10 principles for selection and use of language. These principles suggest that those using disabilities language should: respect longstanding meanings of words; use terms to communicate (and not for other purposes, such as political correctness); be clear (i.e., not euphemistic) when referring to devalued people; observe the rules (e.g., grammatical principles) of the language spoken; not unnecessarily or deliberately degrade people's images; not resort to "term-hopping," abandoning old terms for new ones that may be no better; adopt new terms only if they are clearly an improvement; analyze new terms with an eye to the amount and relevance of the information they communicate; avoid coercive means to change language conventions; and recognize that language and communication are imperfect processes. Realistically, Wolfensberger (2002) concluded, no term is likely to meet his ten criteria; nevertheless, his plea was for clear, honest communication about people and their characteristics.

The use of language intended to be politically correct or euphemistic may actually harm individuals with disabilities Wolfensberger (2002) contended, because if descriptors do not accurately characterize a person, others may expect more or less of the individual, make poor decisions, or even become angry with those providing poor information, and generalize their negative emotions to the person with disabilities. Thus there is danger of exacerbating the already existing tendency to blame victims for their own circumstances (e.g., Finerman & Bennett, 1995), a phenomenon known as defensive attribution (Shaver, 1970). There is an element of defensive attribution, for example, in the phenomenon Wolfensberger (1975) termed "the retarded person as a menace"—resulting in a tendency to blame people with intellectual disability for social and genetic problems and in response to treat them with vindictiveness or persecution.

Despite modern efforts to escape the limitations of labeling, labels have made life difficult for many people with intellectual disability. They have attributed defective traits, often medical in nature, to individuals, creating limiting self-fulfilling prophecies (Dunn, 1969). But the effects of labels are evident not only in the lives of the individuals carrying the labels. They also affect others in the cultural context surrounding individuals with disabilities.

Effects on others

Contemporary authors have recognized the connection between conceptions of intellectual disability and public policy (Shogren & Turnbull, 2010). However, the idea that perceptions of people with disability can influence the actions of others is not new. For example, Édouard Séguin, the French-American physician known for his pioneering work in educational techniques, was generous in his attitudes toward "idiots," but harsh in his views toward "imbeciles" (whom he saw as more capable; Trent, 1994).

Wolfensberger (1975) detailed the ways in which perceptions of individuals with disabilities served historically to determine institutional models of care. These perceptions (and their accompanying labels) included the retarded person as "sick," "subhuman," "menace," "object of pity," "burden of charity," "holy innocent," and "developing individual" (pp. 5–17).

The retarded person as sick It is noteworthy that the organization that would later become the AAIDD was known, at its founding in 1876, as the Association of Medical Officers of American Institutions for Idiotic and

Feeble-Minded Persons. The superintendents who gathered to establish the group were all physicians, and they had been denied membership in the Association of Medical Officers of American Institutions for the Insane—a group that limited itself to the superintendents of lunatic asylums (Trent, 1994). So from its beginning, the major professional organization concerning itself with intellectual disability was responding to intellectual disability as a disease or illness—labels that persisted well past the middle of the twentieth century (e.g., American Medical Association, 1965). As Wolfensberger (1975) noted, facilities responding to individuals as sick were marked by a medical ethos, as evidenced by the pervasive use of medical language (e.g., "hospital," "infirmary," "nursing care," "patients," "disease," "diagnosis," "patient charts") and procedures (medical-style staff uniforms, hierarchical relations between types of staff, physicians as decision makers, medically related disciplines and treatments taking priority over non-medical approaches). As we will see later in the stories of affected individuals, one consequence of this approach in institutions was that there was little time or concern for residents' emotional and psychological well-being (e.g., Sienkiewicz-Mercer & Kaplan, 1989).

The retarded person as subhuman Wolfensberger (1975) related an anecdote in which Martin Luther, apparently referring to a child with severe or profound mental retardation, considered the child a changeling (the offspring of some sort of legendary creature, left in place of a human child) and advocated the child's drowning. When this failed, Luther prayed for the child's death. Vail (1967) described the kinds of dehumanizing practices associated with the subhuman expectation. These included emphasis on indestructible environments (unbreakable glass, heavy-duty furnishings, shielded light fixtures, heavy locked doors, barred windows), environmental control (inaccessible control of water temperature, lights, room temperature), and efficient management of people (drug-based behavioral control, large dormitories, soil- and stain-proof floors and walls, mass showers). Individuals seen as subhuman were not, of course, expected to develop or learn sufficiently to become fully human.

The retarded person as menace Humans have long tended to denigrate or fear the "other," those people who are different in customs, appearance, language, or other salient characteristics. Sumner (1906) coined the term "ethnocentrism" to describe this practice, and noted that it involves not only elevating one's own group, but also seeing the other group as inferior and threatening. In institutional care for people with intellectual disability, such attitudes have resulted in segregated facilities and perceptions of individuals as violent, criminal, or otherwise socially menacing. The label of menace creates in others the perception of individuals with disabilities as an out-group. Further, Gelb (1995) argued that degeneracy—a perspective shaped by Christian religious views—was a contributing factor to the view of the "feeble-minded" as a public menace. According to Gelb, this view arose from two assumptions: first, that humans and animals were different creations, leading to the notion that "primitive" and "savage" people were less than human; and second, that sinful living produced degenerate people. Individuals with intellectual disability were, of course, considered degenerate, and therefore the kind of menace that Goddard (1912) described in *The Kallikak Family* (about which we will hear more in Chapter Three). In Chapter Two we will discuss in more detail the changes that produced the evolution of the "menace" perspective.

The retarded person as object of pity Labeling a person as an object of pity may cause others to see the person as a child who never grows, is not accountable for his or her behavior, and who "suffers" from his condition (Wolfensberger, 1975). Other people may be prompted to behave in paternalistic ways that protect the person and make minimal demands. People may also create environments free of the risks of normal life, with a focus on trying to make the person happy.

The retarded person as burden of charity This label appealed to people whose conscience dictated that individuals with disabilities should receive basic care and shelter, but little enrichment or stimulation. Individuals should be grateful to these people, who would expect (perhaps begrudgingly) to provide basic subsistence needs, with nothing that could be considered a luxury. This view of persons with disabilities comes naturally from the history of some institutions as outgrowths of earlier homes for orphans, paupers, and others (Bartlett, 1967).

The retarded person as holy innocent The term "holy innocent" derives from the story of Herod the Great, who is supposed to have ordered the killing of young boys in Bethlehem to avoid having one of them become King of the Jews and replace him. The legend holds that these children were the first Christian martyrs, and hence "holy innocents." The holy innocent label prompts others to see the individual as a child of God, largely blameless and lacking capacity for willful evil (Wolfensberger, 1975). Unfortunately, this perception of lack of capacity has also encompassed such areas as capacity for moral growth and human development.

The retarded person as developing individual Seeing people as developing individuals is likely to prompt others to respond in optimistic ways, perceiving the possibilities for growth and learning. Programs and facilities are likely to foster interaction, with both environment and other people, and individuals are afforded opportunities for responsibility, dignity, privacy, the amenities of normal home life (e.g., personal control over environment, opportunity for normal life risks, individualized programs and living arrangements; Wolfensberger, 1975). The developing individual label may help others to see the person with disabilities as less deviant and more like other people.

In an effort to further explore the meaning of labels for other people (in this case professionals), Carroll and Reppucci (1978) studied the reactions of teachers and mental health workers to three labels: mentally retarded (MR), emotionally disturbed (ED), and juvenile delinquent (JD). Teachers (more than mental health workers) considered children in all the labeled conditions less likely to finish high school and less motivated for school. Teachers rated themselves as less knowledgeable and willing to work with any of the labeled children (as compared to average children), and mental health workers considered themselves less knowledgeable and willing only with the MR group. The labels were associated with a variety of perceptions that differed from the norm, with some particularly interesting findings for the MR group; the professionals were less motivated to work with children labeled MR, and they thought the MR group unlikely to achieve future skilled employment. Carroll and Reppucci concluded that professionals attach different meanings to different labels, and that different professional groups may respond differently to labels.

Millington, Szymanski, and Hanley-Maxwell (1994), observing that people with intellectual disability are often unemployed or underemployed, investigated the effect of the label "mental retardation" on employers. Millington et al. found not only that a number of skills influenced employer perceptions, but also that the presence of the label of mental retardation lowered expectations of potential employers about the skills of people with the label.

We can conclude that labels not only facilitate the grouping and stereotyping of people based on salient characteristics, but that they also have important effects on the people who are labeled and on others who react in various ways to labels. We can also say that the label that prevailed for a half century—mental retardation—has often been applied to people who are more different than they are alike (Gelb, 1997). Despite the variations in people who have carried the label, the term "mental retardation" has been pejorative and stigmatizing (Smith & Smallwood, 2007), and Danforth (2002), consistent with Wolfensberger (2002), pointed out that changing the words to terms assumed to be free of stigma is not likely to help, in view of the fact that new terms (e.g., intellectual disability) will soon develop the same cultural stigma. This realization naturally leads to speculation about the role of culture and the social context as influences on the recognition and definition of intellectual disability.

Social Construction of Intellectual Disability

Behavioral scientists have long recognized the role of hypothetical constructs in development of theory and explanations for psychological phenomena. Such constructs refer to entities, events, or processes that are not observed, but are "somethings" possessing causal properties (MacCorquodale & Meehl, 1948). Moore (2010), for instance, pointed out that we might explain the breaking of a pane of glass by reference to its "brittleness," despite the fact that brittleness is not an observable entity or process. Sometimes constructs originate as descriptions of behavior, but eventually come to be viewed as explanations; thus, we might say the glass breaks *because* of its brittleness. Human examples might include intelligence, motivation, or creativity, each of which can describe behavior, but which also, in common usage, often serves to explain behavior (Ebel, 1974). Morey (1991) suggested that the classification of mental disorders may be a collection of hypothetical constructs tied not only to description of the disorders, but also to their causes, even though the causes may in fact be unknown.

A difficulty with the use of constructs lies of course in the danger of circular reasoning. For example, we are likely to consider a person more or less intelligent when he or she behaves in a more or less intelligent manner (Ebel, 1974), but it is of course circular to say that the person behaves intelligently because he or she is intelligent. The same logical trap exists for intellectual disability: Is it logical to say that a person's behavioral characteristics or deficits are due to intellectual disability, when identification of disability depends upon existence of those same characteristics? Just as the brittleness of glass may be a construct that exists in the mind of the observer, intellectual disability may be a social construction existing in the minds of professionals or the public (Lea, 1988). The disability construct is not directly observable, but is rather inferred from observable behaviors or characteristics (Wehmeyer et al., 2008). Thus, such general essences as "mental retardation" may be conceptually empty and scientifically and morally dubious.

The changing labels applied over time to people with intellectual disability, reflecting as they do the prevailing social context and attitudes of a place and an era, clearly indicate not only that this is a construct subject to social perception, but also that some writers have considered such individuals less than human (Boddington & Podpadec, 1991). In China, just as female children have been devalued, so too have children with disabilities; thus, despite the traditional one child policy, a change in the law in the 1980s allowed for parents to have a second child if the first had disabilities (Sonnander & Claesson, 1997)—as if the firstborn were not a "real" child. Some philosophers, as we will see, have advocated that selective abortion is morally permissible when the life of an existing disabled fetus is sacrificed in favor of a not-yet-conceived "normal" child. As Bogdan and Taylor (1976) noted, the labels we construct divide humanity into two groups: the "normal" and the "retarded" or "disabled."

However, these groups have not been static; their membership has changed along with the shifting conceptions of those who have defined intellectual disability. For example, in 1973 the American Association on Mental Deficiency removed large numbers of people (many of them ethnic minorities) from the ranks of the mentally retarded simply by changing the foundation of the construct from one to two standard deviations below the average IQ score (Grossman, 1973; Trent, 1994). Most recently the same association (now known as the AAIDD; Schalock et al., 2010) has defined intellectual disability as significant limitations in both intellectual functioning and adaptive behavior (everyday skills). Further, to be considered intellectual disability under this definition, the limitations must have originated prior to the age of 18.

Summary

Are people with intellectual disability today so different from those whom earlier generations labeled idiots, imbeciles, morons, or retardates? People living in more recent times have been able to speak for themselves (e.g., Groulx, Doré, & Doré, 2000; Helle, 2000; Ward, 2000; Williams & Shoultz, 1982), yet still find themselves encompassed by the construct of intellectual disability. As Smith (1995) noted, it is society that instills values and teaches us how to behave, and as we have noted, societies have continually changed the language and the concepts they have used to designate those whom they consider intellectually disabled. We may conclude, with Rapley (2004), that intellectual disability is not an observable fact, but instead a social construction that is a product of the interaction of people in a particular society, with particular aspirations and behaviors reflecting their time and place. Perhaps Blatt (1985) was right in his assertion that the categories into which we group people are our own inventions, and that people have disabilities at least in part because someone said so.

Keith (1990, 2002) argued that individuals' rights and personal empowerment will be restricted so long as they are viewed (by others or by themselves) as clients or wards of service delivery agencies, and that true social integration and quality of life will come only when their labels are those applied to other citizens: *citizen*, *neighbor*, *friend*, and *employee*. Perske and Perske (1980) foresaw a future in which people with intellectual disability will be:

> living in ordinary houses and apartments like yours; passing you or standing next to you on the streets; riding with you on buses, trolleys, and subways; rubbing elbows with you in shopping centers; going to public school with the other kids on the block; working in the same building where you work; making money and paying taxes; seen in restaurants, theaters, and at athletic events; sitting beside you in churches and synagogues (p. 77).

This is a future that will await yet more changes in the social construct we call intellectual disability.

2

The Social Construction of Purgatory
Ideas and Institutions

The mid-nineteenth century marked the dawn of a time both interesting and troubling in the history of Americans with intellectual disability. Beginning with establishment of the first public institution in 1848 in the state of Massachusetts (Wolfensberger, 1975), people with intellectual disability found themselves travelers on a strange, convoluted odyssey that involved a variety of forms of treatment, at least as many kinds of mistreatment and abuse, public display and ridicule, and a veritable building boom in public facilities devoted to their care and confinement. At each juncture, society's representatives—policy makers, physicians, psychologists, and educators—were certain they were doing the right thing. But, as we will see, certainty can sometimes be a dangerous thing.

In the Beginning

Although people with intellectual disability certainly existed in the US prior to establishment of the first specialized institution, and numerous mental asylums had earlier beginnings, 1848 marked the start of development of such facilities by states; within a quarter century seven states had constructed facilities (Braddock & Parish, 2001). In the early days, most of these state facilities (and a few private ones, as well) were called schools, and had as their aim the provision of education intended to make people less deviant (Wolfensberger, 1975) and to return them to their communities (Braddock & Parish, 2001)—an enterprise that was, for a time, rather successful.

Intellectual Disability: Ethics, Dehumanization, and a New Moral Community, First Edition.
Heather E. Keith and Kenneth D. Keith.

One pioneer in development of educational techniques for people with intellectual disability was the French teacher Edouard Séguin (1812–1880), who was an important figure in establishment of "idiocy" as distinct from "insanity" (although, as we noted in Chapter One, British law had made a similar distinction much earlier), and in promoting the development of specialized institutions for the intellectually disabled, both in France and in the US (Simpson, 1999). Séguin met Jean-Marc Itard, the mentor of the famous "wild boy" of Aveyron (Itard, 1962/1801) late in Itard's life, and became convinced that idiots could be educated. Following his emigration to the United States in 1850, Séguin worked at institutions in Massachusetts and New York, and also completed medical training in New York in 1861 (Trent, 1994). Using techniques that he termed the "physiological method," Séguin (1866) employed procedures, including sensory stimulation, imitation, and repetition (although repetition for its own sake, he thought, should be avoided), that Ball (1970) recognized as forerunners of more modern behavioral tools. Séguin's approach emphasized development of intelligence (sensory experience) and activity (physical/muscular), and also encompassed what he called "moral treatment," which involved careful use of reward and punishment to teach appropriate social behavior in its natural context. Séguin (1866) believed, for example that a child could best learn to name foods at mealtime, with the general rule being that "our teaching how to do a thing, is of no practical value if we do not place him in the best circumstances to accomplish it" (p. 217). For Séguin, moral treatment, which he believed educated the will, meant what today we might call socialization—learning how to behave appropriately in various settings and situations. This perspective is not unlike that of the pragmatist philosophers, about whom we will learn more in Chapter Six.

The effectiveness of Séguin's techniques, both in France and after his arrival in the US, gave rise to the views that idiots could learn, and that the specialized institutions could provide the environment and the teaching necessary to facilitate such learning—a legacy that influenced future facility superintendents and others interested in social reform (Trent, 1994). The early training schools were relatively small; the public institutions established by the first seven states to build them housed only about 1000 individuals in total (Braddock & Parish, 2001). These institutions did not initially intend to become permanent homes for individuals with intellectual disability. Instead, they were viewed as temporary schools from which people would return to their families or to ordinary schools after learning the necessary skills for functioning in society (Wolfensberger, 1975). Samuel

Gridley Howe, superintendent of the first state institution, set the early tone in his 1848 report to the Massachusetts legislature:

> Massachusetts admits the right of all her citizens to a share in the blessings of education, and she provides it liberally for all her more favored children . . . The humanity and justice of our rulers will prompt them to take immediate measures for the formation of a school or schools for the instruction and training of idiots (p. 53).

And in its first biennial report the Asylum for Feeble-Minded Children of the State of Iowa recounted the hiring of three teachers (Robertson, Cattell, Russell, & Archibald, 1877), offering instruction in gymnastic exercise, words, colors, reading, writing, arithmetic, music, marching, geography, and "fancy work" (Archibald, 1877).

Figure 2.1 Early building at Glenwood Resource Center (formerly Asylum for Feeble-Minded Children of the State of Iowa). Glenwood, established in 1876, was the seventh such facility in the US, and the first west of the Mississippi River. *Source:* Photo by K. D. Keith

The Growth of Institutions

However, attitudes changed, and the numbers of people with intellectual disability proved daunting for the fledging institutions. Early authorities realized that different people were more or less susceptible to training and, as Wolfensberger (1975) pointed out, there was perhaps a fatal flaw in the reasoning underlying the plan to remove people from society so as to train them for return to society. Maybe, as Herndon (1971) asserted, "An Institution Is A Place To Do Things Where Those Things Will Not Be Done" (p. 110). Thus, even though Howe, speaking in 1886 at the founding of a new institution in New York, counseled against segregation and in support of integration of the disabled with ordinary children and families (Wolfensberger, 1969), by 1880 the training schools had largely become custodial asylums (Braddock & Parish, 2001; Trent, 1994), and the word "school" began to disappear from their names (Wolfensberger, 1975). Although states had achieved some success in placement of residents back into productive community life (Kerlin, 1885; Knight, 1879; Powell, 1887), by the end of the century Johnson (1899) reported that "It has not been found practicable to discharge large numbers of the educated imbeciles to care for themselves and direct their own course of life" (p. 469), that "A belief in the necessity of permanent care for all this defective class is professed by the superintendent of every state school for the feeble-minded in the United States today" (p. 467), and that "the average citizen looks upon the feeble-minded with contempt or indifference" (p. 468).

In the last quarter of the nineteenth century and the first decade of the twentieth, the number of people housed in American institutions multiplied nearly 20-fold, to almost 21,000 by the year 1910, according to the U.S. Census Report (Kuhlman, 1916), with some of the institutions also having long waiting lists. Residents were called "inmates," and the institutions divided the inmates into groups: "educables," "industrials," and "custodials" (Johnson, 1899, p. 470). Despite the apparent indifference of some to the needs of people with intellectual disability, the movement toward custodial care brought with it a protective attitude, with states moving to provide gardens, pleasant grounds, and facilities as homelike as possible (Kerlin, 1877), and the institutions continued to teach practical life skills, even though lifelong institutionalization was becoming the norm for many (Trent, 1994). According to Walter E. Fernald (1893), many family members and guardians wanted their charges to remain in the institutions where they could be safe and happy, and authorities eventually believed that even some of those with higher abilities required lifelong supervision and care. The custodial movement was perhaps epitomized in the 1893 naming, at Rome, New York, of the Custodial Asylum for Unteachable Idiots (Ferguson, 1994). The meaning of the Rome facility's label, connoting as it does the lack of ability to learn, could not be more diametrically opposed to the earlier aims of the schools for people with intellectual disability. Did the *people* so dramatically change from those whom Séguin had optimistically taught a half century earlier, or did the views of society contribute to a new social construction of the notion of intellectual disability?

In any event, attitudes had changed, and people with intellectual disability had become objects of pity and protection (Wolfensberger, 1975). The institutions became "colonies," and rather elaborate plans evolved for their development and maintenance. Johnson (1899), for example, described the ideal "village of the simple" (p. 472), with land for farming, gardens, and orchards, a dairy, and buildings constructed by the residents. High- and middle-grade imbeciles, Johnson reasoned, could be self-sufficient in such a colony, and a thousand acres could support "three hundred adult trained imbeciles and twice as many more of the lower grades" (p. 473). The institutions grew in size as the perception developed that more and more people needed the protection afforded by the idyllic visions created by institutional advocates. The Rome, New York facility, for example, eventually grew, by the middle of the twentieth century, to house more than 5000 people, the Sonoma State Hospital in California would grow to well over 3000, and some supporters of the institutional model believed that increasingly larger facilities were required to properly serve the diversity of individuals requiring care (e.g., Knight, 1891).

As the institutional emphasis changed from that of schools to custodial environments, and as the institutions became larger, so too did the focus of institutional work evolve. Initially, work had the primary aim of training residents in skills and vocations that might be useful upon their return to the community (Kerlin, 1885). However, as it became apparent that most people would be long-term inmates, and as the facilities grew, it became economically important for those living in institutions to contribute to the maintenance and operation of the facilities (Kerlin, 1886; Rugg, 1983). This practice became known as institutional peonage—the "widespread practice of employing residents in institutions for the mentally handicapped to perform productive labor associated with the maintenance of the institution without adequate compensation" (Friedman, 1977, p. 62)—and would continue in such institutions until well past the middle of the twentieth century, when it became a major issue in legal actions aimed toward establishing the rights of individuals with intellectual disability (Gelhaar, 1981). As the institutional population increased, per capita state budgetary allocations decreased, making the work of residents more essential to maintenance of the facilities (Wolfensberger, 1975).

Despite rules forbidding physical force and inappropriate use of punishment by institutional staff (e.g., Kerlin, 1891), along the way reports of abuse and neglect sometimes surfaced, as did concerns about matters of discipline for unruly institutional residents. These problems became more frequent as the institutions experienced rapid growth and underfunding (Trent, 1994). Individuals with disabilities, even in adulthood, were regarded within the institutions as "boys" and "girls," and escapes (euphemistically termed "elopements") were not uncommon (Kerlin, 1891). The earlier image of institutions as idyllic colonies gave way to the reality of physical labor that would be "heart-breaking and unprofitable work for normal persons," but "For this work, the feeble-minded, . . . who have been called waste humanity, seem to be particularly fitted" (Mastin, 1916, pp. 34–35). Once again, attitudes were changing.

The Social Menace of Intellectual Disability

The era of colonies viewed as villages where people with intellectual disability could live in peace and happiness was relatively short lived. Mastin (1916) spoke for many in his beliefs that at least 50 percent of homicides were committed by "mental defectives" and that "feeble-minded women" living in almshouses "give birth to approximately two feeble-minded children each, thus multiplying themselves by two as their contribution to the burden of pauperism in the coming generation" (pp. 27–28). Observers of the time saw the necessity of protecting the country from imbecility and crime (Barr, 1899). Wolfensberger (1975) termed this perspective "protecting nondeviant individuals from the deviant people" (p. 33).

Writing on the topic of prevention of intellectual disability, Fernald (1915) identified some of the reasons for the change in perspective: increased use of mental testing had simplified recognition of disability; the belief that intellectual disability was the cause of such social problems as illegitimacy, crime, poverty, and juvenile delinquency; increased estimates of the prevalence of disabilities; and the belief that intellectual disability was hereditary in nature, thus making it imperative that mental defectives not have children.

Contemporary research (e.g., Holland, Clare, & Mukhopadhyay, 2002) has suggested that, although people with intellectual disability may be somewhat over-represented in some facets of the legal system, their levels of offending behavior are remarkably low in relation to the psychosocial disadvantages and vulnerabilities they often face, but those writing in the early twentieth century projected a very different picture, and Mastin's (1916) estimate that half of homicides were committed by people with intellectual disability was no doubt greatly exaggerated. Wolfensberger (1975) suggested that, in fact, people with intellectual disability are probably more likely to be victims, rather than perpetrators, of crime. Further, in Chapter Three we will discuss some of the shortcomings of both the heredity and testing movements.

Nevertheless, convinced that idiocy and imbecility were hereditary, institutional administrators believed that individuals of all classes of disability, especially women, should be segregated in custodial asylums (Johnson, 1899). Important psychologists of the era, including Goddard (1912), became eugenicists, advocating that mentally defective people should not be allowed to reproduce. It would be only a few years later, in the 1927 case of *Buck v. Bell*, that Supreme Court Justice Oliver Wendell Holmes would write "It is better for all the world, if instead of waiting to execute degenerate offspring for crime or to let them starve for their imbecility, society can prevent those who are manifestly unfit from continuing their kind . . . Three generations of imbeciles are enough." Carrie Buck, an unwed mother, was institutionalized, at age 18, in the state of Virginia, where she became the first person sterilized under state law—the law the Supreme Court upheld in *Buck v. Bell.* Despite Holmes's "three generations" dictum, representing his belief in the hereditary nature of mental deficiency, Buck's daughter grew up to become an honor student (Smith, 1989). Carrie Buck, like tens of thousands of others, became a pointless victim of involuntary sterilization; over the next three decades, the state of California alone would sterilize nearly 10,000 "defective" people (Hunt, 1994).

Within four years 27 states had passed laws to authorize eugenic sterilization of defective people—laws that would not be repealed until the 1960s (Hunt, 1994). Like Goddard (1914), the states had defined the mentally defective as threats to society, giving legal sanction to their status as a menace, and providing another reminder that intellectual disability is a social construction based on value judgments and definitions that can be arbitrary and subjective (Smith, 1989). Numerous writers of the time (e.g., Bullard, 1910; Fernald, 1893, 1904, 1912; Goddard, 1915) described the mentally deficient using such words as *disgusting, menace, immoral, evil*, *irresponsible*, *burden*, and *dangerous*, among others. The evolution of dehumanization (White & Wolfensberger, 1969) was well underway.

Dehumanization

It would be many years before institutions and the broader culture would move beyond the attitudes and practices of the perspective of intellectual disability as menace (e.g., Blatt & Kaplan, 1966); and the problems associated with this period were not limited to the US. Consider the following examples.

Individual cases

Anne McDonald In 1961, in Australia, Anne McDonald was born with a brain injury that resulted in cerebral palsy. Her doctors told her mother that Anne would never be able to "do anything" and that she should be institutionalized. At the age of three years McDonald entered the new St. Nicholas Hospital in Melbourne, a facility with Spartan wards and high brick walls topped with barbed wire and broken glass. In her memoir, co-authored with her advocate and caregiver Rosemary Crossley, McDonald chronicled her time at St. Nicholas, an institution that nearly killed her (Crossley & McDonald, 1984).

Nurses at St. Nicholas were overtaxed and probably underpaid—during the time McDonald was institutionalized, each nurse was required to feed ten children in an hour, resulting in malnutrition, and in some cases death. Children were fed lying down, bird-like, with food piled into their mouths and little chance to chew or swallow properly. Getting enough to eat proved particularly challenging for McDonald, who had difficulty swallowing and, because of muscle tension, had to be propped up by her neck in order to eat. When Crossley met her, McDonald was starving to death.

Children at St. Nicholas fared little better in other necessities of life. Their sleeping, toilet, and other schedules depended on institutional policies designed to accommodate overworked staff members, a familiar theme in such institutions (Wolfensberger, 1975). For example, Crossley and McDonald (1984) reported that children received their evening meal at 3:30 p.m., with no opportunity to eat again until breakfast, and all residents, regardless of age, were on the babies' schedule, with lights out at 5:00 p.m.—making for long nights and for days too short for normal interaction, play, and education. During "play" time, paralyzed children were placed on the same mats in the same positions each day, again for the convenience of staff, and those with noncompliant behavior were tied up or locked in small dark rooms. Nurses were discouraged from cuddling children, and there was little tolerance for crying. Perhaps the most troubling condition that Crossley and McDonald (1984) reported was the doctors' and nurses' practice of talking about the condition of children in front of them, assuming the children could not understand. McDonald, however, could understand, and witnessed conversations about the deaths of other children and the probability of her own death. She claimed that while some people gave up under such conditions, "death never appealed to me; I wanted revenge" (Crossley & McDonald, p. 19).

When Crossley first met McDonald at St. Nicholas, McDonald's muscles had become so rigid that she could only lie on the floor in a sort of backward bowing position with her heels approaching the back of her head. She was starving, not only physically, but also for attention. Eventually, Crossley learned what other caregivers at the institution did not understand: that although McDonald, lacking speech, scored as profoundly disabled on traditional tests, she was capable of communicating with someone who took the time to help her develop an alternative method. First through gestures with her tongue, and then via a visual alphabet, McDonald, then a teenager, learned to communicate; and with that breakthrough came education and the ability to speak for herself. One of the messages she communicated to Crossley was that she wanted out of St. Nicholas. Although one of the communication techniques devised by Crossley (facilitated communication) has been controversial (e.g., Biklen, Saha, & Kliewer, 1995; Wheeler, Jacobson, Paglieri, & Schwartz, 1993), the reality of McDonald's experience is unquestioned.

At age 18, McDonald obtained a lawyer to help her argue, all the way to the Supreme Court, that she had the right to leave the institution. Even though she was of legal age to determine her own fate, she also had to prove that she was capable of making important decisions; otherwise, the hospital would claim the right to keep her for her own protection. After more assessment revealed that earlier measurements of her intelligence were vastly inaccurate, and after overcoming numerous legal hurdles, authorities decided that McDonald had the ability to make decisions for herself. Upon her release from St. Nicholas, she had the body of a small girl, but with improved care quickly grew. McDonald went home with Crossley, eventually earned a university degree, and spent her life as an advocate for others with disabilities, including some of those with whom she was institutionalized.

Ruth Sienkiewicz-Mercer Sienkiewicz-Mercer was born in 1950 in Northampton, Massachusetts. Probably due to nerve damage occurring during an extreme fever when she was an infant, she developed cerebral palsy and was never able to talk, walk, or feed and dress herself, although she appeared bright and alert as a child (Sienkiewicz-Mercer & Kaplan, 1989). Her parents attempted to care for her in their home, but due to strain on the family, Sienkiewicz-Mercer moved, as a small child, to a private facility. According to her report, this care home, Crotched Mountain Rehabilitation Center in New Hampshire, though not as desirable as being at home, was pleasant and met her basic needs.

When Sienkiewicz-Mercer was nine years of age, her parents were unable to afford her continued care at Crotched Mountain, and she returned home, where her family again attempted to care for her. Unfortunately, her mother's back condition made this impossible, and Sienkiewicz-Mercer moved again, this time to the State School at Belchertown, Massachusetts, a facility situated, in the longstanding tradition of such institutions, on more than 800 acres of land. Though others warned her that it would be different from the private facility she had enjoyed, she wondered "how bad could a place be that was devoted to serving the needs of disabled people?" (Sienkiewicz-Mercer & Kaplan, 1989, p. 36). At Belchertown, where Ruth Sienkiewicz-Mercer became #4774, she was about to find out.

According to Sienkiewicz-Mercer, life at Belchertown was miserable. Patients in wards spent most of their time in bed, and staff had little patience with children who, like her, experienced difficulty in eating. Like Anne McDonald, Sienkiewicz-Mercer was fed while lying down, making swallowing difficult and resulting in attenuation of growth. She lived on a ward or in the infirmary with many other patients, and other children and staff members with whom she developed rapport were often moved with little warning. She reported that for a part of her stay at Belchertown, attendants found it convenient to keep her in bed, flat on her back, around the clock. Her "basic activities" during that year were "crying and not eating" (Sienkiewicz-Mercer & Kaplan, 1989, p. 94). Despite being able to use the restroom with assistance, Ruth wore diapers until the age of 20, and claimed that to some staff members, "we weren't people with physical and emotional needs; we were objects that had to be fed, cleaned, and changed, fed, cleaned, and changed, and so on" (p. 100).

In another parallel to McDonald's experience, most Belchertown staff members assumed that, because Sienkiewicz-Mercer could not speak, her physical disabilities were accompanied by severe intellectual disability.

Though she developed complex gestural communication systems with other patients with similar disabilities, staff members did not take note of these abilities until she was well into her teenage years. Eventually, through the use of word boards and the efforts of attendants, Ruth was able to communicate through verbal language, which provided the key for her liberation from Belchertown because she could finally tell people about the conditions of her life.

With communication skills and help from others, Sienkiewicz-Mercer was able to become educated and to move from the institution to a group apartment and then to her own apartment. She was able to deepen friendships and eventually marry, and to become an advocate for transitioning institutionalized people to the community. Following a series of lawsuits dealing with issues of treatment and individual rights, Belchertown closed in 1992, 70 years after its opening and nearly a century following Fernald's (1893) assertion that people with intellectual disability were prone to lead "dissolute lives" (p. 212). In a landmark 1971 ruling, the United States District Court, in an Alabama case known as *Wyatt v. Stickney*, ruled for the first time that people with mental handicaps, involuntarily confined in a state institution, had a constitutional right to habilitation. Other similar decisions in the 1970s affected citizens with intellectual disability in the states of Minnesota, Massachusetts, Nebraska, Tennessee, and New York (Friedman, 1977). Unfortunately, despite the downsizing and improvement of institutions in the US and other countries, residents of such facilities continue to allege abuse and neglect at the hands of staff members (e.g., Duggan, 2012; Elliott & Sandberg, 2007; Mann, 2010; McMillan, 2006). Despite several decades of efforts to normalize the lives of people with intellectual disability (Flynn & Nitsch, 1980; Nirje, 1969; White & Wolfensberger, 1969), there remain obstacles and challenges on the path to humane, integrated community life for all people (Keith, 2002).

Holocaust

The idea of disability as a menace to society and a threat to the future of the human race was fundamental to the Nazi platform of the purity of the human race, leading first to sterilization and eventually to extermination of thousands of people with physical and intellectual disabilities. Fueled by social Darwinism and compounded by the post-World War I economic crisis, totalitarianism and nationalism, and the view of disabled people as nonproductive burdens on the state, Nazi leaders, bureaucrats, and even members of the public shared the view that it was morally acceptable to institutionalize, and eventually to kill, human beings (Sofair & Kaldjian, 2000). Believing in some cases that disabled lives were not worth living, and in others that they were a threat to humanity, physicians were heavily involved in what became a euthanasia program, though most were probably otherwise pillars of their communities, and close to half of all German doctors (including 3000 psychiatrists), the largest proportion of any group, were members of the Nazi party (Dudley & Gale, 2002).

In 1939 a five-month-old "idiotic" infant with multiple physical disabilities whose parents wanted him "put to sleep" became the catalyst for the Nazi euthanasia program (Zoech, 2003). Although the parents of the first child apparently favored his death, that would not be the case for most of the thousands to follow. There is evidence that local citizens knew what was happening in euthanasia centers during the Holocaust, and that foreign governments and people, including in the US, were not in the dark about the mass killing of people with disabilities. Gallup polls and medical articles in the 1930s in America showed, in fact, that "mercy killing" of people with disabilities was not as unpopular among the American citizenry as we might have expected or hoped. For example, a 1937 Gallup poll found that more than 45 percent of Americans supported euthanasia (Yount, 2000), and about half of respondents to one poll favored involuntary euthanasia for "hopeless invalids" (Noack & Fangeroa, 2007).

Facing economic crisis and decades of scientific claims supporting eugenics, perhaps Americans were not much less concerned than the Nazis about the threat of the disabled. And although there were numerous articles in mainstream media about Hitler's euthanasia program early in the war, America was slow to respond, and it was not until 1945 newsreel footage of liberation of camps and asylums that the crimes seemed real (Noack & Fangeroa, 2007).

Freaks on display

Institutions and governments are not the only agents that have subjected people with intellectual disability to dehumanization. At about the same time that states were beginning to establish institutions for people with intellectual disability, J. M. Warren (1851), a physician, described two people characterized as "Indian dwarfs," who had been exhibited in Boston with the claim that they were "descendants of priests from an undiscovered city in Central America" (p. 293). Warren provided detailed physical measurements and descriptions of the two individuals, and compared their communicative abilities to those of dogs and their head sizes to those of "idiotic children" (p. 289). These children were not, of course descended from an Aztec temple, but had instead come to America from St. Salvador through the auspices of a Spanish trader who told their parents they would be cured of their imbecility (Wood, 1868) and in turn sold them to an American who put them on display, both in the US and in England, as "human oddities" (Bogdan, 1986, p. 122).

By the mid-nineteenth century, a variety of people with unusual characteristics—cultural, physical, behavioral, mental—made up exhibits that promoters mounted for profit. When these exhibits became more organized, they were known as "freak shows" (Bogdan, 1988, p. 10), and in about 1840 in New York the entrepreneur P. T. Barnum established the American Museum, which gave the freak show a prominent place in American entertainment (Bogdan, 1988). However, the display of people with unusual characteristics began long before the freak shows of the nineteenth century. In ancient Egypt dwarfs provided comedic entertainment for statesmen, and in seventeenth- and eighteenth-century Europe court jesters and fools were sometimes people who either had, or pretended to have, intellectual disability (Tuan, 1984). In the Middle Ages people with disabilities, including those with mental disabilities, were exhibited at fairs (Gerber, 1992); in the seventeenth century members of the public were allowed to visit Bethlehem Hospital ("Bedlam") to be entertained (Street, 1994); and by the nineteenth century in America people with disabilities were regularly sold to organizers of shows (Bogdan, 1988).

These shows entertained by taking advantage of public attitudes of the time, displaying people with mental retardation and microcephaly (whom they called "pinheads") as "freaks" (Mateen & Boes, 2010). Organizers often fabricated stories about these individuals, calling them exotic, wild (Braddock & Parish, 2001), or of unknown races or civilizations (Bogdan, 1988). Harry Lewiston, a manager of sideshows and freak shows in the early twentieth century, said that:

> none of the things I had said or would be saying about the pinheads were true. They were plain old white American microcephalics, more popularly known as "pinheads," but you can't tell people, "Now we've got these idiots here; take a good look at them" (Lewiston & Holtman, 1968).

In their deceptions and fabrications the freak show promoters were thus producing their own social constructions of disability in an effort to cater to the attitudes and expectations of the ticket-buying public. And the reference to wild or exotic races had a parallel in the work of some nineteenth-century scientists who considered intellectual disability a kind of carryover or regression to earlier races of humans. For example, Langdon Down (1866), for whom the well-known syndrome was named, asserted that "A very large number of congenital idiots are typical Mongols" (p. 260). Down considered his work an "attempt at an ethnic classification" and evidence of "retrogression" (p. 262), believing that Down Syndrome reflected a resurgence of Mongolian traits (Menolascino & Egger, 1978).

Gerber (1992) argued that to understand the appeal of the freak shows one should question whether audiences saw the shows as performance—in which case they might attach value to the participants—or as displays, which may have included "a large dose of contempt, mockery, and hunger for bizarre spectacle" (p. 61). He went on to note the degradation, exploitation, and oppression of the people who became freaks. We might wonder what factors led to the demise of the freak show; one explanation suggests that by the 1930s mental retardation had achieved the status of a disease, with an accompanying change in public attitudes from exotic entertainment to pity (Bogdan, 1988). However, as Gerber (1992) suggested, other cultural forces may have played a role, in the form of increasing awareness of minority rights, development of different forms of media and entertainment, changing recreational interests, and perhaps the "revulsion at the dehumanization that is part of such displays" (p. 61). In any case, as Bogdan (1988) concluded, it was not their disabilities that made people freaks, but rather the perceptions and understandings of the culture that defined them.

Nameless in death

Patricia Noonan Walsh (2000) described an eerie, isolated place, a reminder of the past and of attitudes toward those beyond the mainstream of proper society:

> On the west coast of Ireland, a field stretches under clouding skies toward the Atlantic. This windswept place, removed from the sight of neighbors, is still marked on local maps as "the Infants Burial Ground." Now half-hidden, it is the resting place of a host of outliers—strangers to the nearby villages, unbaptized infants, seamen washed ashore. Even in death, these nameless individuals earned no more than a place apart from the established community (p. 315).

Burton Blatt and his colleagues (Blatt & Kaplan, 1966; Blatt, Ozolins, & McNally, 1979) provided compelling evidence of the ways that institutions could make people nameless in life. Walsh's description of the old Irish burial ground illustrates how the broader culture can, even in death, accomplish the same. The tradition of separate burial for those who deviated from the norm was well established in Ireland by medieval times. Unbaptized infants, unidentified sailors, people with contagious diseases or with different (non-Catholic) religions, suicides, murderers, and people with mental disabilities were among those who were marginalized not only in life, but in death, as well (Finlay, 2000). Known as *cillíní*, the unofficial graveyards of these people, many of them located on the west coast of Ireland, marked their graves with nondescript rocks and remained in use until the 1950s (Doyle, 2000). Although the church considered those interred in the *cillíní* marginal people, their families saw these graveyards as important sacred places (Murphy, 2011).

If the remote situations of the *cillíní* indicated marginalization of outcast people in Ireland, the location of cemeteries in nineteenth-century England followed suit. In that country, the establishment of burial grounds on the premises of asylums was controversial, and the two entities—asylums and cemeteries—proved uneasy neighbors (Philo, 2012). The graveyards were often located in out-of-the-way places, making those who may have been anonymous in life even more so in death. Similar challenges faced the families of people who died in French asylums and were buried in isolation from society and their relatives (Védie & Breathnach, 2005).

American institutions, too, stigmatized individuals not only in life, but also in death. For example, beginning in 1935 tombstones at the Nebraska Institution for the Feeble-minded at Beatrice carried not the name of the deceased, but simply a number:

> For the growing number of individuals at . . . Beatrice, who were viewed as a social menace in life by society and state policy makers, confined in custodial warehouses, forced to labor to support the very institution which denied them their humanity, they became forgotten with their life stories of hope, despair, love, and anguish buried under numbered tombstones . . . Abandoned in life, they had become nameless in death (Center for Disability Rights, Law and Advocacy, 2007, p. 9).

The Worcester State Hospital in Massachusetts followed a similar convention, with numbered concrete bricks serving as gravestones; finding the location of a particular grave required matching the name with the number and then locating the appropriate marker in the cemetery located on the hospital's old Hillside Farm (Dempsey, 2000). The old farm is the site of the state's Department of Developmental Service's Glavin Regional Center where, Dempsey reported, a former director observed that the cemetery was an indication of the way people with mental illness and mental retardation had been treated in the past. At the Glenwood Resource Center (originally the Asylum for Feeble-Minded Children of the State of Iowa), hundreds of brick-sized stones, planted flush with the earth, carry the names and dates of death (but not birth) of the people interred there over a period spanning more than a century. Perimeter markers, numerical on one axis, alphabetical on the other, allow location of graves within the many rows of small stones. And until the 1970s, graves at the Central Virginia Training Center had metal markers bearing a number that authorities recorded in a record book (Smith, 1995).

Figure 2.2 Nineteenth-century gravestone in cemetery of Glenwood Resource Center. Hundreds of these brick-sized stones lie flush with the earth and carry only names and dates of death.
Source: Photo by K. D. Keith

Not all American institutions have preserved or restored the graveyards associated with their facilities. For example, in 2006 at the Eastern State Hospital in Kentucky, a gardener rediscovered a long-forgotten cemetery overgrown with weeds. Authorities had no records for the estimated 4000 to 7000 people buried in the small space, and additional estimates have placed the number of deaths at the facility (founded in 1815 as one of the earliest mental hospitals in the US) in the range of 30,000 to 60,000 people. Although a genealogist has gathered the names of 1000 people who died at the facility, and the cemetery has been recently restored, there is little hope of matching names to the many bodies buried at the long-lost site (Edwards, 2011).

These stories of marginalization, death, and interment of people with intellectual disability provide sobering reminders of the atrocities that are possible in the name of doctrine—whether social, religious, professional, or cultural.

Reflecting on Purgatory: The Danger of Certainty

Many of our forebears were certain of their knowledge. Mastin (1916) was certain that people with intellectual disability were a threat to society, that they were prone to murder and mayhem. Barr (1902) characterized imbeciles and epileptics as enemies of the taxpayer and community. And Goddard (1912) insisted that mentally defective individuals should not be allowed to reproduce. The Supreme Court was sufficiently certain of the validity of these positions to separate Carrie Buck and others like her from their children, and the majority of the states enacted sterilization laws that would remain in place until well beyond the middle of the twentieth century. The result was the period that Wolfensberger (1975) called the *indictment*, an era characterized by the irreversible effects of eugenics, sterilization, and life-long segregation of individuals whose only crime was to be different in some way from the mainstream of other people—people whose attitudes, fears, perceptions, and dogmatic certainty allowed them to define mental deficiency and the purgatory to which they would consign those whom they so labeled.

In a recent sobering reminder of the perils inherent in unbending certainty, officials unearthing a mass grave in the Catholic cemetery of the German town of Menden-Barge found the remains of a large number of adults and children, some of them with apparent disabilities. Local citizens believed that as many as 200 people from a nearby Nazi clinic may have been buried in the grave as a part of the notorious *Aktion* T4 euthanasia program (Lesjak, 2007). Clearly, no one associated with development of the early training schools, the visions of happy villages, or the misguided fears of hereditary nightmares intended to create a hell on earth, although Carrie Buck, Anne McDonald, and Ruth Sienkiewicz-Mercer may well have described their experience in that way. And we have our own graveyards, silent testament to the isolation and dehumanization of the era of institutions.

In reflecting on the inhumanity of the Nazis' treatment of their fellow human beings, Jacob Bronowski (1973) pointed out:

> It is said that science will dehumanise people and turn them into numbers. That is false, tragically false . . . It was done by arrogance. It was done by dogma. It was done by ignorance. When people believe that they have absolute knowledge, with no test in reality, this is how they behave (p. 374).

In the chapters to come we will illuminate other dangerous certainties, as well as alternative views that hold the promise of a more humane and just view of the people we call disabled. There have always been, and will no doubt always be, challenges and roadblocks, but in the words of poet William Kloefkorn (1974), "To say there is always the rock is not to forfeit the harvest" (p. 60). We will examine the work of those whose contributions hold the promise of the harvest.

3

A Failure of Intelligence

In October, 1898, a young boy and his mother made a railway journey across southwestern Iowa to the town of Glenwood, site of the Asylum for Feeble-Minded Children of the State of Iowa. The child, Mayo Buckner, was mild mannered and had a talent for music, but his mother, according to an intake interview, feared she could not care for him, and that he would be bullied in public school (Wallace, 1958). The institution labeled him a "medium-grade imbecile" and admitted him. Thus began six decades of institutionalization for a man who always thought of himself as normal and who, many years later, would achieve a score of 120 on an Intelligence Quotient (IQ) test. Yet, in his 60s, able to play several musical instruments, and skilled in the printing trade, there were serious questions about whether Buckner could survive in the community—his consignment to a "treatment" center where he became patient #822 had precluded opportunity to learn the worldliness and social skills that he would need for life outside the institution. His is but one case in a century or more of use, misuse, and abuse of intelligence and its measurement in relation to the construct of intellectual disability and the people presumed to possess it.

In this chapter we will introduce the construct of intelligence and briefly discuss its history and use. We will see how various scholars have conceptualized intelligence and some of the cultural and social influences that have played a role in our understanding of intelligence. Despite the central role that intelligence plays in modern education and culture, and in our views of ourselves and others, the range and complexity of existing views of intelligence may prove surprising. For many, intelligence may truly be, as Goodey

Intellectual Disability: Ethics, Dehumanization, and a New Moral Community, First Edition.
Heather E. Keith and Kenneth D. Keith.

Figure 3.1 **Glenwood rail station where Mayo Buckner arrived with his mother in 1898. The station adjoins the grounds of the facility that was known as the Asylum for Feeble-Minded Children of the State of Iowa. An early building is visible beyond the trees to the right of the station.**
Source: Photo K. D. Keith

(2011) observed, some people's dream, and its absence can be a nightmare. Further, although intelligence may be, as some contend, "only a matter of appearances," it is also true that "appearances matter" (Goodey, 2011, p. 1).

By the late nineteenth century, Charles Darwin (1859) and his *On the Origin of Species* had become a force in development of the science of psychology. The similarities and differences in mental characteristics of humans and other species had become a point of interest for scientists who believed that humans and the human mind were evolved from the so-called lower species. Within psychology, one development arising from this evolutionary interest was the related study of variations among individual members of the same species—the perspective that became known as *individual differences.* Darwin's cousin, the British scientist Francis Galton, was the leading figure in establishment of this new psychological field of study.

Individual Differences

Although Galton receives credit for development of the study of individual differences, it was not a new idea. Several millennia earlier, the Chinese had used tests to measure verbal ability, literacy, and various work-related, applied, and abstract skills (Anastasi & Urbino, 1996)—perhaps the world's longest history of testing (Higgins, Lian, & Zheng, 2003). Nevertheless, it was Galton who established the field that we now know as individual differences. The product of a well-to-do British family, Galton had a wide-ranging curiosity about a variety of scientific topics, among them individual differences in weight, height, reaction times, strength, sensory capabilities, and fingerprints (resulting in a technique eventually used not only by Scotland Yard, the British law enforcement organization, but also by police around the world). But in the field of intellectual disability, it is Galton's interest in *intelligence* that we remember, along with his belief that intelligence was inherited (e.g., Galton, 1869).

The term "eugenics" (from the Greek for "good birth") was Galton's invention, and he was a lifelong believer in the proposition that the society would be better if it fostered the breeding of superior individuals (Hunt, 1994). Of course, the other side of the coin was that he also believed that people of (in his view) inferior intellect, if they continued to have children, should be seen as enemies of the state (Forrest, 1974)—a rather foreboding notion that foreshadowed the premium people would come to place on intelligence as an important attribute of humanity (e.g., Singer, 1994), later programs of segregation and sterilization of people with intellectual disability (e.g., Trent, 1994), and even the mass extermination of people with disabilities in the Nazi T4 program. Galton (1883) believed that more intelligent people should have more sensory acuity (vision, hearing, tactile sense) than those of lower intelligence, and thus be more alert and sensitive to their environment. He developed an anthropometric laboratory for measurement of the various sensory and physical characteristics that interested him, but his belief that such characteristics would be good indicators of intelligence was not supported by data, leaving to others the task of developing potentially useful measures of intelligence.

One of Galton's admirers was James McKeen Cattell, who had been the first American to complete a PhD in Wilhelm Wundt's famous psychological laboratory in Germany (Goodwin, 2008). Cattell went to England to work with Galton, and was so taken with Galton's ideas about improving humankind through selective breeding that he offered each of his children (seven of them) a $1000 prize if they would marry the children of college professors. Back in the US at the University of Pennsylvania, and committed to the development of measures of intelligence, Cattell continued a program of research involving the testing of various aspects of individual differences (e.g., memory span, strength of grip, reaction time to sound), eventually producing, in 1890, an article titled "Mental tests and measurements." This paper would be the first published use of the title phrase, and it proved a springboard for the mental testing movement (Hunt, 1994). It also led to a decade of further research, at Columbia University, where Cattell became head of the psychology department. There, each year Cattell collected data on a group of entering students, using his battery of tests in the hope of showing a relation between the test results and students' grades. However, in 1901 Cattell's graduate student Clark Wissler reported on analysis of the data, and to Cattell's surprise and disappointment, found no significant correlation between any of the individual measures and student academic ability (Goodwin, 2008).

Despite the failure of Cattell's early attempt at intelligence testing, his experience did not mark the end for either mental testing or the study of individual differences. Galton went on to devise other important measures of individual differences and became the first scientist to evaluate twins as a means to examine the effects of environment and heredity. Cattell, too, continued to contribute to the testing movement, establishing the Psychological Corporation, a test and measurement company that continues today as PsychCorp. Perhaps most importantly, the role of mental testing became dominant in American psychology, and intelligence testing was the vehicle via which Galton's notions about heredity became influential in education and the public realm (Hunt, 1994).

Intelligence Testing: The Measurement of Mind

Late in the nineteenth century primary education became compulsory in France, and the school system found itself in need of a way to identify students who required remedial education (Greenwood, 2009). French psychologist Alfred Binet, working with his colleague Theodore Simon, served on a Paris commission to develop tests that could identify children believed to be unable, due to lack of mental capability, to succeed with standard educational procedures; in other words, their task was to find a way to test children for placement in special education (Cianciolo & Sternberg, 2004). Binet had a somewhat checkered intellectual background, including a history of unsuccessful arguments that intelligence levels could be ascertained from measurements of skull and brain size. But he was aware of Galton's research, and had used his own children as subjects for trials of some of Galton's tests; except for truly cognitive tasks (those involving thought, memory, and language), the children performed very much like adults. This finding led Binet to the conclusion that a real assessment of intellectual ability would depend upon tests of higher mental processes.

Binet's (1903) early tests included such tasks as sentence completion, association, and moral judgment, originally organized in a scale of 30 items arranged in order of difficulty. Binet believed that intelligence involved such skills as reasoning and judgment, and had earlier (Binet & Henri, 1895) criticized the oversimplification of intelligence tests, urging inclusion of various types of judgment, including moral sensibility. Through a series of studies comparing normally developing children and children with intellectual impairments, Binet and Simon devised tests that could differentiate between the two groups. After administering this scale to school children over a period of about three years, Binet and Simon revised the scale to reflect the age-level abilities of the students; thus an average child would score at his or her age level (e.g., a 10-year-old would score at age 10; Greenwood, 2009). This approach, Binet reasoned, would allow educators to know whether a child was completing work at age level or was lagging behind—and how far behind (or ahead) a child might be. Although the term "mental age" has often been associated with Binet, Binet and Simon actually used "mental level" to designate the achievement of a child on their test. It was William Stern (1912) who used the idea of mental age, in the equation Mental Quotient = Mental Age/Chronological Age × 100, to calculate the score that was soon renamed and became the familiar IQ. Thus, a four-year-old performing at the four-year level would have an IQ of 100; a four-year-old performing at the three-year level would have an IQ of 75, and so forth. American psychologist Lewis Terman (1916) of Stanford University then used the IQ as a test score in the translation of the Binet–Simon test that became widely known as the Stanford–Binet Intelligence Scales. As early as 1913 Terman described his test development work in the *Journal of Psycho-Asthenics*, a journal "Devoted to the care, training and treatment of the feeble-minded and epileptic" (Terman, 1913a, b). Thus, it seems clear that, in his earliest work, Terman, as well as Binet and Simon, was considering the implications of his work for intellectual disability.

In its various revisions, the Stanford–Binet test has remained in print and in common use over the past century. Yet from the very beginning, Binet and Simon were cautious in their belief that their scale reflected nothing more than a potentially useful way to identify students who needed remedial education—just as Ayres (1909), in coining the term "retarded" intended it to refer simply to children whose progress in school was slow. For Binet, a low score merely meant that the child might require more teaching. None of these researchers apparently meant to ascribe to children a fixed level of intelligence that would have the power of the IQ scores that today can be so prominent in the lives of people with intellectual disability. The work of Henry Goddard, however, was a different story.

The Mismeasure of Men, Women, and Children

Henry H. Goddard was among the psychologists who were disappointed with Cattell's approach to testing in the US. Goddard created a laboratory in New Jersey at the Vineland Training School for the Feeble-Minded, and in 1908 visited similar institutions in Europe. While there he learned of the Binet–Simon test and took it back to America, where he translated and published it as the Binet–Simon Measuring Scale for Intelligence. He subscribed to Binet's age-level approach, and believed the Binet–Simon test could be useful for identification and classification of people with intellectual disability. He further sought to clarify the classification scheme, which at the time included the terms "idiot" and "imbecile." Goddard contended that idiot should denote a person with a mental age of 1 or 2, and that imbecile should be reserved for those with mental ages of 3 to 7. He then proposed the term "moron" as a label for people with mental ages between 8 and 12. Thus, the link between labels, mental age, and IQ had been established. Goddard also used his tests to support the claim that intellectual disability was a good deal more common than previously estimated (Hothersall, 1984).

For Goddard, however, classification and labeling were not enough. He eventually made a name for himself not only through the use of intelligence testing, but also for its misuse and abuse. Goddard believed, along with Galton, that intelligence was tied to heredity, a theme he pursued to an extreme end in *The Kallikak Family: A Study in the Heredity of Feeblemindedness* (1912). At Vineland, Goddard had come to believe that the family members of "feeble-minded" people were often themselves feeble-minded (i.e., they had low IQs). He then began to study the family history of a Vineland resident, a young woman (Deborah Kallikak, age 22) whose mental age was 9. Like Mayo Buckner, Deborah Kallikak had come to the institution as a child, in part due to concerns that she did not get along well at school. Also like Buckner, she apparently had an interest in music—one of the existing pictures of her shows her in a band. One of Deborah's ancestors (her great-great-great grandfather) was Martin Kallikak, who gave rise to two family lines—one from his affair with a "feeble-minded tavern girl," and the other from his marriage to a Quaker woman from a "good family." The name Kallikak was, of course, a pseudonym comprising the Greek words *Kallos* (beauty) and *Kakos* (bad), to reflect the two lines of the Kallikak family (Plucker, 2003).

Goddard constructed elaborate genealogical diagrams showing the two families—the good and the bad—of Martin Kallikak, emphasizing that the family arising from the "feeble-minded tavern girl" had not only generations of feeble-minded members, but was also plagued with a variety of other social and behavioral problems (prostitution, alcoholism, epilepsy, illegitimacy), whereas the "respectable" branch of the family produced a long line of fine upstanding citizens. These disparities, according to Goddard, were attributable to genetic differences, including intelligence, and he labeled the family members appearing on the numerous family trees with such descriptors as "normal," "feeble-minded," "sexually immoral," and "alcoholic" (Beirne-Smith et al., 1994; Plucker, 2003; Trent, 1994). Goddard supported his conclusions with photographs of members of the Kallikak families (many of them pictures of Deborah)—photographs that others have interpreted as eugenic propaganda (Elks, 2005) or, worse, as fraud (Gould, 1981). The photographs had been selected and retouched in ways, according to Goddard's critics, that enhanced the presumed feeble-minded appearance of the "bad" Kallikaks and the desirable characteristics of the appearance and lives of the "good" Kallikaks.

Goddard termed his work a "natural experiment," despite the lack of control for a variety of environmental and social variables, and his genetic assumptions, by today's standards, were seriously flawed (Greenwood, 2009). And his assumptions about the immutability of intellectual disability stood in stark contrast to earlier views, such as those of S. G. Howe (1851), who had argued, in describing the success of a Massachusetts training program, that "One of the difficulties . . . in the way is the popular error that idiocy is a positive and incurable malady" (p. 101). However, despite the questionable nature of Goddard's research and his portrayals of it, it became widely known and cited (Davies, 1930), Deborah Kallikak became "The World's Best Known Moron" (Reeves, 1938, p. 199), and the work gave support to the eugenics movement. Like Galton, Goddard believed feeble-mindedness could be eliminated if idiots, imbeciles, and morons could be identified, segregated from society, and prevented from having children (Goodwin, 2008). By the 1930s a majority of American states had enacted laws providing for eugenic sterilization of "defective" people (Hunt, 1994). The assumption of low intelligence brought with it the potential for devastating life changes at the hands of those who had a vision of what "desirable" people should be like.

Goddard did not limit his interest in genetic aspects of intellectual disability to the residents of institutions and their families. By the end of the nineteenth century the number of immigrants entering the US had become massive, and many people believed these new immigrants were of lower quality than the earlier generations who had arrived on American shores. Although most of these immigrants were granted admission to the country in a fairly routine way, some received evaluations, and a small percentage were denied admission (Schlereth, 1991). Further, the Congress had, by law, ordered officials to bar idiots and lunatics (Reed, 1913); nevertheless, officials believed that too many such people were escaping notice and entering the country. In response to a government request for assistance in screening immigrants at New York's Ellis Island, and using the Binet–Simon test, Goddard and his assistants began selecting and testing people whose appearance they thought indicated "mental defectiveness" (Hunt, 1994). The result was a dramatic increase in the number of ostensibly feeble-minded people deported in the years 1913 and 1914, to such an extent that nearly 80 percent of Russians, Italians, Jews, and Hungarians received the feeble-minded label (Hunt, 1994). These people may well have been, in the words of poet Emma Lazarus, "tired, . . . poor, . . . huddled masses" (Lazarus & Lazarus, 1888, p. 203), but it seems impossible that four of five of them were feeble-minded. Goddard (1913), however, approached the Ellis Island task with unbridled zeal. He reported the case of a young man whom Goddard suspected was defective. After the young man achieved a very low score on the Binet test, his interpreter reported that, upon his own arrival in the country, he would not have been able to do as well. Goddard, not to be deterred from his beliefs about intellectually deficient immigrants, reported that "We convinced him the boy was defective" (p. 105).

In his zeal to show the utility of the Binet–Simon test, and given his belief that appearances (as in the Kallikak photographs) could indicate limited intelligence, Goddard's claim that he could identify mentally defective people with 90 percent accuracy far exceeded the quality of his methods and data. In fact, by the methodological standards of modern cross-cultural psychology, Goddard's efforts to administer, through interpreters, a linguistically and culturally unfamiliar instrument, would be seen as totally unacceptable. And, although in 1917 he wrote that "the intelligence of the average 'third class' immigrant is low, perhaps of moron grade," (p. 243), by 1928 he had significantly changed his tune, allowing that most morons, with proper education, would not require institutionalization, but could instead live in normal society.

Nevertheless, the die had been cast. Following Goddard's work at Ellis Island the US, in the 1920s, adopted even stricter immigration laws, and the stage was set for the widespread use of intelligence testing. Terman improved the translation of the Simon–Binet scale, and substantially revised it while developing the Stanford–Binet Intelligence Test. This test launched the era of intelligence testing (in the first two and a half years after Terman introduced the Stanford–Binet, more than four million American children took intelligence tests), and became the model for other individual intellectual assessments. For example, the widely used Wechsler test series (e.g., Wechsler Preschool and Primary Scale of Intelligence; Wechsler Intelligence Scale for Children; and Wechsler Adult Intelligence Scale), derived from the work of psychologist David Wechsler (1939, 1955), became the most widely used of the intelligence tests and they remain popular in the twenty-first century.

Intelligence Testing on a Mass Scale

Individual intelligence tests required a trained psychologist to administer them, they took a long time to complete, and they could of course be administered to only one person at a time. But in 1917, facing entry into World War I, the US government needed a way to quickly classify, based on abilities, large numbers of soldiers. Robert Yerkes, a member of the psychology faculty at Harvard University and president of the American Psychological Association (APA), quickly responded. Yerkes formed a special APA committee to aid creation of the necessary psychological tools. With the help of a working group including Terman and Goddard, Yerkes' team set out to develop a group testing program that would meet the needs of the Army (Greenwood, 2009). About 40 psychologists worked on the project, and within a period of only about two months they had developed two versions of a test they could administer to large groups of people. Their aims included not only classification of individuals according to abilities, and selection of the most able for specialized positions, but also to identify and eliminate those who were not mentally competent—the feeble-minded.

The two versions of the Army test were the Army Alpha, a written test, and the Army Beta, a pictorial test for Army inductees (about 40 percent) who were illiterate. The former version used written instructions and items testing such areas as basic reasoning and cultural knowledge, and the latter employed pictorial and pantomimed instructions to guide test takers through tests of perceptual speed, reasoning, and memory. Both tests produced a single intelligence score for each examinee (Cianciolo & Sternberg, 2004), and by the end of the war in 1918 a band of 300 psychologists had administered the exams to more than 1.7 million individuals (Hunt, 1994). Although individuals taking the Army Alpha exam received instructions including the statement that "We are not looking for crazy people" (Yoakum & Yerkes, 1920, p. 53; Army Beta examinees were simply told to follow instructions), estimates have indicated that about 8000 examinees were discharged and deemed unfit, and a larger number (perhaps 10,000) with low intelligence levels received assignment to simple labor roles (Garrett, 1951; Gould, 1981). Goddard argued that 45 percent of all the military recruits had mental ages below 13 years which meant, by Goddard's calculation, that the same percentage of the American population would have been classified as morons (Smith & Lazaroff, 2006). Ironically, however, despite these statistics the Alpha and Beta tests probably had relatively little overall effect on military selection decisions during World War I (Smith & Lazaroff, 2006), with the Army accepting "feeble-minded" recruits with the intelligence of the average eight-year-old child (Bliss, 1919).

Nevertheless, if the Stanford–Binet had launched the testing movement, the Army Alpha provided its fuel, as intelligence testing quickly became a staple in schools, colleges and universities, industry, and the military. It was the era that gave birth to the Scholastic Aptitude Test (now known simply as the SAT). But the situation was not all rosy for the testing advocates. For example, the claims that such tests as the Stanford–Binet and the Army Alpha measured innate mental ability came under fire. For example, in a series of *New Republic* articles titled "The mental age of Americans," Walter Lippmann (1922a, b, c, d, e, f), a famous newspaper columnist of the time, questioned whether the Army tests really measured intelligence and argued that they could not possibly measure hereditary ability. Other critics protested that the tests would label children as inferior, resulting in prejudice against the underprivileged and advantage for powerful people (Block & Dworkin, 1976). It was difficult to argue otherwise in the face of such authorities as Terman (1916), who said that:

> High-grade or borderline deficiency... is very, very common among Spanish-Indian and Mexican families of the Southwest and also among negroes. Their dullness seems to be racial, or at least inherent in the family stocks from which they come (pp. 91–92).

As Gould (1981) argued, the Army tests (as well as others like the Stanford–Binet) asked for responses that were alien to individuals from non-American cultures, and inevitably disadvantaged those individuals, not through lack of intelligence, but simply by virtue of lack of opportunity for test-related cultural experience.

Intelligence and Human Nature

Goodey (2011) posited two ways of classifying the human species: one objective and the other subjective (a distinction we will see again later, in Chapters Seven and Eight). The objective classification derives from natural history and recognition of the place of humans on the scale of nature. The subjective relates to the criteria by which we determine who is human. The criteria attached to the latter, according to Goodey, include the capacity to make abstractions and to reason logically; one who cannot reason in this way is intellectually disabled, and in this context intelligence becomes a dominant trait. It follows then, that if reason is a necessary condition of humanity, it is easy to dehumanize the person who lacks the ability to reason (Wolfensberger, 1975). Yet the intelligence most often appearing in Western research literature—the intelligence of Galton, Goddard, and Terman—is what Robert Sternberg (1996) called "inert intelligence." Inert intelligence, according to Sternberg, is the intelligence people show on IQ tests, the SAT, or other tests that may be correlated with grades in school or with other tests, but it is not representative of the full range of skills that allow individuals to lead successful lives. For example, research examining the correlation between cognitive test scores and job success has suggested that test scores account for only about 4 percent of the variance in job performance (Wigdor & Garner, 1982).

Sternberg (1986, 1996) has therefore advocated for an approach that he has called practical intelligence. Practical intelligence is the ability to adapt to, shape, and select environments in order to achieve a good fit between self and the surrounding context. John Dewey advocated a somewhat similar view, observing that a single test could not possibly be universally applicable to all one's contexts and goals, and that such concepts as superior and inferior ability were meaningful only in such specific contexts (Danforth, 2008). In the moving story of life with his son Walker, Ian Brown (2009) described the ongoing efforts of Walker and his family to find such a fit—a literal and metaphorical effort to select an environment to which Walker could adapt and which he could shape. Despite profound intellectual difficulties associated with a rare genetic disorder, Walker demonstrated the will and the ability to relate to his surroundings in a way that demanded a rethinking of the meaning of cognitive ability and exposed the poverty of the concept of inert intelligence. Robert Perske and Martha Perske (1980) observed that all individuals are developing—at different rates and in different ways, and that intelligence is a multi-faceted construct that does not lend itself to easy or simple definition.

David Myers (2010) suggested that one of the problems with intelligence, as we have so often construed it, lies in the error of reification. That is, if we treat IQ as if it were a real, concrete entity that objectively exists, it then may become a part of the person—something the person actually *has*, and something that we, consequently, seek in our exploration of human nature. William James (1950/1890) called this error in reasoning the "psychologist's fallacy," while Dewey (1988/1929) called it the "philosophic fallacy." In avoiding errors from both disciplines, it is important, Myers noted, to remember that IQ is nothing more than a score obtained on a particular test. This caution is especially important when considered in relation to the fact that all the conceptions of intelligence represented in the work we have reviewed so far in this chapter represent Western culture. Thus, while Western perspectives value speed of intellectual processing and skills related to academic performance, African cultures may value skills that support harmonious relations within the group (Ruzgis & Grigorenko, 1994), cooperativeness, obedience, and social responsibility (Serpell, 1974), and participation in family life (Super & Harkness, 1982) as important components of intelligence. Asian cultures may also value social components of intelligence (e.g., Azuma & Kashiwagi, 1987). Moreover, in Eastern cultures, intelligence may also include not only social skills and some familiar Western traits (comprehension, recognition, understanding), but also effort, determination, feelings, or opinions (Sternberg & Kaufman, 1998).

A key point here is that, although most cultures probably value some shared cognitive abilities, intelligence can be whatever skills a culture may identify as adaptive to life in its own particular circumstances (Sternberg & Kaufman, 1998)—that intelligence is to a significant extent socially constructed. There are also differing conceptions of intelligence *within* cultures, as evidenced by Gardner's (1983, 1999) theory of multiple intelligences, Sternberg's theories of successful intelligence (1996) and triarchic intelligence (1986), and the notion of emotional intelligence (Mayer & Salovey, 1993). An individual found deficient by traditional measures of cognitive ability may have strengths in musical or interpersonal intelligence (Gardner, 1983), may be able to successfully adapt to or shape environments (Sternberg, 1996), or may accurately perceive and express emotion (Mayer & Salovey, 1993). People who perform poorly on traditional classroom work or examinations may be quite successful in everyday tasks employing the same skills in more relevant ways (e.g., Carraher, Carraher, & Schliemann, 1985; Murtaugh, 1985)—a notion consistent with a Deweyan view of intelligence, which we will see in Chapter Six.

An essential message lies in Rapley's (2004) assertion that we must examine what people with intellectual disability actually do in their *lives*—not in the artificial context of evaluations or other circumstances removed from the reality of their day to day existence. It is unlikely that tests, no matter how sophisticated their psychometric properties, can capture the complexity of the everyday knowledge possessed by people (e.g., MacKay, 1974). Gardner (2012), in fact, has asserted that no two humans have precisely the same profile of intelligences; because they have different experiences, they will not have the same strengths, weaknesses, and interactions among the various forms of intelligence.

One might then ask, along with John Throne (1972), "Towards what end is the assessment of intelligence directed?" (p. 9). IQ scores, Throne argued, are extrapolations that are twice removed from real life; they are second-order theoretical values deriving from first-order values (raw test scores) and do not show behavior under average circumstances. Further, Throne asserted, standardized intelligence testing is invalid for individuals whose life experience differs from that of the standardization sample. Rather than regarding the individual as exceptional, he proposed exceptionalizing the environment as a step toward producing more "intelligent" behavior. Such an approach, according to Throne, would render standardized test scores superfluous; a positive (or negative) outcome of environmental intervention would be evident in the behavior and adjustment of the person, and would not require the traditional validation of teaching by reference to testing.

The perspective advocated by Throne gives further support to the notion that IQ is not an inherent characteristic of the person, but is simply a score obtained at a point in time and in a particular circumstance. The reality of this view was suggested in an early report by Skeels and Dye (1939), who found dramatic increases in IQ scores among institutionalized children with intellectual disability after they had been "adopted" by women (themselves residents of the institution) who provided love and attention—serving as virtual mothers to the children. However, the meaningfulness of the IQ scores was of much less importance than the findings of a follow-up study a quarter century later. Skeels (1966) found that all the "treated" children were living in the community, having been generally successful in educational and vocational pursuits; on the other hand, the members of a control group had been much less successful, and nearly half still resided in institutions. The success of the original treatment group suggested that their initial IQs were, indeed, simply a score on a test, and not an enduring personal characteristic. In a later study, Keith and Ferdinand (1984) found that people living in community settings showed increases in intelligence measures that were significantly greater than those of individuals living in institutions (who sometimes actually decreased in IQ). In Chapter Six, we will explore the relationship between emotional attachment and moral development, as well.

However, as Goodey (2011) detailed, there are those in the mainstream and in professional establishments who may see behavior changes in the person with intellectual disability as mere mimicry—the individual may simply be *acting* intelligently. "The disabled person is not *really* interacting, reading, thinking, self-aware, ambitious, in love or expressing opinions, like everyone else, but merely copying surface behaviours he sees around him" (p. 65). This view, according to Goodey, treats intelligence like honor, and is the response of the in-group to protect its status against threat from the out-group. Intelligent, Goodey argued, means better, and is hence a value-laden construct; this is not to say it is wrong to recognize that some people are more or less capable than others in a variety of ways. However, he suggested, professionals have developed a monopoly on the definition of what counts as "intelligent" or "intellectual." Thus, a person who is not skilled at mathematics may be called intellectually disabled, while a person who lacks a sense of humor or is insensitive in dealing with others is not. And although, as we have noted, researchers have made efforts to expand the scope of the traits defining intelligence, this does not obviate the problem—What behaviors will count as emotional intelligence, or interpersonal intelligence? Who will decide?

Intelligence in Perspective

Measures of intelligence and their accompanying IQ scores have served to define people as ineducable (Race, 2002), incapable of reason (Rapley, 2004), and incurable (Blatt, 1987). In short, there is a long history of overvaluation of IQ, as a measure of intelligence, in assessing individual ability and prediction of potential (Menolascino, 1977). Intelligence as we have known it no doubt plays a role in the success of individuals in such contexts as school and job training. However, to equate intelligence with personal worth, or to use the constituent skills of intelligence as criteria for personhood, can lead to dehumanization, and the kind of social policies that characterized the era of eugenics—an era in which one state alone (California) had, by the beginning of 1928, sterilized nearly 6000 people with intellectual disability (Wehmeyer, 2003). The view that mental defects were hereditary led Van Wagenen (1914), in a committee report of the eugenics section of the American Breeders' Association, to say "These are the people of inferior blood, who are so interwoven in kinship with those still more defective that they are wholly unfitted to become the parents of useful and valuable citizens" (p. 187).

Intelligence is the construction of cultures and of people. Some of the people are professionals, the psychologists, educators, philosophers, and others who establish and use criteria for such constructs as intellectual disability. And some of the people are simply ordinary participants in the culture, people who see others as friends, neighbors, and classmates, or as enemies, threats, and dangers. Intelligence is a concept that, as Goodey (2011) said, can serve to define people as members of the in-group or the out-group. Too often, the result has been that individuals with intellectual disability are seen as the "other" (Foucault, 2006/1961) and subhuman or "animalized" (Carlson, 2010). Yet, as Blatt (1981) made clear, "Mental retardation is an invented disease, an untrue and unnecessary story about a large group of people" (p. 185)—a story that can have harmful, or even abusive consequences. For example, Blatt said, the role of the school psychologist should not be to try to find a reason to exclude a child or relegate the child

Figure 3.2 **Street sign at the modern-day Glenwood Resource Center. The street is named for Mayo Buckner, who in 1898, at the age of eight, became patient #822.**
Source: Photo K. D. Keith

to a special class; rather, it should be the psychologist's role to find a way to help the child succeed in the regular class, to make the story one the student would want to live up to. People with intellectual disability have problems, Blatt acknowledged, in such areas as mobility, mathematical skills, speech, and reading—the kinds of skills that might be reflected in measures of intelligence. But those problems, he argued, are surmountable. The more serious problems are those of moral attitudes, rights, and respect. And solutions to those problems are not likely to reside in test scores. In later chapters, we will consider alternative frameworks and practices that aim to celebrate the humanity and potential of people and their communities, regardless of perceived rationality. Mayo Buckner would have gained a great deal more from a different life story than from an IQ score that was too little, too late.

4

The Consequences of Reason
Moral Philosophy and Intelligence

Austria's Hartheim Castle was like a Nazi concentration camp that had no prisoners. There were no barracks, no crowded bunks, and no unsustainable work regime; but there were also no survivors. Hartheim's only purpose from 1939 to 1941 was to exterminate people with disabilities because they were not thought to be productive or genetically useful members of the new Aryan race.

Citizens were pressured to put disabled family members into institutions, their names were put on lists sent to Berlin, and those with a "plus" were eventually put on a bus to Hartheim or one of five other Nazi euthanasia centers that were part of the T4 program (named after the address of the Berlin office that oversaw it). Victims likely thought they were simply moving, so they brought their valued personal possessions with them. Instead, they were stripped of their possessions, herded through an examining room, and then crowded into a small gas chamber with a fake showerhead. Victims with gold teeth received marks on their shoulders so that the gold could be extracted in the morgue. "Interesting" cases were photographed. Usually, victims spent only a small part of a day at Hartheim before they were killed, and the ruthless efficiency with which masses of people were exterminated made its gas chamber the model for those in Hitler's major concentration camps. In the end, 30,000 people lost their lives at Hartheim (C. Dorner, Mag., personal interview, April 17, 2012).

It seems impossible that otherwise normal people, allegedly generous to friends and kind to neighbors, could put thousands of others on lists, drive them to a killing center, take away their possessions, mark them for their

Intellectual Disability: Ethics, Dehumanization, and a New Moral Community, First Edition.
Heather E. Keith and Kenneth D. Keith.

Figure 4.1 Hartheim Castle, Nazi euthanasia site where thousands of people with disabilities lost their lives.
Source: Photo H. E. Keith

gold teeth, turn on the gas, and later go out with their friends to the local pub or an outing in the countryside on the same bus that had carried their victims earlier in the day. Somehow, they must have forgotten the humanity of others, or perhaps their own. Hartheim's museum today invites visitors to ask questions about how otherwise sane and even gentle-seeming people accepted and perpetrated such monstrous actions against other humans. One answer amid the complex economic and political contingencies of the time is, perhaps, that people involved in this mass extermination failed to see their victims as human at all. The propaganda of eugenics, common not just in Nazi Germany, but also in the US and other developed countries at the time, as we saw in the previous chapter, spread a dehumanizing ideology suggesting that disabled people were anathema to a good society and dangerous to the future of the human race.

Philosophically, these ideas were not created in a vacuum. The Hartheim museum traces some of the roots of dehumanization through the history of science, noting that science is subject to racist, classist, and other divisive ideologies. It also suggests that a focus on worker productivity during the Industrial Revolution led people to value physical health and technological acumen as necessary to a good society. Conversely, people with disabilities were nothing more than burdens that would eventually cause human civilization to fail. We show in this chapter that ideas that cause people to be excluded from moral consideration have roots in our philosophical heritage, and that knowledge of this background is essential to developing more responsive and inclusive ethical theories and policies.

Philosophy and Intellectual Disability

In the history of philosophy, the issue of disability has largely been in the margins of ethical concern (Carlson, 2009). When it has been a central concern at all, intellectual or cognitive disability often has been treated in one of two ways: as a nightmarish glimpse of everything contrary to the light of reason and goodness, or as a marginal case to advance logical arguments or other moral concerns (such as animal rights). In response to the first concern, only a very few philosophers, such as Michel Foucault in his *History of Madness*, have explored cognitive difference as interesting and enlightening (see Carlson, 2009).

The concept of disability as a marginal case, however, seems to be increasingly popular, and we find this somewhat problematic. In marginal case studies, we identify some morally relevant attribute of one group (such as the ability to suffer) and show that because of similarity of that attribute to another group, both groups deserve similar treatment. For some ethicists, such as Peter Singer (1975), people with intellectual disabilities serve to advance the argument for the ethical treatment of nonhuman animals because both groups, for example, have the capacity for pain, but lack a certain level of rationality usually associated with humans (but not with nonhumans). It seems inhumane to use dramatic and tragic cases (such as whether it is morally acceptable to conduct medical testing on disabled people) merely to advance an argument about other populations, such as nonhuman animals, as is sometimes the case in contemporary ethical discussions. Further, marginal case studies seem to relegate discussion of disability to concepts such as death or intense suffering. As Wendell (2008) lamented, "at least 90% of philosophical articles" on the topic of disability "are concerned with two questions: Under what conditions is it morally permissible/right to kill/let die a disabled person and how potentially disabled does a fetus have to be before it is permissible/right to prevent its being born?" (p. 826). Though it is useful to discuss, sensitively, end-of-life decisions, most people's moral concerns are largely about how to live well, and this is no different for the topic of intellectual disability.

Even so, it is important to reflect on historical and contemporary philosophy, both to illuminate the problems with our approach to intellectual disability and ethics, and to develop theories and policies that are more humane and accurate in engaging a wider diversity of people. John Herman Randall (1976) wrote about the history of ideas as similar to ancient streets and buildings in Rome that have served countless generations of people, whether or not they understood the history. About the "persistence of the past into the present," he said:

> A ramble through the mind of the modern man would reveal the same juxtaposition of beliefs that have endured unchanged for centuries, with ideas gleaned from the morning paper, all put together in a structure with a shaky enough foundation and with many a makeshift to fill the gaps yet somehow strong enough to answer the demands made on it and to give shelter until it can be improved (p. 4).

In this chapter, we assess the foundation of our ideas with an aim toward improvement as we lay out some of the problems in our theoretical history that are reflected in contemporary views of intellectual disability. Later chapters will explore what we consider to be stronger approaches. In fact, we hope to show that the study of philosophy itself is better (and not nightmarish) when issues of disability are not marginalized. Stainton (2001b) suggested, concerning contemporary issues such as prenatal testing, euthanasia, genetic modification, treatment, and rights, that "for these debates to be resolved in such a way as to recognize the full equality and value of all humanity, including those with intellectual disability, a fundamental reorientation of dominant Western knowledge constructs is required" (p. 459).

Rational Value and the Birth of Philosophy

Though it is widely assumed in philosophy classrooms that Western culture has been dramatically shaped by the insights of ancient philosophy, it may not be as apparent to other readers. In investigating the roots of discrimination, however, we suggest that until we examine the ideas that have so influenced our view of reason, moral value, and the very construction of our definition of humanity, we will not fully understand implicit and explicit dehumanization of people with disabilities. Until we understand dehumanization, we cannot fully effect positive change.

Burton Blatt (1987) and others have noted that key to understanding the construction of moral value and personhood as connected to reason is understanding the view of human nature in ancient philosophy. Stainton (2001b) argued that:

> A core paradigm in the negative construction of intellectual disability in Western society is that human value is directly associated with human reason . . . and that . . . current debates in the field, such as those on consent and capacity, prenatal testing, the abortion of disabled fetuses, access to treatment, euthanasia, citizenship, and self-determination, all have at their heart this association between reason and value, and this association in turn has its intellectual roots in classical thought (p. 452).

Socrates, Plato, and Aristotle, the central figures of classical Greek philosophy, influenced medieval religious thinking, including that of Augustine and Aquinas, and those views of humanity are critical to our philosophical and cultural thinking today.

Although we do not know as much about Socrates's (469–399 BCE) view of knowledge, reason, and value (he did not write books, so we rely on Plato and others to report his philosophy), what we do know may be of some use in our exploration of other philosophers of his time and ours. Blatt (1987) noted that Socrates is influential as a founder of Western philosophy because of his commitment to humility and critical thinking. According to Plato's account of the trial of Socrates in the *Apology*, in arguing with politically powerful but corrupt Athenians, Socrates put his life on the line (and was eventually executed) to show that the key to attaining wisdom is to recognize your own ignorance. Speaking in the voice of Socrates about his encounter with vain politicians, Plato (1981/c. 399 BCE) wrote, "I am wiser than this man; it is likely that neither of us knows anything worthwhile, but he thinks he knows something when he does not, whereas when I do not know, neither do I think I know" (p. 27). Knowing your own ignorance allows you to open your mind to new insights, to hear and consider new arguments, and to respond to the drive to learn more. Socratic wisdom, according to Blatt, implies that knowledge results from imperfection, rather than perfection. If we assume that the mind is perfect, there is no reason to think or learn.

Perhaps intellectual humility, attention to our own imperfection, will allow us to avoid focusing too much on perfect reason as the defining quality making human life valuable.

However, it is also true that Socratic reasoning about knowledge implies a certain level of logical prowess. It is here that it becomes difficult to separate the ideas of Socrates from those of his most famous student, Plato (429–347 BCE), who had much more specific ideas about the pursuit of intellectual perfection as it relates to the value of a human being. As we will see, the ability to think logically and abstractly is integral to a definition of human perfection and, therefore, moral goodness.

Constructing a view of human nature that still influences our ideas today, Plato suggested that reason is essential to human perfection, including moral agency and worth. Stainton (2001b) referred to this as "scaling"—the idea for Plato that humans exist on a scale with God-like perfection at the top and subhuman nature at the bottom. There are clear categories in Plato's thinking of how one can exist at the top of this scale, and reasons to prefer this kind of existence over the subhuman, submoral category. Note that for Plato, this is not really a spectrum of perfection, reason, or moral goodness—the categories we will discuss are rather all or nothing. A prime example of this occurs in the way Plato constructs his perfect society in *Republic*. In Plato's (1950/c. 380 BCE) imaginary but perfectly ordered city-state, citizens are sorted and educated according to their natural gifts, and are assigned appropriate jobs (from farming and tool-making to the ruling class). In this class system, people could expect to be educated only according to their talents in accordance with their place in the intellectual hierarchy. To attempt to educate citizens outside of their natural gifts would likely be a waste of resources in a perfect society.

Evidence of Plato's argument toward categorical hierarchy based on reason can be found in several places. In Book IV of *Republic*, Plato outlined the tri-partite view of the soul in which reason, spirit, and desire are all necessary for human functioning. All three are important (the desiring part of the soul gives us things to wish to do and the spirited part motivates us to enact our goals), but the reasoning part of the soul governs the others and creates harmony and virtue. A discordant soul cannot be virtuous because desires cannot be controlled. Without reason, we cannot be moral; and without the capacity for morality, we are not fully human.

Plato's "divided line" in Book VI of *Republic* further shows the strict categorization of reason with its link to moral goodness and value. He asks us to imagine two spheres of understanding, divided by lines demarcating various parts of our perceptions and knowledge. At one extreme is pure conjecture—beliefs based on sense experience that may or may not be true. On the other side are ideas (*eidos* in Greek, sometimes translated as "forms") that correspond exactly to reality. This abstract thinking goes beyond even mathematical reasoning to thinking about things "in themselves," beyond sense experience to principles and the very blueprint of reality. As we see in other places, this level of abstraction becomes more than just the ability to use reason in a certain way.

In Plato's Allegory of the Cave (Book VII of *Republic*, 1950/c. 380 BCE), in which humanity is trapped underground and only able to see shadows on a cave wall as (mistakenly) perceived reality, the person who can escape the cave and see things as they really are is one who can see reality beyond the divided line—who can reason abstractly and see forms rather than just shadows. This is not just about knowledge; the sun is the metaphor for the "form" of the "good." There can be no ultimate goodness (value, moral worth, or moral reasoning) for anyone incapable of seeing the light.

Writ large, those with high-functioning reasoning and an enlightened soul have political power over others in order to maintain a harmonious society, and it is questionable whether those with less advanced reasoning capabilities have moral worth as humans at all. In his *Phaedrus*, Plato (1995/c. 360 BCE) wrote "But a soul that never saw the truth cannot take a human shape, since a human being must understand speech in terms of general forms, proceeding to bring many perceptions together in a reasoned unity" (p. 36).

Perhaps Plato's own example best illustrates the political and metaphysical hierarchy created by his view of reason. In any political system, there are questions of authority and moral community—who makes and maintains the policies, and who benefits from them. In Plato's ideal justice system in *Republic* (1950/c. 380 BCE), a first class of guardians (the people with high-functioning abstract reasoning skills, with a philosopher in the lead) governs and maintains laws, a second class of guardian soldiers assists the rulers, and other people necessary to the system (craftspeople, farmers, and the like), comprise a third class. Plato even created a "myth of the metals" to convince people of the fitness to rule of some people, and not others. Those in the highest class are said to have gold in their veins, their assistants have silver, and all other members of the community have bronze. This noble lie keeps people in their places by preventing them from believing they can be educated beyond their class or asking questions about the fitness to rule of those in power.

Stainton (2001b) noted that "Plato does take a somewhat sympathetic view towards the mad" (p. 456). Though it is not clear that Plato's views would affect the treatment of those with intellectual disability, he did admit to somewhat lesser responsibility for those who may be "virtually insane," and suggested that this could be a mitigating factor in determining punishment. About Plato's view of people "lacking a certain degree or type of intelligence," Stainton (2001b) observed "they are to be treated with a certain degree of leniency, but at the cost of their agency" (p. 456).

The point here is not that reason and critical thinking are not important or necessary elements of a just society (especially, we might say, in our political leaders); it is that, in Plato's view, there is a fairly strict definition of what reasonable thinking looks like, and the walls between categories of rational and irrational people seem rather impermeable. Reason, and therefore moral agency and community, are matters of natural gifts or talents. To Plato, those lowest on the chain of being have more in common with nonhuman animals than with fellow humans when it comes to education or moral worth.

There are at least two distinct problems with this view. The most obvious is that to be a functioning member of society (including moral community, both as an agent and as a beneficiary), one must be part of a higher-reasoning category of humanity. Although contemporary moral theory may be able to overcome this view simply through egalitarian measures, the second problem is perhaps more insidious. This is the view of reason and intelligence as innate and fixed, which remains with us today in certain types of intelligence testing and views of moral engagement that suggest that moral agency requires a strict capacity for logical thinking. In Chapter Three we saw some of the limitations of this "inert" view of intelligence.

Plato's student Aristotle (384–322 BCE) was not subtle in his view of reason as a necessary component of a good life. In fact, he famously proclaimed in his *Politics* (1988/c. 350 BCE) "As to the exposure and rearing of children, let there be a law that no deformed child shall live" (p. 182). Because this follows Aristotle's admonition against pregnant women exercising intellectually (lest they harm their unborn children), we might assume that Aristotle was particularly worried about the development of rationality. Though Aristotle's support for infanticide would seem horrifying to most people today, making it easy to vilify him, whether to throw out Aristotle's virtue approach to ethics is rather complicated as it relates to intellectual disability. In some sense, the virtue approach may be quite useful when compared with moral theories that rest more explicitly with a strict sense of reason, and we will explore this kind of approach later. However, as a product of his time and training, Aristotle still maintained that the rational part of the brain was ultimately responsible for moral engagement and is essential to human personhood. Without reason, there can be no humanity and no moral community.

Famous for laying the foundation of what we today call virtue ethics, Aristotle viewed *eudaimonia*, human flourishing and well-being, as the ultimate goal of moral behavior. While it is dependent to some extent on good fortune, a rich quality of life in Aristotelian terms comes primarily from rigorous moral effort; a virtuous person may have bad luck in life and still be able to flourish, but a vicious person has little chance of happiness. In the *Nicomachean Ethics*, Aristotle (1962/c. 325 BCE) explored how habits of our behavior in moral situations lead to the kind of character we will develop over time. Whether we have good or bad character determines quality of life as it results in extrinsic concerns such as how others will treat us, the kinds of friends we will have, and how well we will do professionally, as well as the intrinsic value of simply attaining a moral high ground. Habitually attempting a virtuous path in our moral dealings with others leads to generally virtuous character, which leads to even more potential for virtuous action, which in turn ideally leads to a holistic sense of well-being. It is, as psychologists today might proclaim, living well by doing good (Seligman, 2011).

The development of good character via the habits we practice is quite straightforward, according to Aristotle. It is all about finding the mean between extremes, which he outlines in Book Two of his *Nicomachean Ethics*. For example, one of the virtues Aristotle (1962/c. 325 BCE) extols is temperance. Although we obviously want to avoid starvation, Aristotle also warned against the extreme of gluttony. Likewise, in the case of courage, we attempt to reach some middle ground between cowardice and recklessness. In the case of many of Aristotle's examples of virtues, there is a clear connection between personal moral behavior, consequences for others (such as in the case of generosity), the development of a reasonable and good city-state, and even physical health. What connects the practice of habits with the development of moral character is *phronesis*, or practical wisdom, and it is with the concepts of practical and theoretical wisdom that Aristotle ties moral habituation to intelligence.

This connection between rationality and moral goodness is twofold. First, in Book Ten of the *Ethics*, Aristotle noted that the most *eudaimonic* life is that of intellectual contemplation. *Nous*, rational understanding, is the proper end goal of practical wisdom, and supersedes it in value (Stainton, 2001b). Without the contemplative life, human existence is not fully actualized. Second, a certain amount of rational intelligence is necessary to the process of assessing and reasoning about the good in the practice of *phronesis*. As Aristotle noted in Book Six, thinking about how one action achieves a particular goal is part of the deliberative process, but more important is to deliberate more evaluatively and generally "in an unqualified sense" (p. 163), about how our habits and character help us to actualize *eudaimonia*. Without this higher level of reasoning, a person can achieve only practical ends but is not fully acting in accordance with practical wisdom, and is not fully human. Stainton (2001b) argued that "the implication here is that the person without sufficient intellectual capacity cannot become truly good" (p. 457).

Aristotle then, like Plato, established a scale of beings that puts the gods at the top (*eudaimonia* is a reference to god-like goodness), with rational humans next and nonhuman animals further down the line. Humans who are not, due to birth or disease, able to fully actualize a *eudaimonic* life through *phronesis* and *nous* fall somewhere closer to nonhuman animals and certainly outside the range of moral engagement (and apparently outside the range of moral concern, as evidenced by Aristotle's remarks about infanticide). Aristotle (1962/c. 325 BCE) very specifically developed his own scale among humans, with the *theios* (a person of superhuman, god-like goodness) at the top, and the *theriodes* (a person of subhuman depravity, outside the bounds of humanity) at the bottom.

As offensive as Aristotle's political views about intellectual disability (as well as women, children, slaves, and foreigners) may be, many elements of his ethical theory actually could be of some use to the development of theories of moral engagement that are more inclusive. Contemporary virtue theory, pragmatist ethics, and feminist care ethics, all of which we will explore further, have in common with Aristotle concepts such as habit, character, and friendship. With Plato, Aristotle believed that education and practice are the keys to moral personhood, and that a good society supports its citizens (albeit unequally in the case of the Greeks) in striving to lead fulfilling and moral lives.

Aristotle also focused on contextual moral thinking—learning to read situations and to figure out how to respond is not necessarily a matter of adherence to logical principles, but develops as a result of practice and, especially, in learning from the experience of others. For this reason, Aristotle prioritized friendship, devoting an entire book of his *Ethics* to it, as central to the good life and the development of practical wisdom. Friends are important to our emotional well-being, help us to prosper and grow, and give us the opportunity to practice our moral habits, such as generosity. Good friends also model good moral behavior and help us to "avoid error" (1962/c. 325 BCE, p. 215). Without good relationships with others, we would have neither the motivation, nor the opportunity, to grow morally.

If Aristotle's moral theory were only about developing habits, through education and practice within strong relationships with others, toward good character and easier decision making and leading to the end goal of human flourishing, it would seemingly be expansive enough to include all of humanity in the moral community. It closely parallels many views that prioritize education for everyone (e.g., Blatt, 1987); it recognizes the relevance of relationships in habituating moral engagement, and the core values of Aristotle's view do not exclude people from moral education and community on the basis of a strict sense of intelligence. In fact, these general views have influenced heavily more naturalistic views of ethics in the twentieth and twenty-first centuries, such as pragmatism and the ethics of care, which are clear alternatives to ethical theories based on reason alone.

Aristotle, however, was a product of his time, and his views of human nature and morality are difficult to reconcile with the more inclusive elements of his theory. Though philosophers might agree on the merits of Aristotle's contemplative life, his claim that human goodness is tied to rationality contributes to a chain of being that has intelligence closest to the divine—a worldview that has heavily influenced Western thought. Perhaps even the word "retarded," now in disuse by theoreticians and practitioners though still in use among the public, carries with it an Aristotelian teleology—rationality is the norm of completeness and to be retarded is to be held back from actualizing this norm.

Varying categories of being were constructed with a more explicitly religious orientation in the work of medieval thinkers such as Augustine (354–430 CE), who was heavily influenced by Platonism via Plotinus. With God at the top and the stuff of the earth at the bottom, humans are the beings closest to God. Whereas some theologians argue for a more egalitarian view of God's creation, Augustine, and Aquinas after him, suggested a worldview in which intelligence is the attribute of being that most mimics the divine. Created in God's image, not in physical form but in wisdom, humans are most divine in their intelligence. In his *Confessions*, Augustine argued that the very creation itself is "in wisdom" as God speaks the world into rational existence through eternal language (1993/c. 398 CE, p. 217). Our ability to understand and speak the human form of rational language is essential to achieving an appropriately high level on the scale. Though Augustine claimed a certain amount of faith and emotion on his own journey to God, only the wise can understand creation:

> Let him who can hear Thy voice speaking within him; I, relying upon The inspired word, shall cry aloud: *How great are Thy works, O Lord! Thou hast made all things in wisdom.* Wisdom is "the Beginning": and it is in that Beginning that You made heaven and earth (1993/c. 398, p. 217).

Some may argue that religion (or even philosophy) has little import to the scientific study or ensuing practices concerning disability. However, religious beliefs have heavily influenced our cultural conceptions of human nature, including the prioritization of rationality and even the condemnation, as we saw in Luther, of those who lack it. Even if theologians like Augustine never explicitly discussed intellectual disability, the way we conceptualize humanity in philosophy and religion affects even our most scientific study. As Blatt (1987) said, science "follows rather than leads to the dominant beliefs of an age" (p. 10).

Reason and Ethics in the Modern Era

What philosophers call "modern philosophy" (roughly the seventeenth and eighteenth centuries) shares its popular description, the Enlightenment, with Plato's metaphor of wisdom as light and the sun as the form of the good. Attempting a scientific study of human nature in which the very method assumes rational thought as the highest human end, philosophers such as Descartes, Locke, and Kant developed arguments equating the enlightenment of rational thinking with moral goodness.

As we will see in Chapter Five, while René Descartes (1596–1650) did not write about disability or ethics per se, his philosophy of mind/body dualism has heavily influenced a concept of personhood that prioritizes rationality over other human attributes, contributing to later views of people with intellectual disability as more embodied, and thus animalistic. Moving away from religious justification of truth, Descartes sought certainty in his own logical reasoning, a style of philosophy that came to be known as rationalism. Famously proclaiming in his *Discourse on Method* (1952/1637) "I think therefore I am" (p. 24), Descartes equated existence with rational thought. He used this concept in his *Meditations* (1952/1641) to show that the parts of our existence (such as the body) that cannot be proven through rational thought are, at most, mechanical elements controlled by mind. Engaging in an experiment of radical skepticism, Descartes tried to determine the basic foundation of true belief by doubting all things. The very act of doubting led him to believe that something, mind, must exist to doubt, but that everything else was to be treated with further suspicion. Without the rational thought of mind, the body is merely the stuff of existence—a thing. Although not everyone reads Descartes these days, his body/mind dualism, combined with Western religious views of body/soul dualism, permeates our culture and contributes to a view of mind, or rationality, that surpasses every other part of human experience. Without this, we can be little more than nonhuman animals. There are obvious ethical consequences of this view—one cannot be moral without the control of mind over body.

Writing more explicitly about ethics and justice, social contract theorists such as Thomas Hobbes (1588–1679) and John Locke (1632–1704) also relied on rationality for moral experience. The idea of the social contract is that we enter into civic systems with the agreement that cooperation will help us to meet our ends and protect our interests better than would hostile competition. As Hobbes (1973/1660) famously suggested, without such an agreement we would be in a constant state of war and our lives would be "solitary, poore, nasty, brutish, and short" (p. 65). In the social contract, individuals associate with each other, writing agreements (such as constitutions) that ensure a certain level of justice for the stakeholders. Though we will argue in later chapters that social contract theory of the Hobbesian variety may have been mistaken about some aspects of human psychology, the social contract does seem to expand the reach of justice to whole societies.

However, mistaken views of psychology and the dynamics of most social contract construction may lead to the exclusion of some people from both the development and protection of contracts. In *Frontiers of Justice*, Martha Nussbaum (2006) argued that most social contract theory presents a problem in applying justice to people with disabilities (and, at times, other historically oppressed groups). In the case of Hobbes and Locke, though people are apparently social enough to wish to join together under a contract, the primary reason is to preserve one's own property and to ensure mutual advantage. This implies that individuals have rational interests and enough power to have property or social goods worth protecting.

Further, to be involved in the development of a system of justice, such as a social contract, philosophers have widely assumed that people have a certain level of intelligence. In John Rawls' (1999/1971) contemporary and highly influential version of social contract theory, *A Theory of Justice*, it is apparent that those in the position of developing a justice system and choosing leaders are of "normal" intelligence and will act on behalf of others like them. To go beyond mutual advantage for oneself and others like oneself would mean that we have to hope those who construct and maintain our justice system are intellectually astute, but also charitable. In any case, Nussbaum (2006) stated that the traditional idea of the social contract, with its roots in modern philosophy, excludes people with intellectual disability from genuine moral engagement. She wrote, "When we discuss mental disability, we will see that the equation of citizen status with (prudential and moral) rationality is a hurdle that even the best contemporary theories cannot surmount, without losing their formative link to the social contract tradition" (p. 54). We will explore Nussbaum's interesting alternative, the "capabilities" approach, in Chapter Six.

Bridging Enlightenment thinking with contemporary philosophy, Immanuel Kant (1724–1804) is perhaps the most likely philosopher to be read by undergraduate ethics students, but is also one of the most problematic figures in terms of equating moral engagement with purely rational thinking. For Kant, the key to moral engagement and the fullest expression of one's humanity is autonomy facilitated by rationality. One of Kant's most important contributions to moral theory was his movement away from the "heteronomy" (imposed by others) of receiving one's moral code from religious institutions. Instead, Kant (1983/1785) argued that we need an "autonomous" system of ethics that capitalizes on our ability to think logically about our intentions and actions. To avoid being slaves to our culture, beliefs (e.g., from parents, religion), emotions, or other seemingly subjective sources of morality, Kant argued that we need a more objective approach to ethics—one upon which all reasonable people would agree. Kant's now famous "categorical imperative" asks us to consider the universality of our behavior before we act. Using reason to give the moral law to ourselves, Kant suggested that we should never act unless we can "will that my maxim should become a universal law" (p. 14). For example, if we consider breaking a promise, we should ask ourselves whether it would be reasonable for this behavior to be a universal law. Reason tells us that this would be illogical; after all, if people broke promises for any reason, the very act of promising would break down—no one would accept a promise in a world where promises were systematically broken, and therefore even a false promise would not work. The categorical imperative is not about empathy or sympathy, caring for others, or thinking about possible consequences of our actions (as we will see later in utilitarianism); the categorical imperative is an exercise in logic. As beautiful a work of logic as it may be, Kant made it clear that one is incapable of acting morally without the ability to think in terms of logical argument—to use reason. Any other motivation for behavior, such as emotion, is not even on the moral spectrum for Kant (1983/1785):

> there are many persons who are so sympathetically constituted that, without any further motive of vanity or self-interest, they find an inner pleasure in spreading joy around them and can rejoice in the satisfaction of others as their own work. But I maintain that in such a case an action of this kind, however dutiful and amiable it may be, has nevertheless no true moral worth (p. 11).

Only the rational nature of (most) humans, for Kant, guarantees autonomy and universality and thus becomes the moral end we ought to protect. In Kant's practical imperative (to treat all of humanity as an end in itself), one might wonder whether humanity includes all humans, or only those capable of the logic of the categorical imperative. Peter Singer (2010) noted that "Kant's argument for why human beings are ends-in-themselves is that they are autonomous beings, which, in terms of Kantian philosophy, means that they are capable of reasoning" (p. 337). The rational conclusion of this, Singer argued, is that:

> If we really take his argument seriously it means that human beings who are not self-conscious—because perhaps they are so profoundly mentally retarded that they lack self-consciousness or self-awareness—are also merely means to an end, that end being autonomous or self-conscious beings (p. 337).

In this case, there would be no moral prohibition against using people with serious disabilities for activities such as medical testing that would benefit other, more rational and autonomous, humans.

Although Kant most clearly presents the case for making universal human rationality a necessary condition for morality, this view also can be found in many of the most prominent moral philosophies since Kant. Though ethicists tend to consider it the polar opposite of Kant's theory of morality, and it is to some extent more inclusive of diverse intelligences, John Stuart Mill's (1806–1873) utilitarianism and its followers (such as Singer) also prioritize abstract reasoning for the calculation of the good when weighing alternative actions.

The moral philosophy of both Kant and Mill is grounded in the ability to rationally evaluate the effects of our actions. While Kant's theory asks us to review our intentions and their logical consequences, Mill's utilitarianism suggests that we instrumentally use reason to consider the potential practical consequences of our actions. Mill (2002/1861), perhaps the most famous utilitarian philosopher, approached moral questions from the "greatest happiness principle," which requires that we reflect on whether an action promotes the greatest good for the greatest number of people. Using reason, a moral agent attempts to calculate how her actions may affect herself and others, and adjusts them in order to bring about greater (and long term) pleasure and to minimize suffering. Jeremy Bentham (1748–1832), founder of British utilitarianism, argued that though we use reason to calculate the good, the primary question we should ask is whether a being is capable not of thinking, but of suffering (1798). If an individual (or species, as later utilitarians have argued) is capable of suffering, then he or she ought to be part of our moral consideration. Although this view has the capacity for extraordinary and heroic moral actions (such as stories of Holocaust concentration camp prisoners giving their lives for others who had families or seemingly other greater reasons to live; Frankl, 1959), offers a moral guide for many everyday activities, and provides something of a democratic model of moral thinking, it nevertheless excludes people who lack a traditional facility for rational, almost mathematical, thinking from full membership in a moral community. Though the ability to feel suffering may include a vast majority of human beings as subject to moral consideration, moral agency still rests on rationality. This is because while happiness (or at least minimal suffering) is the end goal of utilitarianism, emotion and other modes of human experience are not part of the process.

Further, the concept of happiness itself is problematic as an end to moral engagement, simply because quality of life is malleable and multidimensional (see Chapter Eight). For example, contemporary utilitarian theorists, such as Singer (1994), apply a consequentialist approach based on quality of life to cases such as selective infanticide, stating that only a life with the potential for satisfying interests (rather than increased suffering) is worth protecting and prolonging (see Chapter Nine). Although promoting happiness and preventing suffering seem like reasonable and moral goals, the problem is that we cannot always agree on what constitutes quality of life. Also, even if we can agree on the general parameters of a good life, proponents of the social model of disability remind us that quality of life is affected not just by individual physiology or cognition, but is heavily influenced by the surrounding environment. Minimally, to account for disability (and intelligence) as at least in part socially constructed, utilitarianism would have to be modified so that one philosopher's version of a happy life doesn't negate the potential for well-being that might be actualized with more concern for an accessible physical and social environment. A strictly utilitarian approach, while it reveals certain facts and issues associated with moral questions (such as suggesting the greater good), also hides others, such as whether there are values and virtues beyond a calculated assessment of what will benefit the greatest number. In the contemporary medical landscape of limited resources and a diversity of interests to be fulfilled, utilitarian-influenced philosophies are abundant.

Current Movements in Ethics: Utilitarian Trends and Marginal Cases

The contemporary ethicist Peter Singer, famous for his work on animal rights, took a utilitarian approach to issues of disability, considering the interests of individuals, their families, and wider society. Throughout his work, Singer has discussed questions of abortion, euthanasia, and infanticide through various cases, from families who happily chose to give birth to babies with Down syndrome, to families who asked doctors to withhold lifesaving treatment from disabled infants, allowing them to die, to those who did not and wished they had (prompting Singer, with Kuhse, to suggest that infanticide might be morally correct in some very limited cases; 1985). In applying utilitarian principles to such cases, Singer has humanely sought to minimize suffering for the parents and children. Although utilitarianism does not necessarily strongly prioritize one individual perspective over another, Singer and other utilitarians have attempted to balance the interests of individuals and groups by arguing that in some cases it might be better to selectively abort a fetus, or even euthanize an infant, when it appears that quality of life for the family may be endangered, and Singer has cited many letters from parents of disabled babies wishing that hospitals had been more willing to withhold treatment from (or even euthanize) their children. In *Should the Baby Live*, Helga Kuhse and Singer (1985) wrote that when a "handicapped" child is capable of some enjoyment of life then prolonging life may be in her "best interest;" but "it may not, however, be in the best interests of the parents or siblings. Which should we choose: the family or the child?" (p. 153). Singer (2010) also noted that social services and resources are stretched by caring for people with disabilities, and that the costs (e.g., financial, physical, and emotional) of raising a child with disabilities are great even when parents are positively disposed to do so. However, "it will clearly be much harder to bear if the parents never wanted to bring up the child but were not able to make that choice" (p. 343).

Rejecting notions of human dignity or the sanctity of human life, Singer's focus in utilitarian ethics regarding disability has been on quality of life and what is in the best interest of the various stakeholders. For example, when debating the moral acceptability of infanticide in the case of disability, Singer (1993) noted that in some cases he assumes that parents do not wish to prolong the life of an infant (because of the emotional and physical burden of care). "Parents may, with good reason, regret that a disabled child was ever born. In that event the effect that the death of the child will have on its parents can be a reason for, rather than against killing it" (p. 183).

Critics of Singer have argued that there is a false dilemma between the interests of a child and the interests of family and society, and that Singer has made claims about quality of life without exploring either the real lives of disabled people or existing social structures that could be changed to increase the chance of a good life (e.g., Kittay, 2010). Although Singer was reasonably concerned about the probability of suffering when a child languishes in an institution, he does not seem to have considered the possibility that social views of disability and intelligence, as well as a lack of access to necessary resources for care, may have contributed to parental attitudes about possible quality of life with disabled children. Though theorists such as Singer are valorous in their concern for the well-being of humans, as well as nonhuman animals, utilitarianism does not necessarily cause one to inquire deeply about why someone is suffering, what the nature of that suffering may be, or whether, with social or political changes, the suffering is necessary. Within this theory, we do not unpack the social nature of suffering (or happiness) and ask whether what we perceive as moral evils are in fact socially constructed, and whether that socially constructed image is changeable in more morally positive ways. Further, Sophia Wong (2002) has questioned why authors often compare the abilities of people of extraordinary ability and good fortune with those of individuals with Down Syndrome whose disabilities are the most severe, when high-functioning individuals with Down Syndrome may well enjoy a quality of life similar to, or better than, that of many people without intellectual disability.

In this sense, a calculative approach to moral situations asks us to consider primarily immediate interests of individuals, without examining whether those interests are legitimate, appropriate, or necessary. For example, when a utilitarian considers the moral acceptability (or obligation) of infanticide in order to create a better life for other family members (or society), he or she ought also to consider whether the immediately interpreted interests of those people are based on contingencies of a wider context, such as poverty, lack of resources, public views of disability, or accessibility. Utilitarianism seems more appropriate to a medical model, while a social approach requires that we genuinely discuss the relational nature of even our most individual interests (and whether those interests serve us well). As one tool in our ethical toolbox, utilitarianism can be quite useful, especially in thinking about the treatment of impairment. If we do not investigate the multiple dimensions of quality of life, however, we may not adequately accommodate the complexity of moral engagement in diverse communities.

Harriet McBryde Johnson (2003), the late disability advocate and attorney, and herself a disabled person, wrote a *New York Times Magazine* article about her interesting interactions with Singer, taking him to task on the question of quality of life. Although Johnson respected the logic of Singer's arguments regarding alleviating suffering, she was not sanguine about one ethicist's ability to judge quality of life for others:

> Are we "worse off"? I don't think so. Not in any meaningful sense. There are too many variables. For those of us with congenital conditions, disability shapes all we are. Those disabled later in life adapt. We take constraints that no one would choose and build rich and satisfying lives within them. We enjoy pleasures other people enjoy, and pleasures peculiarly our own. We have something the world needs (para. 34).

And Ian Brown (2011) quoted a mother of two girls with challenges: "I look at the girls, and I think, Who's to say they're not happier in their world than I am in mine? And here I am feeling sorry for them because I'm trying to judge them by the standards of the world they aren't part of" (p. 144).

Critics of Singer and other utilitarians have also argued that they relegate the question of human disability to the ranks of marginal cases.

Licia Carlson (2009) wrote, "Animal rights literature is littered with references to the severely intellectually disabled, a group of individuals that serves to bolster the case for animal rights" (p. 11). Considering rationality as the scale of one's worth, Singer (2009, 2010) claimed that if we are willing to harm relatively intelligent animals (such as great apes or dogs) for medical testing, then we ought to accept this practice for humans who have similar intelligence because it would be "speciesist" (similar to racist or sexist) to assume that there is anything particularly good or dignified in being human. This use of rationality (which, for Singer, seems to be manifest primarily in language use) to judge moral worth is little different than previous ethical theories in their treatment of disability. Carlson (2009) stated, "Here again we find that intellectual disability is assumed to be a self-evident category of individuals about whom philosophical analogies and comparisons can be made" (p. 11). Singer's utilitarian discussion of quality of life versus suffering is perhaps more productive, but there is still the question of the precision of basing moral judgments and social and medical policy on attempts to universalize a qualitative existence.

Jeffrey McMahan (2002) similarly used cognitive ability as the focal point of questions of moral status in a marginal case approach. He argued that psychological capability, as central to quality of life (including for the family), should be a relevant factor in cases such as selective abortion (which we will discuss in detail later) and infanticide. Although McMahan does not consider traditional indicators of moral status, such as universal reason, autonomy, or free will to be relevant factors, his work does stress what mental ability affords, such as one's sense of future potential and life, anxiety about the cause and duration of pain (rather than just the immediate sensation), and other concepts that seem to require higher level reasoning. While most humans fall into this category, those with severe intellectual disability do not, and nonhuman animals do not, leading McMahan to give nonhumans and people with disabilities a reduced status, especially when it comes to the question of whether it would be acceptable to end a life. He wrote, "Finally, we might accept that animals and the severely retarded share roughly the same moral status, though the moral status of neither is quite what it has traditionally and popularly been supposed to be" (p. 206). In his convergence theory, McMahan (2002) proposed that the ethical status of severely incapacitated humans be slightly lowered, while the status of nonhumans is elevated. Neither group, however, could be said to have a full moral status: "Killing animals, and allowing them to die, are morally far more serious matters than we have supposed. But allowing severely retarded human beings to die, and perhaps even killing them, are correspondingly somewhat less serious matters than we have believed" (p. 230).

Though he did claim that there may be times when we express greater concern over the well-being of intellectually disabled humans than is required of us for animals, out of respect for family members, perhaps, the equating of disabled humans with nonhumans seems to some problematic and insensitive (e.g., Kittay, 2010). McMahan's convergence theory implies that any value people with severe disabilities have is as members of other people's families and it may easily allow us to draw moral lines based on questionable measures, such as IQ tests.

Further, critics take issue with both McMahan and Singer in their presentation of people with disabilities as part of marginal case testing, since both philosophers argued that we are guilty of speciesism if we are unwilling to conduct painful or life-threatening experiments on humans who fall below a certain cognitive threshold (while we are willing to do such things to nonhumans). Though we may agree that the treatment of nonhuman animals is in many cases unethical, categorizing nonhumans with humans as primarily a test of logical consistency is problematic to critics because it is advancing the status of nonhuman animals at the expense of humans. Johnson (2003) wrote, "because I am still seeking acceptance of my humanity, Singer's call to get past species seems a luxury way beyond my reach." At times, it seems as though Singer and McMahan are making logical, more than moral, arguments, and it may be that, as Kittay suggested (2010), they are missing something of what it means to be entrenched in human relationships, including with people with disabilities. As consistent and correct as the arguments may be, they do little to expand moral community to include people with intellectual disability.

On the issue of selective abortion, for example, McMahan used a *reductio ad absurdum* argument to prove that ending a fetal life is morally permissible (and, in some cases, morally required). The argument suggests that if we reject the claim that testing or selection against disability is morally correct, then we must also accept that other, seemingly absurd, positions must be the case (such as the permissibility of actively disabling a fetus or engaging in activities that may lead to disability). Logically, this makes sense, but is it possible that logic cannot always capture the dilemma faced by parents who want to choose the best course of action in a complicated and difficult situation? John Dewey (1985/1917) might say that McMahan and Singer are solving the "problems of philosophy" more than they are solving the "problems of men" (p. 46). Although we agree with Singer, McMahan,

Plato, Aristotle, and Kant, that logic and consistency and the best of human intelligence need to be part of our discussions, people who rely only on these tools are building a house of theory that cannot accommodate all the real people who need a home.

Thus, a problematic consequence of rationality as necessary for moral engagement is that, even though a particular theory or policy might require us to look out for the interests of those who fall outside rational norms, our moral theory will never be entirely inclusive. At best, we practice a form of paternalism, acting for the benefit of "moral patients" without their consent or confederation, and often without their knowledge. A moral patient is the object of decisions, passively awaiting the judgments and actions of others. Though we are all, at times, moral patients (McPherson, 1984), we hope also to take a powerful role in our relationships with others and in decisions which affect our lives. While moral patienthood is surely superior to being a victim of mistreatment or malice, even the most beneficent paternalistic acts can be dehumanizing and can prevent people from speaking for themselves and developing, as we all should, the habits and character necessary for moral agency and citizenship. After all, the concept of the moral patient has evolved over recent years to include not only nonhuman animals, but even ecosystems, and once again we are left with the question of whether people with disabilities are any more a part of our moral community than chimps, dogs, rivers, and landscapes (Schönfeld, 1993). Although one may agree with Singer and McMahan that some (or even all) nonhuman animals merit higher status, and with environmental philosophers (e.g., Fesmire, 2010; Light, 1996) who argue that we are not as independent of our physical environment as much of our philosophy suggests, the moral problems of humans and ecosystems may simply require different deliberation.

Moral theories that claim some universal standpoint or principle may be philosophically questionable, as well. Whether we can achieve a fully "objective" perspective (which would require abstract thinking on a vast scale) is a question with which pragmatist, feminist, and postmodernist thinkers have struggled in the last century. Dewey, for example, stressed that moral deliberation always begins from the middle of a context, not from abstract principles, and that even abstract principles (such as suggested by Aristotle, Kant, and Mill) are not inseparable from our lived experience (Pappas, 2008). At most, they are tools whose use, we hope, will help us to live better.

Finally, moral theories based on reason seem to promote a cold and calculated view of moral problems that does not account for the fact that contexts often lack clear edges. Universalist theories allow philosophers to discuss issues such as selective abortion and infanticide with what seems to be objectivity, but which Kittay (2010) worried is actually a perspective lacking both "epistemic responsibility" (genuinely understanding a complex situation; p. 401) and "epistemic modesty" (knowing what we don't know; p. 404). Missing from seemingly objective perspectives is a more sensitive, emotional standpoint, which allows us to see the humanity, and often tragedy, of our moral choices, though it does not always offer us clear or correct responses. Moral theories that require us to choose a single correct response regarding moral obligation, in addition to excluding people who fall outside the norm, also fail to account for the possibility of tragedy—that in the middle of messy and real situations, often there simply is not an entirely correct response. Tragedy is part of our humanity, however, and must be part of our discussion of moral choices.

In the end, with the reminder that our intellectual heritage directly affects our practices (Stainton, 2001b), we might ask whether historic and contemporary moral theories would have prevented or promoted policies such as those that led to the atrocities at Hartheim Castle during the Nazi T4 euthanasia project. Theories favoring intelligence and reason above all else might seem to support a project that sought to amplify this aspect of the human race. Although there are prohibitions against unnecessary killing in most moral theories, there are also obligations to protect and promote human reason, such as in deontology and Aristotle's virtue ethics. Hitler presented himself as a utilitarian, cleansing humanity of disease and deformity, for the greater good of the rest of us. And when it seemed expedient, officials in the T4 program even suggested that the murder of disabled people was a quality of life issue—mercy killing (Strous, 2006).

There is evidence that the Nazis took elaborate steps to prevent epistemic responsibility (cf. Milgram, 1974) and a personal standpoint that would likely have led to more humane actions. The system required that decisions about life or death were made in sterile offices in Berlin, and that care workers often weren't kept in the information loop (when they were, some care workers risked their own lives to prevent the killing). The Nazis, knowing that care workers might be moved to intervene, transferred most victims from their home clinics to Hartheim and other centers, and the transport buses had painted windows so that passengers were invisible and isolated. From faraway offices, Hitler and his people would have argued that they were making objective moral decisions, based on reason, for the greater good (C. Dorner, Mag., personal interview, April 17, 2012).

Hartheim Castle today, while memorializing the victims of T4, offers a glimpse into the real lives of people with disabilities, presenting a human standpoint that celebrates the possibilities of life. People are pictured in love relationships and friendships, working and commuting, and taking an active role in the cultural interpretation of disability. Later, we will explore moral theories that attempt to embrace the joy and complication of real human lives, expanding the moral community to, in the words of Harriet McBryde Johnson (2003), invoke "the muck and mess and undeniable reality of disabled lives well lived" (para. 153) and to "make a world that's fit to live in, a society that has room for all its flawed creatures" (para. 139).

Part II

Out of the Darkness

5

Defining the Person

The Moral and Social Consequences of Philosophies of Selfhood

John is a skilled worker in a small business specializing in refinishing antique furniture. Although John lives in a large American city, he is a native of another state that placed some of its young people with intellectual disability in living arrangements outside the state—in some cases for reasons related to availability of particular human services, and in some cases simply to save money and get people out of the state's inadequate human service programs. Despite the facts that he is a talented employee, has a driver's license, and is capable of living independently, his home state considers John intellectually disabled. On the other hand, to his employer John is a valuable asset, and to his mother he is a capable driver who transports her through city traffic when she visits him. How, we might ask, does John think of himself? Is he confused by the various views others have of him? Does he have a coherent self-perspective that incorporates the views of others, or might he have a view of self formed independently of others' perceptions? Or is he, as Sacks (1984) suggested may be typical of people with disabilities, just trying to be ordinary? The construal of self, the meaning of being an individual, is central to both psychology and philosophy.

In order to fully understand our historic and contemporary thinking about morality and intellectual disability, and to change it for the better, we first must make sense of our conception of the moral agent or individual. Much of our Western intellectual tradition includes a vision of the ideal human self as radically independent, autonomous, and, of course, rational. While this view of personhood is helpful to development of some moral beliefs and policies such as those that promote freedom and other universal

Intellectual Disability: Ethics, Dehumanization, and a New Moral Community, First Edition.
Heather E. Keith and Kenneth D. Keith.

human rights, the assumptions behind such claims may be more the result of wishful thinking than solid psychology. It is noteworthy, for example, that the construal of self may be quite different in non-Western cultures than in the West (Markus & Kitayama, 1991).

Further, a conception of the self as isolated or "atomic" contributes to a view of ethics that requires rationality for full membership in the moral community, while ignoring other types of intelligence, such as practical or emotional. Mark Johnson (1993) argued that traditional moral theories, as we saw in Chapter Four, rest on faulty assumptions "of the way people actually conceptualize, reason, deliberate, and so forth" (p. 19), which causes moral dissonance; a tension between what we value as correct and intelligent action and the way in which we are actually constituted to behave. In this chapter, we explore the intellectual legacy of the isolated individual that is the foundation of moral assumptions that emphasize rationality. We also offer some alternative theories that may be more consistent with what we know today about the self and moral ideals that are inclusive, relational, and more likely to be useful to a moral community that embraces intellectual diversity.

The Self in Isolation

As we saw in earlier chapters, historians (Goodey, 2011) and psychologists (Blatt, 1981) argued that our concept of intellectual disability, like intelligence, has a history, and that using intelligence to put humans into moral categories is dependent on our philosophical and cultural views of human personhood. And as we saw in Chapter Four, this intellectual history has consequences for who falls into moral categories and justice systems, from the Ancients to contemporary ethics. Here, we will look to the modern era in philosophy (c. seventeenth through nineteenth centuries in Europe) to unpack our intellectual heritage regarding the construction of the autonomous and rational self and, in turn, how we construct moral community in regard to disability.

The most famous iteration of rationality as the apex of human existence is perhaps the mind/body dualism of Descartes. In his *Discourse on Method* and *Meditations Concerning First Philosophy*, Descartes worried about human knowledge and whether we can achieve any sort of certainty about things we think we know. As we saw in the previous chapter, he engaged in an elaborate thought experiment, attempting to imagine that all the things he thought he knew, including his own existence and that of the otherwise obvious things around him, were false (perhaps planted in his mind by some sort of trickster) and then attempted to figure out what would be epistemologically responsible beliefs. In this experiment, Descartes started piecing himself and his world back together, not surprisingly ending up with the same assumptions with which he started.

The first thing about which Descartes expressed any certainty was his mind. In the very act of doubting his own existence, he concluded that there must be something that exists to do the doubting and thinking. Thus, we get Descartes' *cogito ergo sum* ("I think therefore I am"): "I must finally conclude and maintain that this proposition: *I am, I exist,* is necessarily true every time that I pronounce it or conceive it in my mind" (1952/1641, p. 82). Although he could not be absolutely sure about the existence of his own body, he could be sure that, because he is able to engage in the thought experiment in the first place, his mind does exist:

> But what am I? A thinking being. What is a thinking being? It is a being which doubts, which understands, [which conceives], which affirms, which denies, which wills, which rejects, which imagines also, and which perceives (1952/1641, p. 85).

And because this thinking thing, mind, is the only thing about which Descartes can be certain, it is epistemologically (and, perhaps, morally) superior to everything else, including the body. What human nature is most, is a rational, thinking, entity, "a mind, an understanding, or a reasoning being" because "thought is an attribute that belongs to me; it alone is inseparable from my nature" (1952/1641, p. 84). McMahan (2002) noted that a version of Descartes' philosophy becomes soul/body dualism because: "According to certain views, personal identity over time is not reducible to or explicable in terms of anything else" (p. 5), and so we posit the existence of nonmaterial substance, the soul, to explain it.

From the perspective of contemporary psychology, there are clear problems with Cartesian dualism, and we now know Descartes was wrong about the physiology of his mind/body dualism (Goodwin, 2008). Damasio (1994) argued that "Descartes' error" is

> the abyssal separation between body and mind ... the suggestion that reasoning, moral judgment, and the suffering that comes from physical pain or emotional upheaval might exist separately from the body. Specifically: the separation of the most refined operations of mind from the structure and operation of a biological organism (pp. 249–250).

Cartesian psychology also contributes to contemporary ethical theories holding that rationality is required for moral considerability, in much the same way that we saw with "scaling" in the works of Plato and Aristotle (Stainton, 2001b). Rather than viewing the experience of being human as a unified whole, "Cartesian dualism has given birth to such alienations as nature/culture, subject/object, substance/extended substance and body/soul" (Iwakuma, 2002, p. 76). Further, dualism that prioritizes mental substance over material substance resulted, for Descartes, in a mechanized view of the body. It is not difficult to imagine a logic in which people with intellectual disability, or any group historically considered to be more body than mind (such as women and people of color), are dehumanized because they are seen as little more than machines. Damasio (1994) worried that mind/body dualism might obscure "the inherent tragedy of conscious existence," causing us to "feel far less called upon to do something about it" (p. 251).

For Descartes, to fully be a person, one must be rational, and the nature of rational mind is to exist separately from other elements of existence. In a Cartesian sense, "the mind is a solipsistic self" (Goodey, 2011, p. 208), and "human reasoning, in the form of the cogito, is itself a 'permanent act of grace"' (p. 160). The view of what makes us most human as static rationality leaves out of the moral community many people with intellectual disability who would benefit more from a conception of personhood that involves learning, growth, and relationships with others.

Following Descartes, other philosophers of the modern era asserted a view of the self as rational and separable from the body and from other selves. John Locke's political philosophy, which, as we noted in Chapter Four, provides the foundation for much of the American system of governance, remains one of the most comprehensive theories of moral personhood. Like a Cartesian view of the self, Locke's philosophy of human nature relies more on rationality than other human attributes, which is problematic for a justice system aimed at genuine equality among members of an intellectually diverse world. Known also as one of the most important empiricists in philosophy, Locke applied his interest in human understanding to his political philosophy. Like Descartes, Locke was concerned with the process of knowledge and in avoiding claims stemming from uncertainty. Locke (1959/1690) warned against extending the limits of what is knowable too far:

> Thus men, extending their inquiries into those depths where they can find no sure footing, it is no wonder that they raise questions and multiply disputes,

> which, never coming to any clear resolution, are proper only to continue and increase their doubts, and to confirm them at last in perfect skepticism (p. 31).

So that we may avoid skepticism and the raising of unnecessary doubts, Locke thought that we must consider carefully the capacities of our understanding that set the bounds for what we can and cannot know. Written in the thick of the emerging Enlightenment scientific era, Locke's work involved an empirical, psychological approach to perception and the subsequent formation of ideas. For Locke (1959/1690) knowledge comes to us through experience:

> Let us then suppose the mind to be, as we say, white paper, void of all characters, without any ideas:—How comes it to be furnished? Whence comes it by that vast store which the busy and boundless fancy of man has painted on it with an almost endless variety? Whence has it all the materials of reason and knowledge? To this I answer, in one word, from EXPERIENCE (p. 122).

All other knowledge claims fall into the category of speculation. About the empirical theory of perception and the subsequent formation of knowledge, Locke stated that "perception is the first operation of all our intellectual faculties, and the inlet of all knowledge in our minds" (p. 191). Locke was clear about what has traditionally been understood as "knowledge," which actually, he believed, falls outside the limits of human understanding. Thus is his rejection of the concept of innate ideas (e.g., Descartes)—ideas that come to us prior to experience, which, to Locke, are impossible ideas. Though the mind has certain capabilities, actualized through experience, there are no ideas that exist prior to our interactions with the world. The canvas of our minds is primordially blank, to be painted with almost endless variety only by experience.

While the rejection of innate ideas might seem to offer a foundation for a view of intelligence that is more expansive and inclusive than that of other modern philosophers, for Locke, the painting of the canvas is possible only through perception processed by reason, and all other ways of knowing are suspect, including insights from emotional or social experience. Though his empiricism seems at odds with his political philosophy (which is characterized by a commitment to what seem to be innate human rights), the rational mind is still at the core of Locke's work, which presents a problem for moral and political opportunities for people with intellectual disability. The "state of nature" allows that, all persons being born equal, we each maintain throughout our lives the natural rights of freedom "within the bounds of the law of nature" (1952/1690, p. 4), which includes "what several rules and canons natural reason hath drawn" (p. 5). We are thus allotted certain particular freedoms innate to our species, such as the right to dispose of our "possessions and persons" (p. 4).

So, though we lack innate ideas, and gain all our credible knowledge from experience, Locke believed that the faculty of reason, which we each have individually, is something innate to humans. And from the "rules and canons" our natural reason has given us, we know that our "possessions and persons" are inalienable in that they belong to us each alone. It is the individual desire for and the ability to create and own property that characterizes subsequent social contract theories and results in a two-tiered justice system with those who possess reason charged with the distribution of resources, and everyone else in their care. Nussbaum (2007) noted that for Locke, the chief end of political association is the preservation of property and not "benevolence and mutual support for human dignity" (p. 45). The politics of Locke's social contract thus excludes those of us uninterested in or unable to accumulate and preserve property, such as people with intellectual disability and even, for Locke, women (Nussbaum, 2007). Once again, human beings are framed as unproductive burdens on society; perhaps moral patients, but certainly not moral or political agents.

Richard Aaron (1971) pointed out that Locke's political theory is just "bad psychology." He wrote, "The free individual tends to be depicted as largely isolated, a mere individual with no social ties. But man is by nature social. The 'unsocial' individual of the pre-political stage is an unreal abstraction" (p. 273). Even so, a Lockean individual does have social moments, at least in the prepolitical stage of human nature (hence the drive to associate, unlike a Hobbesian individual who must associate in order to survive a war-like state of nature). Locke (1952/1690) claimed, after all, that God deemed it ill that humans should be alone and thus put them "under strong obligations of necessity, convenience, and inclination to drive him into society" (p. 44). All social relations, however, are among isolated individuals who reasonably suspect that they would be better off associating with other rational beings. Aaron (1971) continued his critique of Locke: "Moreover, it cannot be denied that he deals too frequently in artificialities. His individual is artificial. He has no family ties. He tends to be conceived as a somewhat isolated being even when he enters into social relations with others" (p. 284).

As we saw in Chapter Four, individual autonomy and innate reason are also central to Kant's universal approach to ethics, and this ability is made possible by a mind free of the constraints of others, or even the body. Johnson (1993) observed that "Kant preserves a dichotomized view of human nature and a conception of reason and will as in no way dependent on human embodiment" (p. 26). Once again, the rational, moral self, that which makes us most human, is utterly independent and isolated.

There are at least a couple of clear consequences for people with intellectual disability of a view of the self that is radically separate from others. First, without faculties that give us the moral status of persons, such as rationality (or any other innate quality), it becomes harder to argue that individuals merit membership in the moral community as moral agents, or even as moral patients. Second, philosophically isolating oneself from others may result in a kind of superficial moral competition for resources, pitting one individual against others. Perhaps this individualism is at the root of contemporary bioethical views which assume that the rights of disabled infants must be weighed against the rights of parents or even of society. Singer (2010) and McMahan (2002), for example, have suggested that it may be less tragic to kill a person with profound intellectual disability (who cannot, presumably, reason about the future or make important human contributions) than someone likely to make more significant lifetime contributions; and the factors to consider, according to Singer, include the views and rights of the person's parents. Such dilemmas, couched in a battle of resources and rights, clearly treat the self of the child as distinct from that of her social context, including her family.

There is no doubt that the European modern era in philosophy has been influential on scientific and cultural views of human nature and moral personhood, and some of the effects are likely quite positive. We will discuss more in Chapter Nine how a rights approach may benefit in a limited way individuals with intellectual disability. Rights concepts tend to be useful on national and multinational agendas that try to gain more resources in order to enhance quality of life, and that single out specific groups of individuals who might otherwise get lost in the competition for limited resources. However, rights often imply moral personhood, and modern conceptions of the self, such as in Descartes and Locke, may actually work against rights for people who seemingly fall below intellectual standards. While the rhetorical use of rights might help to ensure quality of life, we also need moral tools that help to build the argument that rationality is not essential to personhood, and that many human beings who might have previously been excluded because of disability from our moral community may, in fact, be valuable and valued members worthy of rights and resources.

There are theories in recent times that, with the benefit of more knowledge of human psychology, aim to cultivate a moral view of the person who is not an innately isolated rational being, but is natively related to others and develops interests and capabilities because of that relatedness. Many twentieth- and twenty-first-century philosophies, as well as contemporary psychology, have developed the idea of the relational social self, rather than the isolated rational self, as the center of moral philosophy.

Philosophies of *Relationality*: The Social Self

With more knowledge about the human brain and body, recent philosophers have developed theories of personhood involving relational experience rather than rationality. Because our moral theories still rely on philosophy, as well as science, for relevant claims about human nature, it makes sense to explore philosophical views of the self that might be more useful to contemporary ethics and policy. One of the most comprehensive and, for his time, psychologically accurate visions of the self as social, is that of the American pragmatist philosopher George Herbert Mead (1863–1931), about whom the phenomenologist Jürgen Habermas (1991) argued "If we want to release the revolutionary power of the basic concepts of behavior theory, the potential in this approach to burst the bounds of its own paradigm, we have to go *back* to Mead's social psychology" (p. 138). With a background in both philosophy and psychology, Mead contributed to the pragmatist ideal of using the best science and social science research of the time to inform philosophic accounts of human experience.

Influenced by Darwin and schooled in the laboratory of German psychologist Wilhelm Wundt, Mead developed a social behaviorism in which he used the descriptive methods of social science to ground claims about philosophy and ethics. In his work, he focused extensively on the emergence of the self out of social (such as family) relationships, which contradicted most philosophies of human nature since the European modern era. In *Mind, Self and Society* (1934), Mead stated:

> The self is something which has a development; it is not initially there, at birth, but arises in the process of social experience and activity, that is, develops in the given individual as a result of his relations to that process as a whole and to other individuals within that process (p. 135).

In his concept of the self, Mead accounted for the development of individuals within a social setting that includes both interactive communication and reflection. This begins not with an autonomous individual but with the individual's embodiment and environment—a pool of communicative interaction, Mead's "conversation of gestures" (1934, p. 63). This may be the instinctive growl of a dog at the sight of an interloper or the hungry cry of an infant. Human animals, in response to others in their social context, gradually construct more and more complex and meaningful systems of gestures. Otherwise, our world would forever be given to us as "bare thereness," or, as Dewey (1983/1908) might say, "mere sound and fury" (p. 65).

According to Mead, the first signs of social behavior occur during infancy, but these gestural responses are on a more instinctive level and do not yet imply the ability of the child to understand her social environment:

> To the young child the frowns and smiles of those about him, the attitude of body, the outstretched arms, are at first simply stimulations that call out instinctive responses of his own appropriate to these gestures. He cries or laughs, he moves toward his mother, or stretches out his arms (1964a, p. 137).

This imitation of conduct, while devoid of an understanding of any meaning behind a mother's smile, for example, is a step toward meaningful communication and, as such, is a social act. For Mead, sociality does not occur when an individual learns that she exists in an environment full of others; rather, social behavior (and the development of mind or self) begins when one learns, through interaction within an environment of others, that she exists somewhat separately. Self-consciousness is a function of reflective social behavior that extends beyond the instinctive gestural responses to an environment. What is required is a social relationship that draws out the reflection of one individual in another. Mead wrote, "Whatever may be the metaphysical impossibilities or possibilities of solipsism, psychologically it is nonexistent. There must be other selves if one's own is to exist" (1964d, p. 103).

This is a far cry from the isolated individual of Descartes, Locke, and Kant, and the subsequent view of personhood depending on static intelligence. For Mead, when humans cultivate meaning in their interactions, it is not first from the point of view of the individual. What we become conscious of is our own behaviors, selves, or minds, but this is the result of a process that first calls our attention to the attitudes of others. In the response of a mother to an instinctively smiling infant, an attitude is displayed that is gradually understood as meaningful by her child.

To the growing child, the mother becomes a social object separate from the child because the mother is seen in response to the child's behaviors. So it is not the individual organism herself, but the attitude of the other to her behavior that is first perceived. This response to the organism is the first movement toward the conscious discovery of the self and the later possibilities for empathizing with others in the social environment. In effect, we bounce ourselves off others, finding out that we are somewhat substantial and whole, in ourselves different from others (Keith, 1999). As Mead (1964b) said, "the child does not become social by learning. He must be social in order to learn" (p. 122).

Mead (1934) called this ability to envision ourselves from the experience of others "taking on the attitude of the other." He stated, "The individual experiences himself as such, not directly, but only indirectly, from the particular standpoints of other individual members of the same social group" (1934, p. 138). Once the organism begins to understand herself as "other" from the standpoint of another's responses to her, she develops a sense of individual identity. What moves our gestures from being unorganized and reflexive to meaningful and reflective is this ability to take on the attitude of the other, which we now think of as empathy (Snyder, 1994). It is the capacity for empathy that grounds the realization that we evolve out of social and natural relationships and that we, in turn, shape these environments. For Mead, we don't precede society, we are a product of it (De Waal, 2002).

Mead's description of the place of an empathetic individual within a social system carries with it a certain amount of responsibility, not only for an individual making decisions that affect others, but for all members of the group who must recognize that, like any ecology, the health of the environment affects the health of its individuals (Habermas, 1991). Caring about others and the social environment we inhabit is thus imperative to cultivating and preserving rich and healthy experience. But caring cannot occur without a conscious, felt recognition that we are already related. In Mead we have the basic philosophical foundation for a theory of intelligence as social (Snyder, 1994), which may be more amenable to moral theories that include the experience of people with intellectual disability.

Influenced by Mead, Dewey (1988/1927) developed a theory of ethics and politics which reflected the idea that the individual emerges out of social relationships: "To learn to be human is to develop through the give-and-take of communication in an effective sense of being an individually distinctive member of a community" (p. 332). Contrary to theories that isolate the individual political mind from those of others, Dewey (1988/1927) wrote:

> There is no mystery about the fact of association, of an interconnected action which affects the activity of singular elements. There is no sense in asking how individuals come to be associated. They exist and operate in association. If there is any mystery about the matter, it is the mystery that the universe is the kind of universe it is (p. 250).

Mead's and Dewey's colleague Jane Addams (1860–1935), a philosopher and social worker, likewise developed a social ethics grounded in relationships (1902). And contemporary feminist theorists, such as psychologist Carol Gilligan (1982) and philosopher Nel Noddings (1984) see moral deliberation as growing out of family situations.

Hilde Lindemann (2010) wrote about the cultivation of the self in terms of a social narrative structure in developing a conception of identity conducive to caring for people with cognitive disability such as dementia. Like Mead, she argued that the self in its earliest form, including the potential for moral agency, grows out of family relationships; and that identity, as a representation of the self, is a result of the stories we tell and that are told about us. This begins even before birth "as the pregnant woman and other family members call the baby-to-be in to personhood" through "stories of relationship" (p. 162) that will place the baby within the wider family and cultural narratives. As the child grows up, her identity continues to be constituted by the narrative accounts of her family, and then others, as she begins to take on their meaning. "It is third-person contributions, then, that first form a person's identity" (p. 163). This constructivist view of identity has moral weight because these representations of self "function as counters in our social transactions, in that they convey understandings of both what we are expected to do and how others may or must treat us" (p. 163). For Lindemann, the family has a special role not only in forming a child's identity, but also in maintaining it as she continues to grow and develop throughout life. This is important in cases of dementia, where an individual may not be fully able to hold onto her own identity. Bruce Jennings (2010) also noted the importance of interactions with others, in this case semantic relationships, in maintaining the self. In his discussion of "trusteeship" as a model of care aimed at promoting one's agency in the case of dementia, he noted that quality of life depends, in part, on "being re-membered or recognized as a self who is a subject rather than an object and as a self who is (once more and still) a member of an ongoing social web of meaningful communicative relationships" (p. 175). We will explore ethical practices and theories based on a conception of the social self in more detail in the next chapter.

The Self as Culturally Construed

Cross-cultural philosophy and psychology underscore the concept of the self as socially or culturally constructed. Richard Brislin (1993) noted a distinction between the socially constructed concept of selfhood in collectivistic cultures and individualistic cultures:

> In collectivist cultures, people are more likely to downplay their own goals in favor of goals set by a valued group. That group is most often one's extended family, but it can also be one's organization or one's religion. People obtain much of their identity as members of their collective (p. 48).

For example, he continued, "In Japan, a collectivist country, people have to mention the organization to which they belong when talking to someone else who is not already well known" (p. 48). It might not occur to an American, on the other hand, to list her family or work organization when meeting a stranger to whom such knowledge is not immediately relevant. Rather, we seem to pride ourselves on our individuality and independence. As Hazel Rose Markus and Shinobu Kitayama (1991) noted, "In America, 'the squeaky wheel gets the grease.' In Japan, 'the nail that stands out gets pounded down'" (p. 224).

Markus and Kitayama (1991) went on to articulate two distinct conceptions of the notion of self; according to the independent construal of self (common to individualistic Western cultures), the self is bounded and clearly separate from others. The focus, in the context of the independent view of self, is on individual characteristics such as intelligence, personality, or preferences. In contrast, the interdependent self-construal (common to collectivistic non-Western cultures) places emphasis on the connectedness of the individual to others; the self is unbounded or permeable, and overlapping with such relevant others as family, friends, and coworkers. We saw these cultural concepts as low- and high-context in Chapter One. The independent self-construal does not overlap with others, and is thus not context-dependent; attitudes, abilities and other personal characteristics are seen as stable and intrinsic to the person. The interdependent self-construal, on the other hand, defines self in relationships with others, is more context-dependent, and produces self-esteem, satisfaction, and responsibility in the framework of those relationships. The independent view of self may place the rights and well-being of the individual with disabilities in conflict or competition with those of others, including parents or other family members, while the interdependent perspective places a premium on interpersonal relations and the welfare of the group (e.g., family). Interdependent self-construals are common in Asian cultures (Matsumoto & Juang, 2013), as Senoo (1985) illustrated in a description of Japanese services for people with intellectual disability: "All living things should remember that they are sharing their lives with others" (p. 1). The person with intellectual disability is not simply an individual entity possessing (or lacking) certain traits, but a person whose self is defined in interaction with others. Within American culture such interdependent self-construals may be more common among women than among men (Gilligan, 1982), and can also be found in Native American cultures (Morisaki & Gudykunst, 1994), where cultural divergence from mainstream society may produce significant difficulties for children with intellectual disability (Drew, Hardman, & Logan, 1996; Pepper, 1976).

Even an individual's concept of health is affected by culture. People learn culturally acceptable ways of expressing symptoms of distress, including the fact that some types of complaints are acceptable and others are not (Brislin, 1993; Eshun & Gurung, 2009). For example, according to Brislin (1993):

> When encountering significant distress, Americans learn that they will earn more sympathy when they complain about headaches rather than about memory problems. Mexicans learn that complaints about memory are acceptable, and the Vietnamese-Chinese learn that complaints about fullness in the head will be understood by others in their culture (p. 332).

This phenomenon carries with it the implication that what is acceptable as ill health in a culture is internalized by its individuals, no matter what the medical cause for the complaints. What we assume to be the same illness might create certain symptoms in one culture that do not show themselves in others. When we consider the stigma associated with depression, for example, in American culture we might find that more clearly physical symptoms are presented, as they tend to be more socially acceptable; and in a large international study, Hopper, Harrison, Janca, and Sartorius

(2007) found that people with schizophrenia showed differing symptoms, depending on their culture. Americans, for example, showed fewer auditory hallucinations than did Nigerian and Danish patients. Journalist Ethan Waters (2010) reported that syndromes such as anorexia and posttraumatic stress disorder are very real in Western culture but nonexistent in some other places, and Gurung (2011) reviewed a variety of health beliefs and practices that vary across cultures.

Even cognition seems to be dependent on culture and social relationships. Mark Johnson (1987), in his argument against objectivist knowledge, the idea that there is "one universal set of concepts that map directly onto the objective features of the world" (p. xii), wrote that "we have found that the conceptions of space and time upon which certain non-Western languages are structured is radically different in kind from the conceptions on which familiar Indo-European languages are structured" (p. xiii). Jayanthi Mistry and Barbara Rogoff (1994) likewise showed that memory is culturally conditioned as they related the variations on stories children remember in different cultures. Depending on the culture, different aspects of the story are emphasized and even the very style and basic structure of the story is altered according to acceptable modes of speech in an individual's society.

The idea of the self as having its origin in social relationality, from the family situation to cultural history, is reflected also in cross-cultural philosophy. The delicate balance of the individual and her social and natural context is a core theme in Chinese Confucian ethics. Starting from what David Hall and Roger Ames (1998) called the "field," (similar to Mead's "conversation of gestures") the Confucian self emerges out of social relationships and cultural traditions. In fact, we can see a kind of social behaviorism (broadly defined) in *The Analects* (2003). Like Mead, Confucius and his followers believed that individual identity emerges only from the context of social relationships, especially family (Giordano, 2011), and in *Analect* 3:23, we see a musical metaphor for the growth of the self:

> The Master was discussing music with the Grand Music Master of Lu. He said, "What can be known about music is this: when it first begins, it resounds with a confusing variety of notes, but as it unfolds, these notes are reconciled by means of harmony, brought into tension by means of the counterpoint, and finally woven together into a seamless whole. It is in this way that music reaches its perfection" (2003, p. 27).

Like music, the individual starts out tentatively, but in harmony with others. Gradually, she is "woven together into a seamless whole" as she grows into her own identity. Self-cultivation depends on the fundamental idea that our own individuality is an outgrowth of our socialization.

This socialization has its origin not in abstract principles or logic, but in love for one's family. According to Philip Ivanhoe (2002):

> The obligations to one's family were most important because for Kongzi [Confucius] they were the earliest and strongest bonds human beings form. They also were regarded as the source of our social obligations; our obligations to others were developed out of and modeled on the family (p. 1).

The Confucian moral agent grows out of relationships with others and can be said to be "universal" only because socialization is seen as a trait of human nature. Unlike Western Enlightenment reason-based moral agency, "one cannot find any discussion of the nature of reason, nor anything like Kant's arguments linking reason with morality in the *Analects*. We look in vain for an analysis of moral maxims, autonomy, or freedom" (Ivanhoe, 2002, p. 9).

The moral self as social can be seen in both Vedic (Hindu) and Buddhist philosophy, as well, where the relational nature of the self is stressed even more radically. In these traditions, the concept of the isolated agent disappears altogether, based on the assumption that what we call the human subject is merely an aspect of something larger, perhaps Nature or the Divine. In fact, the goal of most philosophies that emerge from these traditions is to extinguish the self in order to gain a kind of enlightenment. Detachment from the ego as a moral ideal can be seen in the *Bhagavad Gita*: "Abandoning all desires, acting without craving, free from all thoughts of 'I' and 'mine,' that man finds utter peace" (Mitchell, 2000, p. 59).

Similarly, in Buddhism the central concept of Conditioned Genesis states that all things, including mind or self, have an origin conditioned by something else. Everything is connected and no one exists separately from others. According to Walpola Rahula (1974), elements of the experience of being human, from perception to thought, "are all relative, interdependent and interconnected, and nothing is absolute or independent" (p. 54). Recognizing this helps one on the path to the ideal of "no self" which is moral and spiritual attunement to the nature of the universe itself. Again, one does not find discussion of rationality as the key to personhood here. On the contrary, mind is merely another bodily faculty and is not "spirit opposed to matter" (p. 21). A metaphysics of interconnectedness, "considered as a circle, and not as a chain" (p. 54), is useful to an ethics of disability that avoids the scaling (Stainton, 2001b) we see in ancient Western thought.

Native American philosophy also offers a worldview consistent with the idea that the self, and therefore the moral person, evolves within relationships with others in the social and physical environment. In fact, the name of one tribe, the Lakota, means "related people" (Pengra, 2000, p. 191). Lavonna Lovern (2008) argued that this has clear consequences for disability theory and supports a multicultural constructionist perspective. She said, "For Native Americans, the worldview is one that involves an understanding of the wholeness of existence," which includes a notion of "the individual as located within the world and as part of the world with the understanding that all things are interrelated" (p. 4). This worldview is flavored by a special emphasis on narrative as not only a record of human experience, but as constructive of it. From stories evoking the creation of the universe to accounts of how individuals came to be how they are, narratives are used to mediate our existence. "Personal narrative simultaneously is born out of experience and gives shape to experience. In this sense, narrative and self are inseparable" (Ochs & Capps, 1996, p. 20). This harkens back to Lindemann's (2010) claim that the self grows out of the collection of stories we tell and retell.

In many cultural perspectives, isolating the self from relationships with others (human and beyond) just does not make sense. Consequently, a view of the moral agent as radically autonomous, free, and having innate capacities, such as reason, does not have much meaning cross-culturally or for people with diverse experiences (such as people with disabilities). John, whom we introduced at the beginning of this chapter, is more likely to find a meaningful perception of self in his relationship to family, work, and community, than in assumptions about his innate intelligence or capacity for reason. Isolated from his connections to others, in a world that judges others only by reference to their individual traits, he might well be lost. In the next chapter, we will explore ethical theories and practices that are grounded in a view of the self as fundamentally related to others and that may prove to offer true moral engagement to a greater diversity of people.

6

Alternative Views of Moral Engagement

Relationality and Rationality

In *The Boy in the Moon*, Ian Brown (2009) painted an intimate picture of life with his son Walker, who has cardiofaciocutaneous syndrome, an "impossibly rare" genetic mutation shared only by about 100 human beings worldwide. Walker's profound disabilities have meant around the clock care on the part of his family and caregivers in a group home. In the book, part biography, part memoir, and part journalistic exploration of disability, Brown detailed this care, the emotional and physical exhaustion of his family, and his attempts to understand his son, all within a wider discussion of the philosophical implications of Walker's life:

> Sometimes watching Walker is like looking at the moon: you see the face of the man in the moon, yet you know there's actually no man there. But if Walker is so insubstantial, why does he feel so important? What is he trying to show me? All I really want to know is what goes on inside his off-shaped head, in his jumped-up heart. But every time I ask, he somehow persuades me to look into my own (p. 3).

Life with Walker, Brown found, of long nights, frustrations with social services, and devastating "what if" questions of whether he and his wife would have chosen abortion had they known the severity of their baby's disabilities, leads not only to despair, but also to acceptance, love, and a greater capacity for empathy. Brown wrote:

> He may be a deleterious effect of evolution as far as a geneticist is concerned, but he has few peers as a route to developing what Darwin himself in *The Descent of Man* called the evolutionary advantages of "the social instincts . . . love, and the distinct emotion of sympathy" (p. 285).

Intellectual Disability: Ethics, Dehumanization, and a New Moral Community, First Edition.
Heather E. Keith and Kenneth D. Keith.

In this chapter we explore moral and political theories that accept and thrive on intellectual diversity and that offer an expansive description of moral community; theoretical approaches that we believe have themselves been marginalized, to the detriment of people of a variety of intellectual abilities. In Chapter Four, we explored the dominant theories in the history of moral philosophy, arguing that most would exclude, at least on some level, people with intellectual disability. While many of these theoretical approaches may be useful tools in various ethical situations, such as utilitarianism's commitment to alleviating suffering and promoting quality of life, it is also helpful to consider positions that value diversity, among both theories and people. We argue here that the boundaries of moral community need to be pressed beyond discussions of rights, intention, utility, and capacities in order to respond to and welcome the capabilities of all people, with and without intellectual disability.

In her criticism of Singer (1994, 2010) and McMahan (2002), Kittay (2010) argued that moral theories ought always to be grounded in epistemic responsibility (knowing what you need to know) and epistemic modesty (knowing what you don't know). Here, we will examine some contemporary ethical theories that have roots in empirical knowledge and in humility, and philosophers and psychologists who adhere to the position that moral theories are tools in our toolbox and that the more tools we have, in quantity and diversity, the more flexible and inclusive our actions will be. And, of course, in the spirit of engaging a diversity of people, the theories we will offer here are grounded not so much in an individual capacity for reason or rational judgment, but in other sorts of intelligence, such as empathy, emotion, and the desire and ability to relate to others. We certainly value rational thought, and think such enterprises as logic and mathematical calculation are at times essential to the development of policy and practices, but we are also interested in advancing other human values that we think should be acknowledged as viable foundations for moral life and community.

In his criticism of ancient philosophy, Stainton (2001b) wrote that "ultimately, a more fundamental debate on the basis of moral status that does not associate reason and goodness is required" (p. 459), and that there are indeed other traditions that do not make a close association between reason and value. However, he suggested that "these alternatives have been, and largely remain, outside the dominant epistemological discourse in Western societies" (p. 459). We believe that this has been changing with the advancement of more pluralistic approaches to both epistemology and ethics, specifically in fields such as pragmatism, feminism, and some recent theories of justice, and even (as we will see in the next chapter) some ancient traditions in ethics from non-Western culture, such as Confucianism and Buddhism.

In abiding by Kittay's call for epistemic responsibility, before we can adequately consider ethical theories that associate goodness with other attributes of humanity, such as emotion and empathy, we need to consider what we know about human psychology in such areas. For example, as we saw in Chapter Three, traditional views of intelligence have sometimes described skills useful in the limited circumstances of academic testing, the kind of intelligence that Sternberg (1996) termed "inert." Although inert intelligence may be useful in some settings, and may reflect the traditional notion of "reason," the construct so highly valued as a criterion for goodness and humanity in much Western thought, it certainly does not reflect all that is important about human abilities. We know that the ability to adapt to and to shape one's environment (practical intelligence; Sternberg, 1986, 1996), form harmonious relationships (Ruzgis & Grigorenko, 1994), be socially responsible (Serpell, 1974), and engage in family life (Super & Harkness, 1982) are all important aspects of intelligence in some contexts. We also continue to learn more about multiple aspects of intelligence (Gardner, 1999, 2011; Sternberg, 1986), and the interpersonal skills that make up emotional intelligence (Mayer & Salovey, 1993, 1997). Our point here is not to critique or to advocate particular views of intelligence, but rather to simply highlight the fact that there exist, within the community of scholars who study intelligence, multiple ideas about what constitutes the human intellect. To base our judgments about humanity and goodness on a single dimension would seem at best short sighted and at worst discriminatory and exclusionary.

American Pragmatism and the Social Nature of Moral Life

In thinking critically about the history of moral philosophy, we are not suggesting that dominant moral theories, such as those of Kant or Mill, are useless to the development of strong moral community; we are merely saying that a single approach that claims to be universal and is grounded primarily in rationality may not account for the whole of human experience. There are theoretical approaches, however, that are more pluralistic and flexible—that aim to cultivate seeds of moral life that grow with people of diverse capabilities in a diversity of situations. Moral theories influenced by and in the spirit of American pragmatism may get us closer to an inclusive approach that values intelligence of all kinds.

Pragmatist philosophy emerged in America in the late nineteenth century with the work of philosophers such as Mead, Charles Peirce, William James, and John Dewey. It is characterized by the integration of theory and practice (Dewey, 1988/1925), a view of human nature as evolving and embodied (James, 1950/1890), and a conception of truth as experimental and fallible (Peirce, 1958/1877). Three aspects of pragmatic moral theory make it a useful framework for discussing intellectual disability. First, pragmatism is pluralistic. There are clear foundations for ethical beliefs and actions; however, a pragmatic perspective embraces the usefulness of many moral systems, such as feminism and even Kantian ethics and utilitarianism, just not absolutely and universally. About pluralistic moral philosophy, Fesmire (2003) wrote, "It functions not to provide a moral bedrock, but to clarify, interpret, evaluate and redirect our natural and social interactions" (p. 57), which is what we aim to do in applying theory to practical contexts. Second, standing in the shadow of Darwin, pragmatism values empirical study. William James, philosopher and experimental psychologist, was a good example of the integration of research with speculative thought, and most other philosophers in the pragmatist tradition, such as Dewey, and Jane Addams, were well versed in the social and natural sciences, which was evident in Mead's social behaviorism. Third, pragmatist moral theory has a functional conception of the self as related to others, as we saw in the previous chapter, and puts this view to work in educational theory and practice.

As we saw in Chapter Five, how we conceptualize the self, as isolated and autonomous or as relational, makes a difference in how, or whether, we categorize people morally. Based on relational views of the self, we will discuss here moral theories that offer a more expansive view of moral community. Common themes among such theories are that ethics is social, both in character and ideals, and the goal of ethics should be increased functionality, both for the individual and the community. Our aim is to explore ethical theory which not only includes moral patients, but considers ways in which a diversity of people, including those with intellectual disability, can participate as moral citizens. Though we will use terminology, such as moral status and community, that is coherent to contemporary analyses, Garret Merriam (2010), from an Aristotelian perspective, warned, "The relevant questions with respect to these issues is not 'what is the moral status of these children?'" but rather "how do we assess their condition in light of the practical circumstances? What emotions, reactions, motives and actions are virtuous in these circumstances?" (p. 140).

Moral Engagement Based on Habit and Character

Though he had some clearly problematic views concerning disability (infanticide, and a strong emphasis on contemplative intelligence), the basic structure of Aristotle's (1988/350 BCE) ethical theory was influential on pragmatist and other contemporary moral philosophy and may be useful in thinking about inclusive moral community. As we saw in Chapter Four, Aristotle claimed that human excellence and happiness resulted from one's ability to practice virtuous activities (such as courage) by finding the mean through avoiding extremes (cowardice or recklessness). However, humans do not have an innate ability to do this—we have to develop the ability to find the mean, which takes education and time. Aristotle (1962/350 BCE) wrote, "the virtues are implanted in us neither by nature nor contrary to nature: we are by nature equipped with the ability to receive them, and habit brings this ability to completion and fulfillment" (p. 34). Moral virtue comes not from nature, as those things natural are impossible to change, praise, or blame. Rather, moral goodness depends on the habits we cultivate in ourselves, as individuals, and the habits we nurture in others, as members of a social group. Habits of *eupraxia* (good action) lead to virtue and happiness, while habits of vice lead to brutishness, gluttony, and an incomplete life. As the conglomerate of habits, character determines present and future tendencies to act: "Hence it is no small matter whether one habit or another is inculcated in us from early childhood; on the contrary, it makes a considerable difference, or, rather, all the difference" (Aristotle, 1962/350 BCE, p. 1103b). A character in accord with virtue and excellence takes hard work and practice.

Influential in both philosophy and psychology, William James likewise viewed practice as central to a well-organized and moral life. Human beings, James believed, are "mere walking bundles of habits" (1950/1890, p. 127).

These habits allow us to live and grow in a mostly coherent fashion in a world that is often precarious:

> Man is born with a tendency to do more things than he has ready-made arrangements for in his nerve-centres... If practice did not make perfect, nor habit economize the expense of nervous and muscular energy, he would therefore be in a sorry plight (p. 113).

Habits, as we know, are not easily changed. Like Aristotle, James believed that we must take great care with the habits we cultivate, especially at an early age. Furthermore, in learning new habits, it is essential that we act on our beliefs at every chance because

> No matter how full a reservoir of *maxims* one may possess, and no matter how good one's *sentiments* may be, if one has not taken advantage of every concrete opportunity to *act*, one's character may remain entirely unaffected for the better. With mere good intentions, hell is proverbially paved (James, 1950/1890, p. 125).

James might have been critiquing Kant's claim that the best of our moral choices are decided only with logic, and not through learning, practice, and growth. For James, intending something without having learned to act on it through habituation would be akin to expecting the stars to change their paths.

In his moral theory, Dewey traced even further than Aristotle the importance of habit in moral growth. In *Human Nature and Conduct*, Dewey (1988/1922) claimed that habits are the means by which we act—means that are inseparable from the final act, which will itself reinforce the existing habits in such a way that the end becomes a means to further action. He considered habits to be active, "energetic and dominating ways of acting" (p. 23).

Habits are not merely integrated into single acts. They are trends in responding that, in collection, lead to more general tendencies according to experience, a continuity of response to various stimuli. This continuity is what both Dewey and Aristotle referred to as character, the general tendency to act that calls for us to make functional moral decisions or those which lead to vice and dysfunction. Our decisions, as well as our character, depend on our experience and practice in a variety of situations, rather than rational power alone.

Like Aristotle, Dewey (1988/1922) viewed character as the "interpenetration of habits" (p. 29). Because habitual responses to a relatively stable and "overlapping" environment are responsible for conduct, there is a unity of action that makes up character. Without character as the expression of the interpenetration of habits, an individual would be "simply a bundle, an untied bundle at that, of isolated acts" (p. 29). From a Deweyan perspective, this is the empirical problem with modern philosophers' view of the individual—an isolated individual relying only on intention would simply be incapable of any kind of coherent action, moral or otherwise. Such a person would lack integrity and self-identity.

A strong and integrated character, according to Dewey, relies on the compatibility of habits. Habits should "embody one another" for the "solidity of a habit is not its own possession but is due to reinforcement by the other habits" (1988/1922, p. 30). For example, in Aristotelian terms, an individual who has become accustomed, through education and habit, to being generous with her resources is much more likely to help a friend or practice charitable giving when presented with such an appeal (1962/350 BCE). However, Dewey (1988/1922) wrote, "A weak, unstable, vacillating character is one in which different habits alternate with one another rather than embody one another" (p. 30). A character made up of radically conflicting habits not only will lack the ability to make sense of goals and desired ends, but also will not be able to withstand the precarious nature of a constantly changing environment outside of that character.

This is similar, perhaps, to Johnson's (1993) "moral dissonance," the attempt to apply universal moral traditions to novel situations. As James referred to how the road to hell is proverbially paved, attempting to apply even the best-intended moral rules to variable contexts might result in unpracticed and clumsy action. A person of strong character, cultivated from practiced habits, however, will be able to intelligently mediate desires, even those generated by novel events. She will rely on her experiences of the consequences habits can bring about to find the course of action that is most likely to end in further integration of habits within a strong character. She will cultivate a character that has integrity and stability.

Note that Dewey's version of habits and character as the foundation of moral action rests on education, social experience, and practice, rather than isolated intentions or logic. A strong moral character is something that is cultivated and maintained; it is not native, and it does not necessarily rely on a certain IQ or universal reason. Moral character based on social experience and practice is accessible to most humans, with or without intellectual disability (and even some nonhumans; De Waal, 2009), because it relies on a multiplicity of traits and influences and not just reason alone. Moral engagement as the process of developing character through learning and habituation fits well with theories that focus on relationships and emotion as the impetus to be a good moral citizen.

Moral Engagement Based on Emotion

As we saw in the last chapter, a conception of the self that is relational rather than isolated offers a view of morality that may be more inclusive than theories based on reason. Empathy and caring as motivations for action rise naturally out of human relationships, such as the family context, according to some philosophers and psychologists (Gilligan, 1982; Mead, 1964a; Noddings, 1984), and the potential for an emotional response to others is a viable foundation for moral citizenship (Harris, 2010; Jaworska, 2010; Lindemann, 2010). Even Aristotle (1962/350 BCE) noted the importance of friendship and role modeling to the cultivation of virtue.

Mead's concept of taking on the attitude of the other (1934) as the development of self-identity is the root of empathy as an emotional response to others, and can spur action. Although Mead primarily attempted simply to describe the process of the genesis of the self, his ideas are also useful to theorists working toward normative accounts of the way we ought to behave in relationships.

Moral theories based on empathy claim that socialization processes are the foundation for both empathy and moral selfhood. The cultivation of a moral theory (or practice) from empathy stems from the process of socialization itself, and begins during childhood as the self emerges from interaction with others. Perhaps the most important stage of empathy as it relates to moral deliberation is that which occurs when the child first discovers that her actions affect others. Evidence of this stage is seen in the daily activities of children. For example, Hoffman (1979) noted that what starts in young children as a general emotional response to the distress of another (such as an infant crying with another in distress) later becomes a more habituated awareness of the inner lives of others and how our actions help or hinder them. With cultivation, Hoffman (1979) suggested, empathy for individuals could become an understanding of the plight of classes of people (such as oppressed ethnic groups or people with disabilities), which is similar to Mead's (1934) concept of taking on the attitude of the "generalized" other.

Whether toward individuals or groups, the ability to help those in distress, or to foresee possible consequences empathetically through the eyes of others, is intensified by the fact that we not only guess at how others will be affected, but we feel it with them as we try out different possibilities "in mind" (Mead, 1934). Empathy, as opposed to sympathy or pity, allows us to be affected by our own interactions in the same way that others feel and perceive our responses and we are then able to understand how we affect others in a genuine and sometimes painful manner because we are affected by our own behaviors at the same time. For example, Mead (1934) explained:

> One starts to say something, we will assume an unpleasant something, but when he starts to say it he realizes it is cruel. The effect on himself of what he is saying checks him; there is here a conversation of gestures between the individual and himself (p. 141).

A child learning to interact in social situations might not at first understand how his cruel language will hurt a friend's feelings, but with enough experience of another's distress, he will learn to respond to it himself. Eventually, he should be able to gauge these reactions in a general enough way that he will be able to foresee another's reactions in an abstract, imaginative sense. He will be able to imaginatively project himself into novel situations and check his language (or change his language habits) before he is at risk of hurting another's feelings.

This talent an actor has to construct his own character based on the ability to take on the attitudes of others, is what Mead refers to when he says that an individual, "responds or tends to respond to his own social stimulus, as another individual would respond" (1934, p. 243). When we take on the attitude of another, we see ourselves from that person's point of view and therefore respond to our own conduct as she might respond. It is important to note that this is vastly different from the "golden rule" in Christianity and the categorical imperative of Kant. In an ethics of empathy, we should not treat others as we would have them treat us (as children of God or as universal reasoners); rather, we should treat others as they would have us treat them, with their individual attitudes, needs, circumstances, and impulses constantly in our minds. For Mead, treating others in terms of their own circumstances was not a matter of duty, universal rights, or absolute rules, because we are actually able to feel the effects of our own conduct with them. As we will see, this idea is consistent with other moral theories that emphasize emotion as central to moral deliberation (Dewey, 1922; Gilligan, 1982; Noddings, 1984), and is supported by social science research suggesting that moral behavior is rooted in empathy (Hoffman, 1979, 2000; Skoe, 2010).

Gerdes and Segal (2011) argued for a comprehensive framework of empathy consisting of three components: the affective response to another, the cognitive processing of that response, and the process of converting that response into some kind of action. There are multiple ways of investigating the fact that humans have evolved a way of relating to one another through empathy. From a Freudian claim that children adopt their parents' response to themselves (Hoffman, 1979) to Mead's (1964c) description of taking on the attitude of the other to functional Magnetic Resonance Imaging (fMRI) studies of the activation of mirror neurons, which cause us automatically to respond to others "as if we were the 'actor' and not just an observer" (Gerdes, Lietz, & Segal, 2011), there is little doubt that humans have an affective response to the experiences of others that does not depend on static intelligence.

The more controversial claim that empathy is involved in morality, contrary to the theories generated by most historical traditions in Western philosophy, is also supported by contemporary social science research as well as recent moral theory. Gerdes et al. (2011) argued that once someone responds emotionally to the distress of another, she is compelled to act by the awareness that she is feeling the experience of another (rather than her own distress) and the conscious decision to act. Although there is much social science research (Hoffman, 2000) highlighting the second step (self-awareness, role-playing, and regulation of emotions), the third component of an empathetic moral response, what moves us to action, is more speculative and benefits from an interdisciplinary approach.

One outcome of an interdisciplinary approach is that we are likely to avoid the "is/ought" distinction in moral theory that psychologists (is) and philosophers (ought) often tend to make. This distinction assumes that moral action is separate from how human beings actually are—that we are able to make moral principles that do not reflect the facts of our existence, such as human psychology or evolution, and that those facts should be morally neutral. For example, consider Kant's claim (in Chapter Four) that social dispositions such as amiability and kindness are not what should compel us to act; it is only in logical intention where we find true moral worth. However, what we now know about the relational development of identity suggests that we would be mistaken in leaving out of the moral equation further compulsion toward relationships and the development of pro-social dispositions. Dewey (1983/1908) noted the is/ought problem in his discussion of moral deliberation and argued that "It is not an ethical 'ought' that conduct should be social. It is social" (p. 16).

Moral Engagement Based on Care

One of the most important contributions to a view of emotion as central to morality comes from feminist psychology and philosophy. As we will argue here and in Chapter Seven, feminist theory and disability studies may be mutually beneficial in developing theoretical frameworks aimed at improving quality of life for socially disadvantaged groups (Garland-Thomson, 2011a; Wendell, 2008). In feminist psychology, Gilligan (1982) famously accused Lawrence Kohlberg (1981) and his reason-based theory of moral development of neglecting to account for the genetically and environmentally conditioned "different voice" of women.

The main argument Gilligan had with Kohlberg was that his theory implied that women may not be able to reach as high a level of moral development as men, which Gilligan attributed to the possibility that Kohlberg's levels were masculinist. Kohlberg's work assumed a hierarchy of moral stages of development resting on an ideal of universal morality based in reason. Using stories with hypothetical moral dilemmas, Kohlberg categorized subjects into stages of moral reasoning based on their responses to questions about the dilemmas. From these studies, he determined that children start at a preconventional cognitive stage, based on rules and threat of punishment; move as young adults to a conventional stage based on loyalty to cultural norms and expectations, such as laws; and eventually (ideally) end up at a postconventional level, characterized by adherence to autonomously generated abstract principles (Bruess & Pearson, 2002). As individuals advance up the levels, they move from heteronomous to autonomous moral capabilities, consistent with the way Kant thought that adult humans should be able to give moral laws to themselves using rationality rather than relating to laws or the ideas of others.

Gilligan (1982) argued that many women seemed stuck in the conventional category, which led her to claim that the categories themselves were biased against women (Bruess & Pearson, 2002). In her adaptation of Kohlberg's study, Gilligan (1982), like Kohlberg, presented subjects with the "Heinz dilemma," in which a man must decide whether to steal a drug to save his sick wife's life. Gilligan presented the examples of two 11-year-olds, "Jake" and "Amy," whose responses seemed to differ according to gender. While Jake worked mathematically through the dilemma, stating that moral responsibility is "one-fourth to the others and three-fourths to yourself" (p. 35), Amy was concerned with what Gilligan referred to as a "web of relationships," seeing a human life as not good in itself, but valuable in relation to others, and wondering where Heinz's family and friends were in his time of trouble and what Heinz's sick wife would do if he was arrested for stealing. Rather than using logic to work through the problem to support Heinz's actions, Amy, whom Gilligan believed to be representative of the way many women have traditionally responded to moral dilemmas, seemingly stayed at a conventional level of moral reasoning as she tried to understand what the effects of Heinz's actions would be on others, concluding that moral responsibility "depends on the situation" (p. 35).

From this, Gilligan concluded that Kohlberg's stages of moral development simply did not account for the experience, whether genetic or socially conditioned, of women. Even though a host of studies (Buess & Pearson, 2002) contests the gender differences that Gilligan claims are evident in Kohlberg's theory, her work at least stressed that the experience of many women (and men) expresses a social view of ethics as empathetic and caring, a view popularized in moral philosophy as the ethics of care.

In philosophy, Nel Noddings (1984) adopted Gilligan's concerns that standard moral theory was masculinist and she developed a theoretical approach that emphasized care over reason as an appropriate foundation of moral life. Like Gilligan's claim of a different voice, Noddings argued that women experience an alternative moral domain. Assuming that women, as mothers and caretakers, offer the world an ethic that grounds moral decisions in traditionally feminine qualities such as mothering, Noddings expanded Gilligan's descriptive claims by creating an ethical theory based on the web of relationships rather than rules or principles.

Noddings (1984) suggested that with moral theory's traditional emphasis on principles, justice, and justification instead of practice, ethics has been largely discussed in paternal, rather than maternal, language. This is not to say that all men will disagree with her view or that all women should accept it; Noddings's ethics of care merely prioritizes the social experience of caregivers, who, at least in family life in many cultures, have traditionally been women. Noddings and other care ethicists have noted that this theory is feminine in the sense of reciprocity, responsiveness, and empathy, though not exclusive to women (Keith, 2008). We similarly will argue that care ethics is not exclusive to people with traditional intelligence.

Similar to Mead's and Hoffman's claims that empathy emerges from social relationships, what begins with the experience of being cared for becomes "a felt concern for the good of others and for community with them" (Baier, 1995, p. 47). From this, an individual cultivates morality by imagining, developing, and maintaining other caring relationships—by becoming the "one-caring" (Noddings, 1984, p. 24). Ethical caring is cultivated via natural experience (the feeling of being cared for) and learned experience (developing the habit of extending care to others). One bases her ability to care for others in the natural responses she feels in close relationships. The extension outward from already existing caring contexts to potential relationships is the result of our ability to imagine such relationships based on our own past experiences and to empathize with others: "To be touched, to have aroused in me something that will disturb my own ethical reality, I must see the other's reality as a possibility for my own" (Noddings, 1984, p. 14).

In this moral philosophy, what Noddings suggested as the "ethical ideal" has its source only within the web of relationships. To learn to care is to imply a specific kind of response to another—one that acknowledges, from experience, that the desire to feel cared for is reciprocal and shared and to purposefully habituate this response. From this, the "best self" (1984, p. 80), the moral agent within the relational context, emerges, much in the way that strong moral character was cultivated in Aristotle's virtue ethics.

Consider the difference between ethics based on caring and theories more traditionally construed. Noddings (1984) wrote that the only universals in the ethics of care are the remembered feelings and attitudes of caring that are available to all human beings. The theory merely "refers the moral agent to her own memory of caring and her commitment to act in accordance with it—as one might refer to conscience for moral guidance" (p. 107). On the other hand, Kant's (1983/1875) moral theory represents the more traditional Western view in espousing universalizable principles and a moral law based on reason that has no need for emotion of any kind.

The ethics of care has been expanded to account for gender bias. For example, Joan Tronto (1989) favored a feminist, rather than a feminine, theory of caring to avoid traditional gender distinctions. While a feminine perspective implies traditional gender roles, a feminist theory is by definition reconstructive, and so examines the usefulness of our existing and potential relationships. And Noddings suggested that the feminine as a foundation for ethics is merely a useful metaphor based on the alternative experience of women, one that denotes reciprocity and can be practiced by both men and women. As gender roles change, "parenting" might become a better metaphor than "mothering," and any caring relationship, whether family or friendship, can facilitate the best self. Further, though Noddings (1984) claimed that ethical caring applied only to humans, other philosophers have expanded this view to include care for nonhuman animals and the natural world (Held, 2006; Keith, 2012).

Recent scholars have also explored whether caring and empathy might be useful to creating a more inclusive moral community for people with intellectual disability. For example, Jaworska (2010) argued against both minimal rational capacities (McMahan, 2010; Singer, 2010) and reason (Kant, 1983/1875) as inclusive enough to provide people with disabilities full moral standing. Instead, she suggested that the ability to care about and for people and things would expand moral status to include most human beings (with or without intellectual disability, though probably excluding psychopaths) and some nonhuman animals (such as great apes that, via sign language, seem to demonstrate the capacity for caring; De Waal, 2009). Caring as a moral foundation affords one not only status as a moral patient, but also assumes that one may be capable of moral growth and decision making as a moral agent.

Supported by research on the development of empathy (as the ability to respond to others) versus reasoning (which is dependent on mental age), Harris (2010) similarly argued that the empathy-based approach

> is the more pertinent of the two models of moral development when considering moral personhood in persons with intellectual disability. Successful moral education for people with an intellectual disability utilizes emotional sensitivity to provide a sense of membership in a viable family or social group . . . The consequences of emotional empathy are compassionate behavior toward others, moral agency, and pro-social behavior (p. 67).

That pro-social behavior emerges from native tendencies is evident in both ancient philosophy, such as Aristotle's (1962/350 BCE) view that virtue stems from a desire to be happy and is learned through relationships, especially friendship, and in contemporary psychology, such as positive psychology's claim that we desire to associate with others. For example, Haidt (2003) showed that morality is learned within a social context, and that it is motivated by an emotional response to others. In Haidt's studies of college students, he asked subjects to report emotional and physical effects of witnessing good deeds, both in person and on video. Students reported warm, pleasant, or tingling feelings, and, perhaps most importantly, a desire to "help others, become better people themselves, and to affiliate with others" (p. 282). Recalling a situation when she witnessed a friend in her carpool ask to be dropped off to help when he saw an elderly woman struggling to shovel snow from her driveway, one student responded

> I felt like jumping out of the car and hugging this guy. I felt like singing and running, or skipping and laughing. Just being active. I felt like saying nice things about people. Writing a beautiful poem or love song. Playing in the snow like a child. Telling everybody about his deed (Haidt, 2000, p. 3).

As Haidt (2000) suggested, "A common theme in most of the narratives is a social focus—a desire to be with, love, and help other people" (p. 3). What Haidt called *elevation* (both mental and physical) upon witnessing or hearing about good deeds seems to be cross-cultural (Algoe & Haidt, 2009), and can be a powerful motivator of subjective well-being, which can in turn motivate compassionate and pro-social behavior.

A care-based perspective, grounded in social science research on the development of empathy, has clear implications for moral community. If we focus on the richness of relationships as an aspect of morality, then minimally, people with intellectual disability qualify as moral patients and are deserving of our care and protective action. This would prevent parents of disabled infants, or even fetuses, from feeling as though the question of whether baby should live is steeped primarily in the moral tension of a competition of rights (of the baby, the parents, and even society), as Singer (1993) suggested. And, ideally, a care-based perspective expands our community to include moral education for many people previously excluded, allowing them to grow into more agency and to become more active members of moral communities.

Moral Engagement Based on Intelligent Growth

If moral engagement is based on *relationality* rather than *rationality*, then it follows that morality is something that can be grown and cultivated. Aristotle, Hoffman, Noddings, and many other theorists posited this idea, and it was central to Dewey's theories of ethics and education. Danforth (2002) argued that Dewey's philosophy would be useful in bridging the gap between the social and medical models of disability that seems to polarize groups working toward good educational practices.

In Chapter Four, we saw some of the problems with traditional notions of intelligence as contributing to a vision of moral community based solely on rationality. Dewey (1991/1935) offered an alternative conception of intelligence that supports morality based on social context and a caring response to others. For Dewey, intelligence was not something native or static. Rather, it was a product of growth and education, habituated and maintained through practical experience, and had as its aim "the mediation of problematic situations" (Fesmire, 2003, p. 38). According to Eldridge (1998), for Dewey, intelligence was both the means and the end of associated living, involving education and creativity: "As a creative practice, it is the use of one's fund of experience to modify practices that have become dysfunctional" (p. 179).

Dewey was quite critical of standardized intelligence testing, though he left the door open for intellectual testing that might help us to measure one's individual growth and ability to solve problems, to "[interpret] the fullness and richness of individuality" (Danforth, 2008, p. 38). For Dewey, the goal of intelligence was not to achieve an exam grade, but "ordered richness," which Eldridge (1998) interpreted as "a situation in which the individuals involved are able to lead rich, expanding lives" (p. 87).

Growth as ordered richness was, for Dewey, dependent on healthy and functional associations with other people. Lekan (2009) noted that

> Deweyan growth, although primarily about individual well-being, is not just the growth of any capacities in any social situation. It is the growth of capacities that promote rich social integration and that are nourished by that same social integration. An individual is growing to the extent that he or she contributes to the shared interests of a wide variety of social groups (p. 223).

Lekan (2009) applied growth as ordered richness to special education, arguing that a more social view of the goals of education would benefit both abled and disabled individuals. He noted that both the social and medical models of disability accept a notion of personal autonomy and a consequent view of education in which resources appear limited and students must compete for teachers' attention. For example, Lekan wrote, often parents believe the accommodations given to students with disabilities result in lesser education for their own, "normal" children. This view assumes an isolated individual "vying for his or her fair share of resources" for whom education "is a set of discrete episodes between individual students and teacher" (p. 219).

However, Lekan (2009) argued, growth as ordered richness in a Deweyan sense "states that the best, richest kinds of human experiences arise from the development of cognitive, affective, and imaginative capacities, which are expressed in shared, self-directed activities" (p. 222), and that education ideally should result in a continued interest in and capacity for learning and growth. In this view of learning and intelligence, teachers focus on the specific capacities and goals of individual students (for which standardized measurements may sometimes be inadequate), students see themselves as members of a community, and students with disabilities are offered a social setting to which they can contribute in important ways. Diversity, in this case, enhances a community's ability to grapple with novel situations and increases the likelihood that individuals can grow in a rich and pro-social sense.

Danforth (2008) argued that the concept of moral equality was also integral to a Deweyan view of intelligence as the capacity for growth. Rather than conceptualizing intelligence as something measureable that can be compared across isolated individuals and equality simply as the right to compete for resources in order to enhance one's status, "Moral equality involves a shared, active ethic that acknowledges differences between individuals without constructing those as differences within schemes of hierarchical gradation" (p. 55). With a social conception of the individual, the goals of education, and morality, Danforth claimed that the dilemma of the social and medical models of disability could be mediated. He wrote that a Deweyan theory of intellectual disability would avoid the extremes of the two models, including

> naturalistic essentialism that frames the biophysical or psychological constitution of the individual as a deterministic factor in human activity, on the one hand, and a radical social constructionism that overlooks individual growth, learning, and agency amid notions of overwhelming cultural constraint, on the other (p. 57).

With a Deweyan view of intelligence as growth and morality and education as social, there is appreciation, or perhaps even a necessity, for people with diverse capabilities.

Moral Engagement Based on Capabilities

The contemporary philosopher Martha Nussbaum emphasized a variety of capabilities in her approach to political theory and intellectual disability. As we saw in previous chapters, social contract theory, a position that assumes we associate politically because it is in our self-interest to do so (and not because we are innately driven to relate to others), is problematic for a couple of reasons. First, it rests on a conception of the individual as isolated and autonomous, a view that is empirically weak and ethically exclusive. It also assumes that people are "characterized by a rather idealized rationality" (Nussbaum, 2006, p. 98) in that those creating the laws and policies of the social contract are by default seen as the primary citizens under its protection and "morality emerges (to the extent that it does) from the constraints of having to bargain with others who are similarly situated" (p. 103), and this similar situation traditionally implies that there is the opportunity of reciprocation. Bérubé (2010) added that social contract theory "has no way to build into its foundations an account of why we should agree to create forms of social organization that will support and nourish some people who will never be capable of repaying the favor" (p. 99). Because social contract theory is so much a part of modern democracy, just as the Cartesian isolated individual is still so much a part of our ethical theory, it makes sense to explore approaches that might work better toward expanding the moral reach of political theory.

Similar to Dewey's view of intelligence as growth toward ordered richness for individuals always within relationships, Nussbaum's (2011) "capabilities" approach (following Amartya Sen, 1985) "takes each person as an end, asking not just about the total or average well-being but about the opportunities available to each person" (p. 18). The approach emphasizes comparative quality of life assessment based on individual potential and capabilities and calls on government to improve well-being. Nussbaum (2006, 2011) promoted ten capabilities, minimally at a threshold level, which she believed ought to be supported in every person, regardless of ability. Some capabilities are reminiscent of traditional ethical theories, such as life, bodily health, and bodily integrity (Lock, Kant, and Mill, for example, would agree to these as rights), but Nussbaum did not highlight in her list traditional social contract or individualistic ethics interests such as rationality or the right to own property. While these are not excluded from the capabilities list, Nussbaum (2011) chose instead to focus on capabilities that promote quality of life and the potential for human association, such as "senses, imagination, and thought," "emotions," "practical reason," "affiliation," "play," "control over one's environment," and even "being able to live with concern for and in relation to animals, plants, and the world of nature" (pp. 33–34). As we will see in Chapter Eight, there is ample evidence to suggest that many of these capabilities are likely to enhance quality of life in various abled and disabled populations. For example, emotional well-being, individual control, self-determination, and social inclusion are well-recognized dimensions of quality of life that have received extensive study in a number of groups, including people with intellectual disability (Schalock et al., 2002).

An important feature of an approach based on capabilities is that, like Jaworska's focus on care, it bases moral and political practices on functional opportunities for growth, rather than on static capacities, such as rationality or language use. In a letter to Singer, Bérubé (2010) wrote "You're looking for things people with Down syndrome can't do, and I'm looking for things they can" (p. 108).

In keeping with other ethical approaches based on the potential for emotional responses to others, Nussbaum (2011) noted that with her capabilities approach it is "quite easy to make the role of care in a conception of justice as fundamental as it ought to be" (p. 168). This includes both for the cared-for and the caregiver, and Nussbaum argued that good public policy would support the above capabilities, which should include making resources available to individuals, families, and groups not only for the physical health of people with disabilities, but also for nurturing their particular capabilities. Good care implies that relationships are secured (especially by supporting caregivers), individual potential is acknowledged and supported (even for people with severe disabilities), and all citizens are afforded opportunities to grow, learn, and flourish. Consistent with Hoffman, pragmatism, and care ethics, good care as public policy supports moral relationships and growth.

Caring Capabilities and Disability

Caring for others, caring about ideas or things, enjoying the company of other people or sports or art or music, and having a sense of ownership over one's living conditions are capabilities that we might agree humanize us and make us unique. Many theorists and practitioners note that a diversity of people display capabilities that would seem to plant them firmly in the realm of full moral status. Lekan (2009) mentioned Temple Grandin whose autism makes it possible for her to relate to confined animals, leading her to be one of the most vocal advocates for more humane slaughterhouse conditions. Sophia Wong (2002) has noted that she and her brother, who has Down syndrome, share achievements and sorrow together and that she believes that "the struggles he faces at home with Down syndrome are not so terribly different from my frustrations as a cognitively 'normal' woman starting to make my own home. It is a difference in degree, perhaps, but not of kind" (p. 114). Bérubé (2010) has written about his son, also with Down syndrome, who is learning French, is interested in science fiction, and "knows more about the Beatles oeuvre than most people who don't study the Beatles for a living" (p. 98). And Kittay (2010) has stated about her daughter, who has severe intellectual disability, that "she is enormously responsive, forming deep personal relationships with her family and her long-standing caregivers" (p. 403) and that she loves classical symphonic music, especially Beethoven. "So much for the assertion that persons with severe mental retardation cannot experience aesthetic pleasures!" (p. 403).

Some people categorized with intellectual disability may even be especially suited, more so than many "normal" people, for moral growth and status because of intense capabilities for caring for and associating with others. Kittay (2008) contrasted people with intellectual disability, including her daughter who brings "joy to all whose lives she touches," with Nazi doctors who "employed rationality of a highly developed sort" (p. 151). She noted that "we can see that having the capacities of rationality and autonomy are neither necessary nor sufficient for avoiding harms or for bringing good into the world" (p. 151).

Williams syndrome also provides an interesting case study for ethics, especially as we consider foundations for moral engagement beyond rationality. Though they score on average 30 or so points lower than the norm on traditional IQ tests, people with Williams syndrome are genetically disposed toward pro-social behavior, or at least a genuine willingness to affiliate (Dobbs, 2007). Though people with Williams have a lesser ability in some areas (such as spatial thinking), they often have an increased ability in language and in affiliatory, gregarious behavior. While they sometimes have a lesser ability than normal for what psychologists call a "theory of mind," making it difficult for them to know when others tire of a conversation or have competing interests, people with Williams have a desire to connect and care. Oliver Sacks (2007) wrote that people with Williams are "extraordinarily responsive to music" (p. 321) and have "unusual social attention and friendliness" (p. 324). Minimally, this may be an interesting suggestion that some people have less traditional reason but a more advanced sense of the pro-social and the basic building blocks for moral engagement than many "normal" people. In the *New York Times*, Robert Sapolsky noted that "Williams have great interest but little competence. But what about a person who has competence but no warmth, desire or empathy? That's a sociopath. Sociopaths have great theory of mind. But they couldn't care less" (Dobbs, 2007).

In his discussion of Dewey and intellectual disability, Lekan (2009) noted that, in addition to clear benefits for the growth of students with disabilities, there are clear advantages to everyone of having people with a diversity of intellectual ability in the classroom (and, we argue, everywhere). Likewise, Ian Brown, in *The Boy in the Moon*, observed that his son Walker's own growth contributes to the moral lives of many others, and he found this to be true for other parents of profoundly disabled children. For example, he interviewed Lana Phillips, mother of Jaime:

> "I live my life less from fear now," she told me. "I just feel that I am becoming the person I've always wanted to be in life," she said. "I work with small children, I have learned patience, and empathy, to reach out for people no matter what they look like. And that has all been because of Jaime" (Brown, 2009, p. 140).

And Shelly Greenhaw spoke of her daughters Kinley and Kamden: "I really believe that they're not a genetic mistake. Maybe they are mistakes in our minds, sometimes, because of the artificial boundaries we human beings create" (Brown, 2009, p. 143). Greenlaw added that "we all have genetic mutations, they're just not obvious in our clinical presentation" (p. 143), and that her girls changed her own pro-social behaviors for the better.

We have proposed in this chapter, with Brown (2009), that our moral community needs to be expansive enough to embrace people of a diversity of abilities, for their sake as well as for ours:

> So you can perhaps forgive me for thinking, some days, that Walker has a purpose in our evolutionary project, that he is something more than an unsuccessful attempt at mutation and variation. For thinking, probably vainly, that if his example is noted and copied and "selected," he might be one (very small) step towards the evolution of a more varied and resilient ethical sense in a few members of the human species. The purpose of intellectually disabled people like Walker might be to free us from the stark emptiness of the survival of the fittest (p. 233).

7

Culture and Intellectual Disability

Raymond Loomis lived at the Beatrice State Home in Nebraska for 15 years, from 1953 to 1968. While at the institution Ray attempted on several occasions to escape, and upon his eventual release the superintendent predicted that he would fail in the community. Although he did indeed experience numerous problems living in the community, Ray not only eventually succeeded, but also became a leader and a legend. Realizing that people in his situation needed advice and support, he worked with local community service staff and volunteers to establish a group. Although only three people attended the first meeting, their numbers grew to 40 within a year, and Ray gave the group a name, Project Two. He chose the name for a logical reason: the community service system in Omaha was a project arising from local initiative, and he wanted a second project.

As Ray developed leadership skills Project Two grew and took direction, and members learned to rely on Ray and on themselves to plan and direct activities. Then, in 1977, they learned of another group, People First, that had formed in Oregon. The members of Project Two learned to raise questions and to talk about their own experiences and needs. They received an invitation to speak at the state convention of the Nebraska Association for Retarded Citizens, and then to local communities across the state. They formed committees and planned their own People First state convention. The planning committees prepared resolutions that Ray Loomis read to the assembled group, and more resolutions came from participants. Those resolutions dealt with basic rights in areas that remain timely today, 35 years later: education, housing, employment, economic well-being, freedom of

Intellectual Disability: Ethics, Dehumanization, and a New Moral Community, First Edition.
Heather E. Keith and Kenneth D. Keith.

expression, marriage, and others. The list began with this statement: "We believe that we are people first, and our handicaps are second. We wish people would recognize this and not give us a tag like 'handicapped' or 'retarded'" (Williams & Shoultz, 1982, pp. 223–224). Ray Loomis continued working on behalf of others with intellectual disability, learning to present programs on self-advocacy and becoming the subject of a television program about his life and work. When Ray died following complications of open-heart surgery in the autumn of 1979 he left an extraordinary legacy and a group of friends who had learned to value and to stand up for themselves.

Any analysis of human nature and ethics is inevitably cultural. As we saw in earlier chapters, even our perception of ourselves is connected to other human beings. Conceptions of intelligence and disability are no different, and there are ample examples, especially around the turn of the twentieth century, of the public perceiving intellectual disability as decidedly exotic (Bogdan, 1988), reflecting an interest in geographic discovery when they believed the people displayed in freak shows were from exotic lands. On the other hand, for more than two centuries the population of Martha's Vineyard Island included a high proportion of congenitally deaf people who were integrated into the community in exceptional ways, because people of the local culture did not consider deafness a disability (Groce, 1985). And homosexuality, considered abnormal in American culture until the 1970s, when the American Psychiatric Association and the American Psychological Association decided otherwise, remained a psychological disorder in China until 2010 when the Chinese Psychiatric Association changed its classification (Matsumoto & Juang, 2013). In the twenty-first century, we recognize that our global era requires that we think of disability studies from cultural and global perspectives. In this chapter we explore a sampling of cultural issues and analyses of intellectual disability.

Race, Ethnicity, Gender, and Disability

The relation between people with intellectual disability and the experience of other marginalized groups is important to address both because of its relevance to developing best practices concerning a diversity of people, and because of possibilities for enhancing disability studies by including insights from previously marginalized groups. Chris Bell (2010) laid out the problem of marginalization of race and ethnicity in disability studies, pointing to the dearth of people of color in documentaries and conferences on disability. In the first half of the twentieth century, race, ethnicity, and "feeble-mindedness" were linked by the mark of impurity and the threat of eugenics (Stubblefield, 2010). Licia Carlson (2010) noted that the concept of intellectual disability was racialized during Victorian times, as in the terms "Mongolian" (Down, 1866) and "Mongolism" (Menolascino & Egger, 1978), which were offensive to both people of Asian descent and people with disabilities (because of negative Victorian attitudes toward the non-Colonial world). These terms, and others like them, reflected the view that other races and ethnicities were inferior to those of Western culture, the kind of attitude that Sumner (1906) called *ethnocentrism* and that exemplified the belief that intellectual disability was a throwback or retrogression to inferior races (Down, 1866).

School segregation has long been an issue for both people of color and people with disabilities (Ferri & Connor, 2005), and there is evidence that children of color are overrepresented in American special education settings (Heward & Cavanaugh, 2001), despite the fact that there is significant controversy about what race really is (Anderson & Nickerson, 2005) and the possibility that distinctions between races may be both dubious and arbitrary (Zuckerman, 1990). In the eyes of government agencies, for example, people often belong to whichever racial or ethnic group they choose (i.e., they self-identify; Beins, 2009); Phinney (1996) reported research in which only 20 percent of people in self-identified ethnic groups could confirm that they belonged in those categories. Nevertheless, some authorities (e.g., Arthur Jensen, 1968) have argued that there are innate differences in intelligence between ethnic groups, despite evidence that IQ among racial groups may vary according to region and culture within the US (Matsumoto & Juang, 2013). Further, as we saw in Chapter Three, there is a long history of questionable use of tools such as intelligence tests against a wide array of marginalized groups, such as immigrants, people of color, and people with disabilities.

Likewise, there are multiple connections between feminist theory and disability theory, from similarity of experience to common philosophical concepts. Women and people with disabilities share the unfortunate historic experience of oppression due to cultural assumptions about both embodiment (Wendell, 2008) and intelligence (Carlson, 2010). An example may be found in the centuries-old belief that because of hormonal changes, women experienced cognitive and emotional impairment during a part of their monthly cycles—an idea debunked by the research of psychologist

Leta Stetter Hollingworth (1914). Hollingworth's findings showed that the previous notions about women and their presumed disability had simply been the construction of male-dominated perceptions. The experience of women and people with physical disabilities has included the problem of bodies not being well-fitted to the environment. Rosemarie Garland-Thompson (2011a) wrote about embodied "disjunction," when "the built and arranged space through which we navigate our lives tends to offer fits to majority bodies and functioning and create misfits with minority forms of embodiment, such as people with disabilities" (p. 594), a problem for women living in cultures prioritizing maleness, and for people with disabilities living in social and built environments more appropriate for able-bodied people. Garland-Thompson's concept of the "misfit" is interesting because it reflects both individual embodiment (including pain and impairment) and the social structures that contribute to the construction of disability, offering a path for navigating the theoretical divide between the medical and social models.

A cultural emphasis on intelligence and mental ability (especially as exemplified by white males) renders both women and people with intellectual disability invisible, and Carlson (2010) noted that this has been doubly the case for women with disabilities. Karen Warren (2000), though writing about nature, argued that there is a "logic of domination" based on intelligence that allows us to believe that those who epitomize rationality (usually men) are morally permitted to dominate other beings (women and nature). Warren's assertion can find support in the fact that the men who developed intelligence tests—men such as Henry Goddard and Lewis Terman—assumed that women, as well as nonwhite ethnic groups and the poor, were less capable intellectually than were white men (Stubblefield, 2010). This logic has no doubt contributed to the history of oppression of people with intellectual disability, especially women.

Within a logic of domination, there is a double bind that subjugates women with disabilities. Carlson (2010) suggested that "feeble-minded" women were subject to institutionalization and involuntary sterilization because they were thought to be morally weak (lacking intelligence) and because they posed a genetic threat to civilization. Incapable of fending off the advances of predatory men, and believed to be at risk of giving birth to feeble-minded children (as, Carlson noted, in the case of Goddard's [1912] focus on Deborah Kallikak as responsible for the "defective line" of that family), women were institutionalized to avoid this genetic threat: "Thus not only were women incarcerated at childbearing age due to the

Figure 7.1 **Girls' Cottage, built at Asylum for Feeble-Minded Children of the State of Iowa in 1912, the year Henry Goddard published *The Kallikak Family*, in an era when institutions assiduously segregated the sexes.**
Source: Photo by K. D. Keith

dangers of procreation, but they were refused parole because of their feminine vulnerability and passivity" (p. 60). And in the 1960s when involuntary sterilization became difficult to obtain (by parents or guardians on behalf of people with intellectual disability), it was the parents of women who most often went to court to attempt to have their daughters sterilized (Diekema, 2003). Leonard Davis (2010) suggested that the association between intellectual disability and criminality, such as sexual license, "established a legacy that people with disabilities are still having trouble living down" (p. 11).

Women and disability have also been historically connected by the fact of dependence, and the United Nations Committee on the Elimination of All Forms of Discrimination Against Women has seen fit to issue a general recommendation regarding the rights of women with disabilities (World Health Organization, 2004). In what political philosophers have called the split between the public and the private, Wendell (2008) wrote that "women (and children) have been relegated to the private, and so have the disabled, the sick and the old (and mostly women take care of them)" (p. 831). This connection between being cared for and caregiving, while at the theoretical root of the feminist ethics of care, can be oppressive when it is only or primarily seen as the private work of women. When such caregiving is private and gendered, workers are often underpaid and people who are cared for are alienated from social structures such as education, meaningful employment, and other aspects of citizenship. Differences in embodiment and experience have led both women and people with disabilities to be marginalized and treated as "other"—as objects rather than active subjects (Carlson, 2010; Wendell, 2008).

This shared oppression, however, has led to interesting theoretical approaches aimed at the liberation of both women and people with disabilities. In their introduction to a special issue on disability of the feminist philosophy journal *Hypatia*, Eva Kittay, Alexa Schriempf, Anita Silvers, and Susan Wendell (2001) wrote that philosophers of disability "find ready-made conveyances in several of feminist philosophy's signature themes" (p. viii). For example, feminist theory has been instrumental in development of the social model of disability, with the conceptual difference of sex (body) and gender (culture) giving a logical structure on which to hang the difference between impairment and disability (Shakespeare & Watson, 2002; Wendell, 2008).

Sophia Wong (2002) used the structure of sexism to discuss discrimination against people with intellectual disability, such as Down syndrome. In her discussion of genetic testing and disability, she wondered whether society would find selective abortion acceptable if we were selecting based on gender, rather than disability. Although some may argue that because there are clear economic and social disadvantages to being a woman in many cultures, this is more a function of society than it is of sex. Similarly, if there are disadvantages to having Down syndrome, it is a result of social discrimination and not necessarily the syndrome itself. If the majority of women and people with disabilities are able to live healthy, meaningful, and productive lives, then it would be morally problematic to abort based solely on assumptions about quality of life.

Wendell (2008), Carlson (2010), and Kittay (2010) have all argued that women and people with disabilities have also shared the unfortunate experience of having their voices silenced. Wendell wrote, "Like women's particular knowledge, which comes from access to experiences most men do not have, disabled people's knowledge is dismissed as trivial, complaining, mundane (or bizarre), *less than* that of the dominant group" (p. 837). From this oppression, however, comes the view that the knowledge generated by this difference in experience might be interesting and transformative, even to the "dominant group" as it becomes part of a "shared social life" (p. 838).

In particular, feminist standpoint theory, an epistemological approach that emphasizes individual experience in generating knowledge, has been useful to disability scholars as well as theorists of race, ethnicity, and gender. Philosophers such as Nancy Hartsock (1998), Sandra Harding (1991), and Mary Mahowald (1998) developed this movement in philosophy to highlight the idea that what we conceptualize as knowledge consists of the contextual and particular standpoints of individuals. Rather than asserting knowledge as objective truth, standpoint theory assumes that knowledge is social and that marginalized people often have insights and truths that do more work than dominant beliefs. Standpoint theories are universal in the sense that they apply individual experience and knowledge to normative claims, especially about political and justice issues regarding marginalized people.

Because people of color, women, and people with intellectual disability have been historically marginalized, standpoint theories have been useful to scholars, especially in criticizing objective claims about personhood, ethical practices, and what constitutes intelligence and knowledge. For example Kittay (2010) argued that while philosophers such as Singer and McMahan make tight analytic arguments, they neglect the real experience of people with disabilities or their caregivers in constructing knowledge about disability ethics. Mahowald (1998) explored the ways in which people with disabilities are different from others, including others with disabilities, from etiology to duration, because all these differences make up the context of an individual's experience, which contributes to her unique standpoint. Mahowald noted in particular that people with cognitive disability must be included in discussions about ethical issues and care because their standpoint is often marginal even within the wider disability movement: "Reduction of the inevitable nearsightedness of those who are cognitively able regarding those who are cognitively disabled requires recognition of our myopia and desire to reduce it" (p. 230).

Standpoint theory offers a view of knowledge that is inclusive of a diversity of people, and is an appropriate addition to any ethical theory regarding disability, especially those that claim that our best moral ideals and practices emerge from social relationships, such as pragmatism and the ethics of care. Standpoint theory is more about methods of inquiry than about practical ends, but it ensures that caregivers, educators, and ethicists reflect on the particular circumstances of real individuals by preventing the tendency to prioritize theories over people. Garland-Thomson (2011b) reframed standpoint theory as "sitpoint theory" to add the experience of life in a wheelchair, an apt reminder to standpoint theorists that even our best efforts at inclusion reflect only some of our knowledge and experience. We also note that the idea of seeing anything from any kind of "point" is itself an ocular metaphor, thus highlighting the dominant experience of sighted people.

Intellectual Disability, Language, and Contemporary Culture

As we can see, language is an important indicator of how we conceptualize disability. We noted in earlier chapters that our way of categorizing and discussing intellectual disability is constantly evolving, from "feeble-minded" to "retarded" to "people with disabilities." This is important because there is ample evidence that the language we use affects how we think and act (e.g., Kreiner, 2011), including toward others, and that how we speak is another example of our contextual, ethical lives (Holtgraves, 1997).

In their work on metaphor, George Lakoff and Mark Johnson (1980) argued that the concepts governing our thinking "structure what we perceive, how we get around in the world, and how we relate to other people" (p. 3). They used the example of argument as war to show that we do not just talk about arguments in terms of war, such as winning or losing an argument, attacking a position, or shooting down another's claims. In fact, perceiving argument as war actually affects how we interact with others. An argumentative victory becomes the end goal at the expense of others. A partner in inquiry becomes an enemy. If we thought of argument as dance, however, our view of our language partners would be much different. Word choice makes a difference in how we frame an issue (Lakoff, 2002).

This knowledge is applicable to our cultural use of language regarding intellectual disability. Because we know that language drives our beliefs and actions, we are increasingly careful about the words we choose to describe ourselves and others. It is clear in the context of the work of Lakoff and Johnson (1980), that terms such as "feeble-minded" or "retarded" convey beliefs about people that are discriminatory, and also serve to reinforce that discrimination in our thoughts and actions. "Retarded," for example, has come to be an insult in our language, used against people without regard to whether we intend to categorize them according to intelligence. There is currently a popular movement sponsored by the Special Olympics, in television advertising and on the Internet, to "spread the word to end the word," which calls to our attention the detrimental effects of using the word "retarded." In hard-hitting brief public service announcements, actors, athletes, young people, and other citizens denounce the use of "retarded" as just another slur used to hurt people. People with disabilities and their advocates relate that they feel devalued and angry when they hear such language. According to Lakoff and Johnson (1980), there is even more at stake because our linguistic conceptualization of intellectual disability (as feeble-minded, retarded, moronic, and the like) shapes how we actually see and treat people.

On a more positive note, self-advocacy groups, recognizing the power of language, often refer to "people first" (Williams & Shoultz, 1982) as in *people* with disabilities, in order to emphasize the commonness of our humanity. Robert Groulx (Groulx, Doré, & Doré, 2000), of People First of Montreal, noted the problem of labeling for employment, education, and, mostly importantly, self-esteem and self-confidence: "One has the impression that attached to the label 'mentally retarded' is the idea of 'burden on society' or 'burden on parents and on professionals.' That does not help you to feel good and to have a positive self-image" (p. 28). Avoiding over-categorization and labeling by putting people first, however, can be empowering (Ward, 2000). Self-advocate Ray Loomis understood the power of language when he said "If you think you are handicapped, you might as well stay indoors. If you think you are a person, come on out and tell the world" (Williams & Shoultz, 1982, pp. 23–24). Another self-advocate, Ollie Webb (2002), succinctly summarized the importance of language and its role in formation of attitudes and perceptions:

> [P]eople should be known by their names [and accomplishments,] not by their disabilities. I ain't different from you. I am the same as you. I got a name, and I want you all to call me by my name. My name is Ollie Wayne Webb (p. 57).

With the power of language in mind, we note that discussing people with disabilities, or disabled people, is also fraught with the potential for problematic meaning. Even using the words "disabilities" or "disabled," of course, emphasizes difference and otherness, and exchanging "disability" for other words, such as "difficulty" changes public perceptions about people's abilities (Schneider, 2009). "Disability" as used in disability studies, or the social model of disability, however, can also help people to identify with a movement, and to develop a clear standpoint from which to challenge dominant beliefs and policies. Tobin Siebers (2010) argued that "disability creates theories of embodiment more complex than the ideology of ability allows, and these many embodiments are each crucial to the understanding of humanity and its variations, whether physical, mental, social, or historical" (p. 317). Perhaps we should have a dream similar to Nancy Ward's (2000): "[M]y dream for the future is to work myself out of a job, because there will be no need to have organizations that work with people who have a disability" (p. 36). Our dream might be to write about disability in order to contribute to the extinction of the idea and the label.

In addition to the language we use, every day and in our theories, our conception of disability, including intellectual disability, is shaped by mass culture, such as film and television. Actors and athletes working on television campaigns to "spread the word to end the word" appear in a far more positive and realistic light than in previous decades. The public perception of intellectual disability for many people was associated with freak shows in circuses and carnivals. As we saw in Chapter Two, people with disabilities were hired (or sometimes bought from their families) to entertain the public with tours across the US and Europe. Bogdan (1988) argued that though many "exhibits" became wealthy in such shows, such as the famous William Henry Johnson ("Zip," the man-monkey), who apparently owned land in New Jersey and a home in Connecticut, the attitudes of the viewing public reflected mistaken beliefs regarding the origin and nature of disability: "How we view people with disabilities has less to do with what they are physiologically than with who we are culturally" (Bogdan, 1988, p. 146). Thus, when people with microcephaly were exhibited as "Aztecs" or other creatures that sounded exotic to audiences of the time, the language created a particular public perception. However, when intellectual disability was "medicalized," and the causes more scientifically understood, fewer people were interested in seeing the exhibits.

In more recent times, people with intellectual disability have had leading roles in major films and television shows. However, whether these media depict disability in a more realistic light remains open to question. According to a Special Olympics policy paper on the media portrayal of people with intellectual disability (2005), although more people with disabilities are evident in the media, they are increasingly depicted as vulnerable, as victims, and in ways intended to elicit pity. If the public is misinformed about the real lives of people with intellectual disability, then it will remain difficult to cultivate more useful ethical theories and practices.

Cross-Cultural Perspectives

Culture—the shared values, beliefs, and behaviors of a group—is the foundation from which people of different heritage, customs, and traditions develop, and it influences self-concepts, language, worldviews, and connections to others (Matsumoto, 2000). Recent trends in the study of intellectual disability in the global cross-cultural context include a refocus from a concentration on individual people with disability to an understanding of them in the social context in which they live, recognition of the powerful influence of family and society on the lives of individuals with intellectual disability, and a move away from the emphasis on specialists and specialized disability services to an emphasis on empowerment and mainstream service provision (Emerson, McConkey, Walsh, & Felce, 2008). In other words, the evolving international view is that intellectual disability is not simply an invariant characteristic of the person (Devlieger, Rusch, & Pfeiffer, 2003; Schalock, 2011; Switzky & Greenspan, 2006), but also a social–ecological construct reflecting the person–environment interaction, the role of environmental supports to enhance personal functioning, and pursuit and understanding of identity (including such factors as well-being, self-worth, and pride; Schalock, 2011).

In contrast to longstanding earlier views of intellectual disability as a medical or hereditary personal condition, the modern international perspective acknowledges biomedical causal factors (genetics, parental age, nutrition, maternal conditions), but also places emphasis on social, behavioral, and educational influences in the framework of a multifactorial understanding (Schalock, 2011). And according to Wehmeyer et al. (2008) and the World Health Organization (2001), the limitations normally considered as "disability" can occur not only in the areas of intellectual ability and adaptive behavior, as traditional definitions have suggested, but also in health (including social and mental well-being); participation in the social life of home, work, education, and culture; and the interrelated context of a wide variety of personal factors and the individual's environment.

Intellectual disability is compounded by poverty in much of the world, with wide gaps between the richest and poorest nations along such dimensions as rights and judicial protections, services (and access to services), government benefits (and financing), and availability of information (Mercier, Saxena, Lecomte, Cumbrera, & Harnois, 2008). The scope of the discrepancy between services/supports and levels of need in developing countries was clear in India nearly four decades ago, when institutional services were available for about 4000 of the estimated 22 million people with intellectual disability (Sen, 1975). Two decades later, prevalence surveys in China placed the overall rate of disabilities at 4.9 percent, two-thirds of these being people with intellectual disability, and a prevalence rate for intellectual disability in children under age 14 of 1.8 percent. These numbers, according to Sonnander and Claesson (1997), gave China at that time more people with disabilities than any other single country. Estimates of worldwide prevalence rates for intellectual disability are 1–2 percent, with higher rates among children and adolescents in poor countries (Maulik, Mascarenhas, Mathers, Dua, & Saxena, 2011). Research has consistently shown a correlation between poverty and the incidence of developmental disabilities, probably due to two major factors: (i) poverty is associated with a variety of environmental and psychosocial risks that in turn cause disability, and (ii) families and individuals with intellectual disability are at increased risk of poverty due to costs of care for families and workforce discrimination against potential workers with disabilities (Emerson, 2007). There thus seems to be a reciprocal relation between poverty and intellectual disability.

Poverty also affects availability of information on people with intellectual disability in much of the world, to the extent that extensive information is available primarily from English-speaking countries with high income levels (Emerson, Fujiura, & Hatton, 2007). Ninety percent of the world's children under age 14 live in countries with low or middle income (World Bank, 2012), and fewer than half of such countries have reported provision of support (in such avenues as in-home support, advocacy, or respite care) to people with intellectual disability (World Health Organization, 2007).

Although people of different nations experience different cultures, and cultures vary in many ways around the world, research has shown characteristic sociopsychological dimensions of disability (De Clerck, 2010), and Rapley (2004) has argued that culture has no reality independent of descriptions of it. To the extent, then, that individuals with disabilities share attitudes, perceptions, beliefs, values, and the like, they may also share a culture defined not by national boundaries, but by their social and psychological commonalities (e.g., Conyers, 2003), creating a pan-ethnic culture that reaches beyond the values and beliefs associated with ethnicity, religion, racial, or gender (Eddey & Robey, 2005).

Comparative Philosophy and Intellectual Disability

In Chapter Five, we briefly explored comparisons between Western and Asian philosophical conceptions of personhood with the idea that theories coming from some Asian thinkers, such as Confucius, express the kind of relationality that is indicative of pragmatist social ethics. There are similarities with social ethics in some of the ethical ideals from Asian thought, as well. In thinking about global issues of intellectual disability it may be useful to develop a social ethics of disability from a comparative position. We offer examples of Asian philosophy, with the understanding that non-Western traditions are far more diverse and fruitful than we can explore here.

As we saw in Chapter Six, social ethics is contextual, emerging from social relationships. The basic element of morality is our habitual response to situations, and we learn from our best interactions with others what habits will be integrated into good character, a "best self" (Noddings, 1984). Asian ethical theories, such as those in the Confucian and Buddhist traditions, also emphasize a moral agent natively related to others. Mencius, an early Confucian ethicist, for example, thought that development of a good moral character was like the growth of sprouts into healthy crops (Ivanhoe, 2002). This growth is fully dependent on a variety of other conditions, such as a nurturing environment, and much of the responsibility of being human is to contribute to moral growth, in ourselves and others. In a Confucian sense, when we achieve what Roger Ames calls "co-creativity" (2011) we become most human.

Clear support for the care of others as part of our own well-being can be found in the Buddhist ethics of compassion. As we saw in Chapter Five, Buddhist metaphysics posits that all things are conditioned by others, including human selves. There is no human ego that transcends relationships with others, and any success, ethical or otherwise, that we may enjoy is shared with others. This deeply felt relationality leads to compassion for all living things in Buddhism (Harvey, 2000), not because we feel pity for others, or see them as moral patients to whom we are obligated, but because we recognize our connection to them, in a manner similar to Mead's (1934) idea of taking on the attitude of the other. In particular, Darla Schumm (2010) argued that Buddhism "teaches that 'your' suffering/healing and 'my' suffering/healing are not inherently different" (p. 134) and so compassion compels us to act to alleviate suffering in all bodies.

The doctrine of "no self" further enables us to envision embodiment in a way that may be healthy regarding disabilities. With metaphysical underpinnings of conditioned origination, which implies constant change, Buddhism conceptualizes the body as always evolving. Schumm (2010) argued that "the idea of a whole and stable body is incommensurate with the Buddhist perspective because there is nothing constant that can be categorized as stable or whole" (p. 134), which changes the focus of embodiment from stability and wholeness to an acceptance of transformation and difference. We could apply this to the concept of mind or intelligence, as well. If the mental self for Buddhism is simply a conglomerate of conditioned and evolving states, then there is no one measurable state (such as intelligence quotient) that is any more or less human or good. Those of us who enjoy, now, "normally-abled" bodies and minds can learn from this worldview that those states are constantly changing, which is simply part of what it is to be human. Fear of change or the unknown is not useful or healthy in this case. In both Confucian and Buddhist ethics, the interconnectedness of ourselves with others also widens the circle of moral agency without requirements such as measurable intelligence.

Disability and Academic Culture

Finally, we note that the environment which most affects what we learn about disabilities in our classrooms and from books such as this, is academic culture. Consistent with standpoint theory, social ethics, and any other theory aiming to be responsive to and engage the real lives of individuals, the voices and views of people with intellectual disability need to be moved from margin to center. This is not solely for the sake of best practices in disability ethics, though that should be prioritized; but the value of widening the scope of what constitutes knowledge is that it serves to enhance the "neurodiversity" of our academic pursuits, as well. Maeve O'Donovan (2010), writing about learning disabilities, noted that though philosophers of mind have an interest in studying disability, they tend to do so only to understand more about the "normal" mind, again relegating intellectual disability to the domain of marginal cases. This is harmful not only to people with disabilities, but it is also problematic for the wider academic culture because it reflects an Enlightenment view of knowledge that does not suggest the actual range of human intelligence. O'Donovan wrote that exclusion "is not only harmful to certain members of the academy, it prevents the academy from developing new knowledges and new conceptions of how knowledge is generated. *It is harmful*" (p. 181).

To remedy the lack of diversity in epistemology and other studies of knowledge, O'Donovan argued that more academically successful people with learning disabilities should be involved in conducting research about intelligence, knowledge, mind, and disability. This inclusion would help to challenge some of the assumptions of current philosophy of mind, such as the idea that "normal" minds are universalizable and all others are marginal cases. O'Donovan used the structure of feminist standpoint theory to show that a more inclusive academic system would embrace and emphasize voices from the margins, strengthening our academic study of intelligence and mind, and fortifying ethical positions that enhance quality of life. In the next chapter, we will explore the dimensions of a good life and the contributions to quality of life of home, community, relationships, competence, and speaking for oneself.

Part III

Disability Ethics for a New Age

8

Quality of Life and Perception of Self

Mary was a woman in her 50s who had lived in a large state institution nearly all her life. The institution was one of the many that had originally carried the term "feeble-minded" in its name—a name that underwent several changes along with the evolution of societal and professional attitudes. Like many other residents of the institution, Mary held a job within the facility—a job ostensibly providing her with job training and preparation for a normal life in the community. According to such traditional measures as IQ tests and culturally appropriate social behavior, she was a good candidate for successful community placement. In Mary's case however, the benefits of the job were complex and not quite what they seemed. Mary's job placement was in the on-campus home of the institution's superintendent, where Mary was assigned to work as a housekeeper. She was skillful in her job, providing the superintendent and his family with reliable, competent service and helping to keep the household running in a pleasant, predictable way. However, despite her obvious abilities and her desire for a life in the community, Mary could not succeed in gaining an opportunity to leave the institution; after several attempts to assist her departure from the facility, her social workers realized that the superintendent, quite happy with her service to his household, would never approve her move to the community. After all, he said, she had a good life at the institution. Why should she want more? This question echoes the words of the early institutional leader W. E. Fernald (1902) who, while extolling the virtues of the outdoor activities, including baseball and football, available to residents of the Massachusetts Farm Colony for the Feeble-Minded, asked "What more can a boy want!"

Intellectual Disability: Ethics, Dehumanization, and a New Moral Community, First Edition.
Heather E. Keith and Kenneth D. Keith.

(p. 489). The superintendent's desire to keep Mary as an institutional worker reflects the kind of peonage and exploitation that was far too prevalent in such facilities (Bartlett, 1964) and the tendency for such places to be built for the convenience of staff rather than residents (Wolfensberger, 1969).

Questions about what people want from life, and the quality of that life, have existed since prehistoric time. However, even a brief review of such reports as Blatt and Kaplan's (1966) *Christmas in Purgatory* or Wolfensberger's (1969) *Origin and Nature of Our Institutional Models* reveals the terrible conditions to which society consigned people with intellectual disability, even within the last half century. In the same era, Blatt (1969) reported that zoos spent more *per capita* for the care of large animals than some American institutions did for the care of people with intellectual disability. Only a few years later, in the 1970s, individuals with intellectual disability began to organize and advocate for their own needs and life quality, in part due to recognition of the need for support for people leaving institutions (Williams & Shoultz, 1982). Landesman (1986) challenged researchers to take up the task of defining and measuring quality of life and, although some writers (e. g., Luckasson, 1990) expressed misgivings, Schalock (1990) foresaw that quality of life would be the dominant issue of the 1990s in the field of intellectual disability.

As Rapley (2003) noted, some of the dangers associated with the movement were identified with efforts to quantify quality of life, leading to concerns about the use of quality of life data to justify decisions about medical treatment for life-threatening conditions (Nord, 1999), physician-assisted suicide for those whose lives might be considered less than worthwhile (Sheldon, 2000), or selective abortion for particular kinds of cases (Kuhse & Singer, 1985). These fears were not totally unfounded; Brown (2000) characterized the relation between economic rationalism and quality of life as a collision course, and Taylor and Bogdan (1996) described a study (Gross, Cox, Tatyrek, Pollay, & Barnes, 1983) including a formula for determining quality of life in decision making about treatment of infants with disabilities. In recognition of some of these concerns, various writers (e.g., Goode & Hogg, 1994; Keith, 1990; Kozleski & Sands, 1992; Schalock & Keith, 1993) have proposed that quality of life of people with intellectual disability should be related to that of other people as a step toward integration of individuals with disabilities into the life of the broader community. In its emergence in the 1980s, quality of life served as a construct sensitizing people to what individuals wanted in their lives and as a guide to human service practices and policies; more recently however, it has become a framework for delivery of services, a foundation for evidence-based human service practices, and a mechanism for implementation of approaches to quality improvement (Schalock, 2010).

Defining Quality of Life

By 1995 Cummins reported the existence of more than 100 definitions of quality of life; Hughes, Hwang, Eisenman, and Killian (1995) identified more than 1000 measures of different dimensions of quality of life; and between 1992 and 1995 more than 2500 references to quality of life appeared in the psychological literature (Antaki & Rapley, 1996). Eventually, Schalock and Verdugo (2002) reported that beginning in 1985 the number of published articles with "quality of life" in their titles numbered more than 20,000. Schalock's (1990) prediction about the importance of quality of life as an issue proved prophetic, and some (e. g., Keith, 2007) suggested that quality of life was the *raison d'être* of the various organizations, services, and supports developed to aid people with intellectual disability.

Researchers have not come to agreement on a single definition of quality of life that seems appropriate for all people (Hensel, 2001) and some authors (e.g., Schalock, 1996) have suggested that a single unitary definition may not be appropriate. Some have seen quality of life as a correlate of personality or temperament (Edgerton, 1996), a product of person–environment interaction (Rapley, 2000), a result of personal feelings and experience (Taylor & Bogdan, 1996), and as a construct influenced by psychological, sociological, and anthropological forces (Brown, 2000). Despite long-held beliefs that objective factors (physical and material well-being, housing, income, and especially elimination of poverty via increased economic status) would improve individual well-being, it seems clear that both objective and subjective (individual perceptions and interpretations) indicators are necessary for an understanding of quality of life (Campbell, Converse, & Rodgers, 1976). Although most evidence has suggested that personal experience of quality of life of people with intellectual disability does include both the tangible, objective conditions of life as well as the person's subjective perception or interpretation of those conditions (Keith, 1996), Edgerton (1996) raised a cautionary concern, suggesting that objective aspects of life or program quality and subjective factors may not be highly related. Nevertheless, there are no truly objective standards for assessment of quality of life, and it is likely that some individuals may be quite happy (a subjective characteristic) in objective circumstances that others would find unacceptable—an observation consistent with findings of weak relations between objective and subjective indicators of quality of life (e.g., Hensel, Rose, Stenfert Kroese, & Banks-Smith, 2002; Parmenter, 1992). Because of the differences between objective and subjective factors, researchers have commonly taken both into account (Cummins, 1995, 1997; Schalock & Keith, 1993), and the earlier emphasis on material aspects of quality of life eventually gave way to a broader concern for social indicators (Veenhoven, 1996).

Despite the efforts not only of researchers, but also of individuals with intellectual disability (e.g., Groulx, Doré, & Doré, 2000; Helle, 2000; Ward, 2000), a clear definition of quality of live has remained elusive. However, Cummins (1997) provided a description consistent with much of the work in the field; he described quality of life as both objective and subjective and comprising seven domains (material well-being, health, productivity, intimacy, safety, and community and emotional well-being). This model has considerable similarity and overlap with one put forth by Schalock (1996), which has produced a significant international consensus (Schalock et al., 2002) around eight core domains of life quality: emotional well-being, interpersonal relations, material well-being, personal development, physical well-being, self-determination, social inclusion, and rights. Thus scholars have placed emphasis not on a singular definition, but on the multidimensional nature of the construct of life quality.

A Multidimensional Construct

Schalock et al. (2002) described the international consensus around the eight quality of life domains noted above. Earlier, Keith, Heal, and Schalock (1996), in a study of seven cultures, found broad agreement on ten quality of life concepts (rights, relationships, satisfaction, environment, economic security, social inclusion, individual control, privacy, health, and growth and development). Writing in the same year, Felce (1996) described six essential aspects of quality of life (physical well-being, material well-being, social well-being, productive well-being, emotional well-being, and (civic) rights well-being), and Hughes and Hwang (1996) collected numerous definitions of quality of life that, in aggregate, provided 15 dimensions including, among others, community integration, well-being, satisfaction, civic responsibility, and personal competence. The multifaceted nature of quality of life is well established in the research literature of the field.

In addition to the dimensions identified by researchers, it is important to recognize the efforts of people with disabilities and their advocates to identify meaningful aspects of life quality (Felce, 1996; Goode & Hogg, 1994; Keith, 1990, 2001; Renwick & Brown, 1996; Renwick, Brown, & Raphael, 2000; Taylor & Bogdan, 1996). Thus, in pursuit of the common values underlying quality of life, the views of individuals with intellectual disability have been significant in shaping our conceptualization of the multidimensional meaning of the construct (Amado, Conklin, & Wells, 1990; ARC of Nebraska, 2002, 2003; Bonham, Basehart, & Marchand 2000; Keith & Bonham, 2005). The result has been recognition of the importance, for all people, of feelings of well-being, positive social involvement, and opportunities for achievement of personal potential (Schalock et al., 2002). Efforts to measure quality of life have occurred in the context of five key assumptions that serve as working principles underlying our understanding (Schalock et al., 2002):

1. Individual personal circumstances (the contexts of life, work, and play) are crucial aspects of quality of life.
2. Different people experience life differently, and individual people experience life differently at different times.
3. Quality of life is a holistic entity such that the different domains interact in reciprocal ways.
4. Individual control, choices, and empowerment are important contributors to quality of life.
5. Quality of life is significantly colored by the subjective perceptions of the individual; life quality truly lies in the eyes of the beholder.

Measuring Quality of Life

We have seen that researchers have been generally agreed that quality of life is a multidimensional entity—a fact that led to recognition of the usefulness of multifactorial approaches to life quality assessment (Brown, Brown & Bayer, 1994; Heal, Borthwick-Duffy, & Saunders, 1996; Schalock, 1996). These approaches have readily lent themselves to development of quantitative multidimensional scales. However, researchers studying quality of life have employed a number of other approaches, some of them quantitative (e.g., direct behavioral observation; McGill, Emerson, & Mansell, 1994) and others qualitative, including grounded theory (Strnadova & Evans, 2012), interviews (Alderson, 2001), ethnographic studies (Edgerton, 1990), and conversation analysis (Antaki & Rapley, 1996). Qualitative approaches can be particularly useful in understanding quality of life from the perspective of a particular individual or locale, as opposed to an understanding based on presumed universal norms or large group comparisons (Rapley, 2003). Here we will briefly review some of the viewpoints and research representing four perspectives: multidimensional scales, ethnographic studies, discrepancy analysis, and direct behavioral measures.

Multidimensional scales

An early multidimensional scale, the Lifestyle Satisfaction Scale (LSS; Heal & Chadsey-Rusch, 1985) included four subscales measuring Community Satisfaction, Friends and Free Time Satisfaction, Satisfaction with Services, and General Satisfaction. The LSS later underwent revision and expansion, eventually including additional dimensions such as recreation and leisure, job satisfaction, and satisfaction with interpersonal interactions (Harner & Heal, 1993; Hawkins, Kim, & Eklund, 1995; Heal, Rubin, & Park, 1995).

Another early instrument designed to measure individual quality of life was the Quality of Life Questionnaire (QOL.Q; Keith, Schalock, & Hoffman, 1986). In its initial form, the QOL.Q assessed Environmental Control, Community Involvement, and Social Relations. Subsequent revision (Schalock, Keith & Hoffman, 1990; Schalock & Keith, 1993) produced a QOL.Q with four scales (Satisfaction, Productivity, Empowerment, and Social Belonging), numerous translations, including Chinese, Japanese, Polish, Spanish, and French, among others (Keith, 2007), and a factor structure sufficiently robust for cross-cultural application (e.g., Caballo, Crespo, Jenaro, Verdugo, & Martinez, 2005; Kober & Eggleton, 2002; Otrębski, 2000; Rapley & Lobley, 1995).

Another widely used scale for measurement of quality of life is the Quality of Life Scale—Intellectual Disability (ComQol-ID), developed by Cummins (1991) and subsequently revised several times (e.g., Cummins, 1997). The ComQol-ID assesses quality of life across seven domains (material well-being, physical well-being, productivity, intimacy, safety, community, and emotional well-being) and also allows for evaluation of individual acquiescence (the tendency for a respondent to comply or agree with an interviewer), which is an issue that has concerned some scholars studying quality of life (Heal & Sigelman, 1995; Perry & Felce, 2002; Rapley, 2000). In development of the ComQol-ID, Cummins (1991) stressed the role and weighting of individual values as determinants of the importance of quality of life domains for each person.

In their effort to assess quality of life for individuals with severe disabilities, Ouellette-Kuntz and McCreary (1996) developed the Quality of Life Interview Schedule (QUOLIS). The QUOLIS incorporates measures of 12 domains: health services, case management, transportation, social-recreational, religious-cultural, family guardianship, income maintenance, education-employment, advocacy, counseling, aesthetics, and housing and safety. In order to evaluate quality of life for people who cannot be independently interviewed, the QUOLIS uses proxy informants to report on behalf of individuals with severe disabilities.

According to Schalock and Verdugo (2002), the QOL.Q and the ComQol-ID are the most frequently implemented scales in studies of quality of life of people with intellectual disability. These instruments share four characteristics that, according to Schalock and Verdugo, contribute to their widespread use:

1. Both are multidimensional and tap the most commonly studied life quality domains.
2. They include items that assess both objective and subjective aspects of quality of life.
3. Both possess good psychometric properties.
4. They have both been extensively studied in empirical research.

Townsend-White, Pham, and Vassos (2011), in a review of 24 quality of life assessment instruments, found that the various instruments each had strengths and weaknesses, and that most were lacking in at least some important psychometric characteristics.

Most of the foregoing material has its basis in study of quality of life of adults with intellectual disability, and quality of life of school-age children has received limited attention in the literature (Schalock & Verdugo, 2002; Watson & Keith, 2002). Researchers have designed a number of quality of life measures focused on health-related issues of children (Zekovic & Renwick, 2003), while others, including the Quality of Life Profile: Adolescent Version (QOLPAV; Meuleners & Lee, 2005; Raphael, Rukholm, Brown, Hill-Bailey, & Donato, 1996) have been used mainly with mainstream groups (i.e., students without intellectual disability). Keith and Schalock (1994, 1995) designed one scale, the Quality of Student Life Questionnaire (QSLQ), using groups of children with and without intellectual disability. The QSLQ measures quality of life via four scales—Satisfaction, Well-Being, Social Belonging, and Empowerment/Control—and has proven useful in applied research with both groups (Watson & Keith, 2002). More recently, other researchers (Emerson, 2010; Emerson, Honey, Madden, & Llewellyn, 2009) have discussed the use of human rights instruments (e.g., United Nations Convention on the Rights of the Child) to identify social indicators of the well-being of children.

Measurement of quality of life is a process that has its pitfalls and its critics. Edgerton (1990), for example, expressed the concern that attempting to measure quality of life using typical psychometric scales would risk oversimplification of a complex construct, and Hatton (1998) questioned whether the aims embodied in individual quality of life are incompatible with the aims of standardized measurement. Taylor (1994), writing in a similar vein, pointed out the risk that a standardized approach might impose lifestyle aims inconsistent with those of the individual. It is indeed important to recognize the danger in the assumption that quality of life is a single thing that can be defined by a particular instrument, especially if that assumption comes at the cost of an understanding of the individual nature of personal judgments about life quality (Rapley, 2003). These concerns are among those that have given rise to alternative approaches to quality of life research.

Ethnographic study

Ethnography is a qualitative research approach to the study of people in their cultural context. In a long-running program of research using unobtrusive naturalistic observation Edgerton (1990) and his colleagues studied the lives of individuals with intellectual disability. These studies have involved extended contact, at irregular intervals, with people in the natural settings of their everyday lives and without use of structured psychometric or interview techniques (Edgerton, 1996). The intent of this approach has been a full, rich picture of the life satisfaction of these individuals, often producing personal accounts of people's lives in their own voices (Edgerton & Gaston, 1991).

Taylor and Bogdan (1984) also showed the value of qualitative techniques to the study of people in their natural settings, giving an intensive, focused picture of the lives of individuals. Similarly, Hutchison (1990) used open-ended interviews of people with intellectual disability, as well as their family, friends, advocates, and service providers, to develop an understanding of the friendship patterns of individuals living in community settings. Ethnographic approaches, and other related techniques aimed toward illuminating the lives of people in their own cultural contexts and through their own words and behavior, may produce very different understandings of such complex constructs as life quality than do the standardized approaches emanating from the professional human service disciplines (psychology, psychiatry, social work) that Rose (1999) called the "psy-complex." As Rapley (2003) observed, ethnographic approaches are grounded in the "emic" (context-specific) views of the respondent, rather than the "etic" (universal) perspective of the professional—a distinction that can be important in evaluation of quality of life (Bowd, 1989).

Discrepancy analysis

Heal et al. (1996) discussed a discrepancy model of quality of life that emphasized the goodness of fit between the needs of individuals and personal satisfaction of the needs—in essence, the nature and quality of the fit between person and environment (Parmenter, 1992). As Schalock, Keith, Hoffman, and Karan (1989) suggested, the underlying assumption here is that a better person–environment match would lead to better quality of life. Rimmerman and Crossman (2004) found that quality of life of adults with severe disabilities was higher in people whose self-perception suggested milder disability and who used their sheltered work site only for work (not unrelated leisure and recreation activities)—apparently reflecting their own view of their match with the environment. In other words, individuals who saw themselves as *mildly* disabled (even though they had received the label of "severe disability") reported a higher quality of life. Their personal subjective perceptions of their circumstances and their relation to their environment were better predictors of quality of life than the "reality" of their disability.

Another important determinant of goodness of fit seems to be the capacity of the environmental context to provide support for individual skills and for the personal choice and control essential for reduction of discrepancies between individual needs and goals (Heal et al., 1996). The significance of opportunity for personal choice in living environments has found support in the research of Strnadova and Evans (2012), Wehmeyer and Schwartz (1998), and Lachapelle et al. (2005), who reported positive correlations between self-determination scores and quality of life measures among adults with intellectual disability. In other words, people with greater control over their own lives experienced greater quality of life. These findings provided empirical evidence consistent with Ward's (2000; Ward & Keith, 1996) assertions concerning the relation between quality of life and personal empowerment.

Murrell and Norris (1983) proposed a model that would make quality of life the central element in determination of goodness of fit between individuals and their environments. The model is based on the notion that the characteristics of people interact with the various resources and stressors present in the environment to produce a resultant level of quality of life. This is an approach that can reduce the discrepancy between personal perceptions of current and desired life conditions (Goode, 1997), it has been demonstrated in aging individuals (Stevens-Roseman, 2007), and would have significant public policy implications (Dennis, Williams, Giangreco, & Cloninger, 1993).

Direct behavioral measures

Ultimately, quality of life depends in some large measure upon the behaviors available to the person—in terms of both environmental opportunity and individual behavioral repertoire. In recognition of this reality, some researchers have employed direct observation of behavior as a quality of life indicator. Rawlings (1985), for example, used observation of engagement in appropriate social behaviors and activities as a way of relating such behavior to judgments of autonomy and personal freedom in community settings. As individuals move from institutional to community living, changes in occurrence of challenging behaviors can serve as an indicator of improving quality of life (McGill, Emerson, & Mansell, 1994), and, using the Index of Participation in Domestic Life (Raynes, Sumpton, & Pettipher, 1989) as a behavioral measure, Rapley and Hopgood (1997) found significant correlations between productive behavior and quality of life measures.

Jones et al. (1997) studied the effects of staff training in "active support" on the behavior of individuals with intellectual disability. Active support is a planning process that directs staff time and effort toward involvement of people with disabilities in meaningful behavioral activities and toward being responsive to the activity preferences of individuals. Such activity can be systematically observed and research has shown that it contributes to quality of life of people with intellectual disability (Felce, 2000). Other similar approaches to improvement of adaptive behavior have also produced desirable quality of life outcomes (Felce, Lowe, & de Paiva, 1994). These efforts remain important in view of the reality that the lives of people with challenging behavior may differ significantly from those of other people (Cummins, 2005), that service providers have used very restrictive methods (e.g., physical restraints, chemical controls, neglect) to control behavior (Deveau & McGill, 2009; Sanders, 2009), and that service programs can effect behavioral changes that are reflected in quality of life (e.g., Bonham, Basehart, Schalock, Marchan, Kirchner, & Rumenap, 2004).

Results of Quality of Life Measurement

At the beginning of this chapter we met Mary, who lived and worked in an institutional setting. What is quality of life like for an individual such as Mary? Was she happy with her life in the institution? Would she be more satisfied with life in an ordinary community? Or would she simply find herself isolated and unhappy in the community? Could she speak for herself in describing her own perceptions and wishes, or would someone else need to speak for her? These are the kinds of questions researchers have attempted to answer in a large number of studies investigating quality of life of people with intellectual disability.

In their efforts to measure quality of life, researchers have found that it is correlated with a number of other measures, including personal characteristics, conditions of life, and the attitudes and perceptions of other people (Schalock, 1994). And although quality of life remains fundamentally a product of the subjective experience and perception of the individual, studies have highlighted a number of important objective aspects of quality of life affecting people with intellectual disability. For example, people moving from institutions to community settings typically experience increased quality of life (Chowdhury & Benson, 2011). Nevertheless, individuals with intellectual disability are more likely than their fellow citizens to experience social exclusion and socioeconomic disadvantage (Emerson & Hatton, 2007), their community participation and employment rates are lower (Verdonschot, deWitte, Reichrath, Buntinx, & Curfs, 2009), and they are more likely than their nondisabled peers to be victim of abuse (Horner-Johnson & Drum, 2006).

Quality of life of people with and without disabilities

Despite the fact that for some time a variety of authors (e.g., Cummins, McCabe, Romeo, Reid, & Waters, 1997; Keith, 1990; Kozleski & Sands, 1992; Williams & Schoultz, 1982) have stressed the importance of the relation of life quality for people with disabilities to that of other citizens, studies have generally revealed that individuals without intellectual disability enjoy a better quality of life than those with disabilities. Kishi, Teelucksingh, Zollers, Park-Lee, and Meyer (1988) reported that adults with intellectual disability who were using community-based services had fewer decision making opportunities than did their fellow community members. Kixmiller, Keith, and Schalock (1991), in a study of quality of life of people with intellectual disability living in community settings in two towns, found that those with disabilities liked their towns as much as other residents, but had less interaction with neighbors and believed they were treated less favorably by neighbors. Sands and Kozleski (1994) found people with disabilities to be generally satisfied with their lives, but they were also less likely to experience such other quality of life indicators as self-determination; recreational, community, and leisure activities; and independence.

Keith and Ferdinand (2000), in a study involving more than 3000 people in 37 communities, collected data on nine dimensions of quality of life (satisfaction, productivity/competence, empowerment/independence, social belonging, rights, relationships, economic security, growth/development, and overall perception of well-being). For all nine dimensions the average scores for people with intellectual disability ($n = 2699$) were lower than those of people without disabilities ($n = 442$). There were some exceptions to this pattern, most notably in productivity/competence and growth/development, for which the differences between the groups were not statistically significant. The largest differences (significant across all 37 towns and cities) occurred in the dimensions of empowerment/independence and rights. In 36 of the 37 locations overall perceptions of well-being were higher for people without intellectual disability.

Hensel et al. (2002) investigated objective and subjective aspects of the quality of life of adults with and without intellectual disability. The results for objective and subjective measures differed somewhat, consistent with other researchers' findings that objective and subjective aspects of quality of life may not be highly correlated. Hensel et al. found significantly lower scores for the group with disabilities on four of seven objective measures (health, productivity, community, and emotion). However, on subjective measures, people with intellectual disability indicated significantly greater satisfaction with their productivity and material well-being than did nondisabled controls, and those with disabilities rated five of eight domains (material well-being, productivity, community, safety, and emotion) as more important than their nondisabled counterparts. The researchers suggested that these greater estimates of importance may have been due to stronger aspirations on the part of people with disabilities to improve their lives.

In a study of school-age children, Watson and Keith (2002) found that children with disabilities reported lower scores than those without disabilities for all scales and for total scores on the QSLQ. Bramston, Bruggerman, and Pretty (2002), in another study of adolescent quality of life using the QSLQ, reported that children with intellectual disability showed significantly lower social belonging and empowerment than their nondisabled peers, and were also less likely to use some community facilities. Using different methodologies, D'Eath, Walls, Hodgins, and Cronin (2003) found that Irish adolescents with intellectual disability were likely to experience social isolation, few opportunities to meet friends outside of school, and increasing (rather than decreasing) dependence on family. These studies would seem to suggest that the findings typical of the quality of life of adults with intellectual disability may well prevail for children as well.

People with intellectual disability

Within groups of people labeled with intellectual disability, studies have shown correlations between quality of life measures and a variety of individual characteristics, attitudes and perceptions of significant others, and personal life conditions (Schalock, 1994). However, research has also suggested that quality of life is not related to age within the range of 15–55 years, or to sex (Schalock & Keith, 1993). On the other hand, Keith, Schalock, and Hoffman (1986) found, in a relatively large sample (about 800 individuals), an inverse relation between individual service needs and quality of life scores (greater need levels were associated with lower quality of life scores), and in a sample of 312 people Schalock and Keith (1993) reported a significant correlation between quality of life scores and IQ scores. However, within need-level groups, Keith, Schalock, and Hoffman (1986; $n = 455$) and Schalock, Keith, and Hoffman (1990: $n = 552$) found differences among people receiving services in different employment and residential programs, generally indicating higher quality of life associated with service delivery approaches more nearly resembling "normal" settings. In other words, people living in apartments had better quality of life than those in small group homes, those in small group homes had better quality of life than those in large group homes, and so on. Similarly, as noted above, a recent review of the literature on deinstitutionalization (Chowdhury & Benson, 2011) suggested that individuals moving from institution to community tend to experience increased quality of life fairly soon after relocating (although the effect seems to reach a plateau within the first year following relocation).

Recent evidence (Perry, Felce, Allen, & Meek, 2011) has indicated that movement to the community can improve the lives even of people with severely challenging behavior, if appropriate services and supports are in place, and that adults with intellectual disability who live in the community in out-of-family placements may participate in more household and community activities than those who live in their family homes (Felce, Perry, & Kerr, 2011). Somewhat parallel findings exist for older people with intellectual disability, who fared better in terms of quality of life measures (including meaningful activity and community access) when living in community disability homes than in the homes of other older people (Higgins & Mansell, 2009). An exception to the generally desirable outcomes of community placement may be found in those cases involving community placement of individuals with intellectual disability in areas removed from their local area; in these cases the affected people are at risk of reduced family contact, community alienation, and failure to have personal needs (e.g., cultural) met (Perry, Shervington, Mungur, Marston, Martin, & Brown, 2007).

Speaking for Oneself: Proxies, Self-Advocacy, and Quality of Life

One of the most commonly used methods to assess quality of life is the individual interview, and when people with intellectual disability cannot be interviewed, researchers and professionals have often asked proxies who know individuals well to respond on their behalf (Stancliffe, 1999). Hence, according to Zekovic and Renwick (2003, p. 30), "Who should be asked?" is among the most frequently raised questions concerning assessment of quality of life of people with intellectual disability. The answer, according to scholars (e.g., Heal & Sigelman, 1996; Raphael, 1996), depends upon such factors as the ability of the individual to respond to inquiries, congruence of others' perceptions with those of the person with intellectual disability, and the extent to which the individual may be dependent on the other person. Although some investigators (e.g., Rapley, Ridgway, & Beyer, 1998) have reported that proxies (generally service staff or family members) overestimate some aspects of individuals' quality of life, Stancliffe (1999) pointed out the possibility of other factors (e.g., individual response bias, including acquiescence) that might account for discrepancies between the perceptions of individuals and their proxies. Nevertheless, researchers are agreed that proxy reports of individual quality of life are less desirable than are first-hand reports from people themselves (Cummins, 1998; Rapley, 2003; Schalock & Keith, 1993; Stancliffe, 1999), and that multiple sources of information, including of course the perspective of the individual, are valuable (and necessary) to understanding life quality (Zekovic & Renwick, 2003).

The importance of the voice of the person with intellectual disability is central to the notion of self-advocacy—the process by which individuals or groups speak on their own behalf about issues that affect them and their life quality (Williams & Shoultz, 1982). As Ward (2000) asserted, "Our responsibility is to help change the situation and that is the connection between self-advocacy and quality of life. We have to learn to speak up for ourselves and help make our lives better" (p. 35). In speaking for themselves, individuals with disabilities can inform others, including researchers, about their views of such important issues as friendships, intimacy, relationships, aging, and grief (Knox & Hickson, 2001). This issue is significant in view of the fact that, as Boxall (2002) noted, much of the literature dealing with the social model of intellectual disability originates with people *without* disabilities. If, as we have suggested earlier in this book, intellectual disability is in large part a socially constructed notion and, as Morris (1993) contended, "People are disabled by society's reaction to impairment" (p. x), it is imperative that the society hear the voice of individuals and their views of their own quality of life. It is, after all, these people whose perceptions of self and relation to community context define what it means to live with the disability label.

Quality of Life in Perspective

As the research suggests, quality of life occupies a central place in discussion of the construct of intellectual disability. Although service programs espouse a variety of goals and intended outcomes, their ultimate aim is to improve and maintain the quality of lives of their consumers. This is a very different aim from those of the institutional superintendent who stood in the way of Mary's aspiration for a life in the community or of the numerous facilities whose abuses of residents have come to light in legal actions (Menolascino, 1977).

Keith (2007), drawing on the work of Edgerton (1996) and Schalock et al. (2002), summarized several principles that provide a framework for an understanding of the concept of quality of life and its relevance to the lives of individuals:

1. Quality of life evaluation must be multidimensional.

   It is true that quality of life can be assessed objectively, but it is always experienced subjectively. Thus, efforts to measure quality of life must take account not only of the multiple domains of quality of life, but also the role of such other factors as family, friends, life settings (work, home, community), personal control, and the rhythm of daily life. Some of the ethical approaches we have reviewed (e.g., Kuhse & Singer, 1985; McMahan, 2005) seem to attend mainly to medical and other individual dimensions of quality of life. A more pluralist pragmatist view, however, also emphasizes social, political, and other relationships (e.g., Dewey, 1985/1918, 1988/1927; Lekan, 2009). Further, the pragmatist view, in concert with recognition of the importance of the rhythm of daily life, sees quality of life as an evolving, aesthetic process, and not a static product.
2. Assessment of quality of life should be meaningful and comfortable—not a "testing" situation.

   Antaki and Rapley (1996) showed that an examiner or interviewer can easily direct or select the responses of individuals in such a way as to obscure the intent and the voice of the person. Evaluation of quality of life, when accomplished in an interview setting, should take the form of a conversation, jointly engaged, that provides opportunity for expression of and respect for individual desires and perspectives. Thus, it is essential that quality of life assessment avoid the problems inherent in the earlier intelligence testing movement, particularly the perspective that Sternberg (1996) identified as the construct of inert intelligence.
3. The voices of others, whether they are informants, proxies, advocates, family members, or friends, are not an adequate substitute for the individual's voice and viewpoint.

   Keith (2007) described a community scenario in which individuals lacking verbal skills sampled two forms of Sunday morning activity: religious services and televised reruns of *The Lone Ranger* (a TV series). The service provider, not wishing to impose either activity on service users, arranged to observe the behavior of individuals as they experienced each activity, and to take their behavior as an indicator of their preference. In this way, individual wishes could be respected and, although they did not have a literal voice, their "voices" were heard—an outcome that might not have been possible if assessment had been limited to quality of life interviews or questionnaires.

4. It is not always necessary to compare individual quality of life data to those of other people.

   The subjective nature of quality of life means, among other things, that individuals need not always try to be like others. Although data can be universally important if they indicate dangerous living conditions, denial of rights, restriction of autonomy, or other truly perilous circumstances, the fact remains that, as we noted earlier, quality of life and personal satisfaction really are in the eye of the beholder. A pragmatist conception of quality of life (Dewey, 1934; Kupfer, 1983) prioritizes the personal aesthetic experience of everyday living; further, as Perske (1972) showed, exposure to prudent, normal risk may well enhance quality of life.

5. We must go beyond superficial judgments based on standard social values such as community integration.

   Although evidence suggests that life in the community is desirable for most people, we also know that too many people live in isolation and loneliness in the community (Rapley, 2000), and that being physically present in the community is not necessarily the same as having a meaningful life in the community (Bramston, Bruggerman, & Petty, 2002). A key point here is that a pluralist approach acknowledges that while we can measure elements of quality of life, there is no single right moral claim that can universally account for the contingencies of every life.

6. Living standards do not, in themselves, establish quality of life.

   Gardner, Carran, and Nudler (2001) found, in a variety of types of service organizations, that health and safety measures did not reliably co-vary with quality of life indicators, and Edgerton (1996) suggested that individuals may be more or less sensitive to various aspects of the environment, meaning that better places to live or work may not necessarily result in persistent changes in personal well-being.

We saw, earlier in this chapter, that researchers have not agreed on a single definition of quality of life. However, we might now be able to say simply that quality of life is a human aspiration that encompasses success and satisfaction with the experience of life, and includes happiness and contentment in all its dimensions—social, emotional, physical, financial, and professional (Keith, 2007; Watson & Keith, 2002). This notion is consistent with the perspective of American philosopher Joseph Kupfer (1983), who discussed how the everyday activities of life—work, education, relationships, decision making—present opportunities for aesthetic experience. Put another way, the aesthetic permeates experience (Dewey, 1934; Alexander, 1987), a notion we will explore further in considering ethical cases in the next chapter. Thus, a life of quality is a life lived with as much beauty, grace, and dignity as possible—a metaphorical dance that each individual carries out for a lifetime. Let the dance begin.

9

Application and Best Practices
Rights, Education, and Ethics

Life in the real world for people with intellectual disability, perhaps more than for many others, is complex and challenging. A portion of the challenge is of course occasioned by the individual characteristics, whether cognitive, medical, or behavioral, of the person. But much of the challenge is also associated with the kinds of social, cultural, and perceptual factors we have discussed in preceding chapters. We saw, for example, in Chapter Seven that people with intellectual disability are more likely than others to live in poverty, and that discrepancies in judicial treatment of those with disabilities are great between rich and poor countries. In Chapter Eight we learned that quality of life is likely to be poorer for people with intellectual disability than for other people, and data from the US Equal Employment Opportunity Commission (EEOC, 2011) suggest that only 31 percent of adults with intellectual disability are employed, even though many more would like to work. Advocates and authors, including Jacobus tenBroek (1966), in his often-cited *The Right to Life in the World*, have argued for policies of full integration for people with disabilities, but the reality of life for many remains not mainstream, but marginal, and far too many people, although residing in the community, continue to lead lives of isolation (Rapley, 2000). Among children, only 17 percent with intellectual disability and 13 percent with multiple disabilities spend most of their school days in general classes (National Center for Education Statistics, 2012). We have come a long way since the age of indictment, but we clearly have a long way remaining to go.

Intellectual Disability: Ethics, Dehumanization, and a New Moral Community, First Edition.
Heather E. Keith and Kenneth D. Keith.

Justice for All

For too much of America's past people with disabilities lived out a history that Burgdorf and Burgdorf (1975) characterized as dismal. Unequal treatment prevailed in state laws, public education, institutionalization and other living conditions, opportunity for employment, voting rights, and protection from abuse. Here we review some key examples of important rights provisions enacted on behalf of people with disabilities.

Education

Ironically, education for students with intellectual disability received impetus from a 1954 court case widely recognized as a mandate to eliminate racial segregation, *Brown v. Topeka, Kansas Board of Education.* In its decision in the *Brown* case, the Supreme Court used language indicating that *everyone* should have equal access to education (McDonnell, Hardman, McDonnell, & Kiefer-O'Donnell, 1995). However, widespread changes in education would await further court action, in the 1970s in Pennsylvania and in Washington, DC, resulting in rulings that all children with disabilities were entitled to free, appropriate public education and leading to passage of Public Law 94-142, the Education for All Handicapped Children Act (Beirne-Smith et al., 1994).

Subsequent amendments led to the Individuals with Disabilities Education Act (IDEA) in 1990. IDEA required that all students, without regard to type or extent of disability, must receive public educational services essential to meeting their needs, including assessments, involvement of parents in their programs, service in the least restrictive appropriate environment, and an individual education program (McDonnell et al., 1995). IDEA continues today to mandate free special education and related services for children with disabilities between the ages of 3 and 21 years, and a 2010 change included the adoption of Rosa's Law, named for Rosa Marcellino, a girl with Down syndrome. Rosa's Law required replacement of the words "mental retardation" with "intellectual disabilities" in federal statutes affecting people with intellectual disability, including IDEA (Klotz, 2010).

Employment

Another law dating from 1990, the Americans with Disabilities Act (ADA), included provisions to protect the rights of workers with disabilities. This law too has been revised from time to time (e.g., 2008; EEOC, 2011), prohibits all forms of employment discrimination against qualified workers with disabilities, and applies to employers with 15 or more employees (US Department of Justice, 2012). ADA also requires employers to make reasonable accommodations (modifications or adjustments) to allow workers to successfully complete the application process or to do the job.

Enacted in the 1970s, Section 503 of the Rehabilitation Act of 1973 also provides safeguards for workers with disabilities by prohibiting discrimination in employment by federal contractors and subcontractors. Its companion, Section 504, prohibits discrimination against people with disabilities in programs and activities conducted by the federal government or who receive federal financial assistance (United States Department of Labor, 2012).

International rights initiatives

In 1948, on the heels of the atrocities of World War II, the United Nations General Assembly passed The Universal Declaration of Human Rights. The Declaration asserted that basic rights and freedoms should be extended to all persons, without regard to any of a number of personal characteristics such as race, religion, sex, color, place of origin, or political views. It did not mention disabilities, although language throughout the document suggested that it applied to *all* people.

Later, in 1971, the United Nations General Assembly passed the Declaration on the Rights of Mentally Retarded Persons calling for, so far as feasible, the same rights for people with mental retardation as for other people; the right to appropriate care, therapy, and education; the right to economic security, decent living standards, and opportunity for productive employment; life with family or in the most normal possible settings; protection from abuse and exploitation; and, in cases in which rights must be restricted, freedom from abuse in that process. Then, in 1975 the General Assembly passed a more generically titled Declaration on the Rights of Disabled Persons, encompassing a list of provisions similar to those of the 1971 Declaration. A further Declaration on Intellectual Disabilities resulted from the Pan American Health Organization/World Health Organization Montreal International Conference on Intellectual Disability in 2004, calling for basic rights and freedom from discrimination. It is important to note that a Declaration is a document reflecting the views of member countries about a particular topic, but that governments are not bound to follow the provisions of the Declaration; a Convention, however, is more like an international law, and countries agreeing to it are expected to comply and are encouraged to include the provisions of Conventions in their national laws (Inclusion International, 2012).

It was thus noteworthy when, on December 13, 2006, the General Assembly of the United Nations enacted the Convention on the Rights of Persons with Disabilities by resolution A/RES/61/06. The stated purpose of this document is to "promote, protect and ensure the full and equal enjoyment of all human rights and fundamental freedoms by all persons with disabilities and to promote respect for their inherent dignity" (p. 4). The Convention is much more detailed than the earlier Declarations, with 30 articles describing desired state actions in a broad range of rights areas, based on the following general principles:

1. respect for inherent dignity, individual autonomy including the freedom to make one's own choices, and independence of persons;
2. non-discrimination;
3. full and effective participation and inclusion in society;
4. respect for difference and acceptance of persons with disabilities as part of human diversity and humanity;
5. equality of opportunity;
6. accessibility;
7. equality between men and women;
8. respect for the evolving capacities of children with disabilities and respect for the right of children with disabilities to preserve their identities (United Nations, 2006, p. 5).

As we write this book, 153 nations have signed the Convention, meaning that they intend to take steps to ratify the Convention at a later date. Of these nations 118 have ratified the Convention, meaning that they have taken the additional step of indicating their intent to undertake the legal rights and obligations contained in the Convention. The US has signed but not ratified the Convention, although the National Education Association (2012) and other organizations have urged the US Senate to do so.

In Europe, the Fundamental Rights Agency (FRA, 2012) established a project in 2009 to gain better understanding of both rights safeguards and rights violations for people with mental health problems and intellectual disability within the European Union. While studying all aspects of equality and anti-discrimination, the FRA project is particularly concerned with efforts of European Union nations to incorporate the UN Convention into national laws.

Rights challenges

Despite the presence of the laws and declarations we have briefly described here, significant challenges remain for people with intellectual disability around the world. According to the United Nations (2006; Al Thani, 2005) 80 percent of people with disabilities live in developing countries, and 90 percent of children with disabilities in those countries do not attend school; the worldwide literacy rate for adults with disabilities is 3 percent (1 percent for women); and 98 percent of people with disabilities in developing countries have no access to healthcare or rehabilitation services.

Attention to rights, Young and Quibell (2000) argued, is not enough. Even if rights can provide basic minimal standards (which, as we have seen, they often do not), they said, the rights perspective fails to address the root causes of inequities—the misunderstandings that require philosophical and sociological analysis that may help to develop alternative solutions. Assertions of rights, important as they may be, are not likely to effect immediate change in the sociological context of any people, including those with intellectual disability, and are solely dependent (as in social contract theory) on those making political policy. A potential explanation may lie in the philosophical assumptions inherent in our rights-based approaches.

Such efforts as the ADA, as Lekan (2009) and Silvers et al. (1998) have suggested, embody a kind of formal justice that has its basis in the social model of disability. The social model sees disability as the product of social environments that discriminate against the individual and thereby prevent effective or normal functioning. This, Lekan said, necessitates equalizing opportunity for people with disabilities by changing environments in order to remove socially created barriers. Danforth (2008) contrasted the social model with the medical model, which construes disability in terms of a mental or bodily abnormality (e.g., sensory deficits, deficient intelligence, maladaptive behavior). This model, which gives rise to what political philosophers refer to as the distributive approach to justice (Lekan, 2009), requires of society compensatory responses intended to correct or mitigate the "defect." Lekan characterized both the formal and the distributive approaches as "liberal" views of justice in the sense that either requires rather extraordinary compensatory steps to offset injustice to the person with disabilities. Further, the medical approach may engender attitudes resulting in marginalization of individuals with disabilities and the distributive perspective may result in a variety of moral dilemmas surrounding fairness in allocation of resources—not only monetary, but in the form of such social resources as teacher time and attention (Lekan, 2009).

In attempting to chart another, more productive, course toward a just view of education and intellectual disability, both Lekan and Danforth drew upon the philosophy of John Dewey and his conceptions of growth and intelligence. In this Deweyan perspective, intelligence is not defined in terms of contextually disconnected testing (what Sternberg, 1996, called inert intelligence), but in the range of experiences required to enhance the individual's interests and abilities. Education, then, should offer a diversity of opportunities that allow students to prepare themselves for numerous life activities (Danforth, 2008). In other words, individual growth and well-being depend upon development of individual capacities through rich social integration in settings that foster "each person's very particular capacities" (Lekan, 2009, p. 223). The Deweyan perspective attempts to avoid extreme views about both justice and the causes of disability, asking instead "why individuals engage in effective or ineffective activity in specific social and material circumstances and how pedagogy can be devised to increase and expand the range of effective, goal-satisfying activity for each student" (Danforth, 2008, p. 58). The ultimate justice, then, lies in "rich, meaningful social integration" (Lekan, 2009, p. 225). As we saw in Chapter Six, this promotes greater justice for all, rather than the distribution of limited resources in a competitive setting, because all people benefit from the opportunity for growth in a social setting that values diversity and cooperation. This view, of course, has implications for human rights not only in education, but also in other contexts, such as employment and citizenship.

Engaging Moral Community

As philosophers such as Dewey knew, the real test for our best theories is in putting them to work. Though ethical issues are likely more complicated than we often imagine for people adept at grappling with them, they grow in complexity in cases where it is not clear what an individual would want, when there are seemingly competing interests (such as family or even the state), and when moral challenges are partnered with despair and tragedy and a "right" answer seems impossible. Though these cases may seem difficult to imagine, some will touch most people's lives in an age of enhanced technology.

Selective abortion and moral status

In recent years, prenatal testing has become far less invasive, safer, cheaper, and more accurate (Parens & Asch, 1999), and in 2007 the American College of Obstetricians and Gynecologists recommended Down syndrome screening for all women, regardless of age (Rabin, 2007). While most people view technologies that help to birth healthy babies as an ethical no-brainer, the ease by which we are able to predict disability and to abort fetuses behooves us to consider the ethical ramifications of such actions. Even a robust pro-choice position, embracing the legality of abortion, benefits from a critical look at the morality of our decisions regarding disability and selective abortion.

The most common framework within which ethicists tend to discuss selective abortion is that of individual rights. We ask whether fetuses are persons (to whom we have moral obligations) and whether their moral status is on the same level as existing persons. In some sense, we end up with a competition of rights, exacerbated by limited resources (for families, communities, and even nations). As we saw earlier regarding education, there are problems with an individual rights perspective that seeks a clear delineation of moral status based on capacities, categorization, or even species membership.

To abort or not to abort as a matter only of individual rights assumes the metaphysics of an isolated individual. Consistent more with Enlightenment views of the self, or soul, as radically separate, this position requires that we consider the fetus to be an individual agent in a moral competition. It either does or does not have rights, such as the right to life, and it therefore either is always morally acceptable or always unacceptable to end a fetal life. The wider abortion debate tends to make the individual rights assumption, making it difficult to suggest that it may be sometimes acceptable and sometimes wrong to abort, which would be consistent with a more pluralistic, contextual approach.

Further, proponents of an individualistic approach, such as Singer (1993), point out that if we are looking for some element of humanity that makes us morally protected persons, such as rationality, language use, or self-awareness, infants do not fare any better than fetuses, making infanticide just as acceptable (or unacceptable) as abortion because "the most plausible arguments for attributing a right to life to a being apply only if there is some awareness of oneself as a being existing over time or as a continuing mental self" (p. 183). Looking for individual faculties also leads logically to the discussion of whether nonhuman animals with similar capacities have rights. While we may be sympathetic to the plight of nonhuman animals, many ethicists are concerned first with whether we treat our human companions ethically.

An extreme version of the individualistic approach asks whether it is any less ethical to end a human infant's life than that of a fetus, under any circumstances. If infants are not categorically different in capacities than fetuses, and if we accept the permissibility of abortion, what keeps us from determining that infants have no right to life (e.g., Wilkinson, 2006)? In a controversial article, Giubilini and Minerva (2012) argued that newborns, like fetuses, lack moral personhood, which makes killing a newborn ("afterbirth abortion") acceptable in any case where abortion is acceptable. Logically, this makes sense if we determine moral personhood by individual capacities such as reason or language use, but it is dependent on a particular metaphysical view of the self as unrelated to others. Interestingly, the concept of infanticide here provides support for the claim that the concept of moral status itself (especially based on mental capacity) is problematic.

Viewing abortion and infanticide from a primarily individualistic perspective causes us to conceptualize these issues as competitions for limited resources. Singer (1985, 1994) noted that parents have a right to make decisions for their unborn sons and daughters based on family needs and access to resources. Although Singer gave examples of many family situations in which children with disabilities seemed to tear apart relationships, these cases highlight not only the impairment of individuals, but also the lack of social structures that might improve family life. We can accept that there are impairments that make family life more difficult, but it is a fallacy to assume that current conditions are the way things ought to be. Families may be more likely to give birth to, and successfully raise, educate, and love children with disabilities if they had better access to social services and support networks that make financial, emotional, and physical commitments less burdensome.

Singer and other philosophers (e.g., Hare, 1976) have even suggested that disability results in a competition of rights between a fetus and potential children who are not yet conceived. Kuhse and Singer (1985) argued that parents of disabled children are less likely to procreate further (impinging upon their own right to have "normal" children and even on the potential rights of not-yet-existing offspring): "we are offsetting the loss of one possible life against the creation of another life with better prospects" (p. 158). According to this view, we should weigh the future possibility of normalcy against the impending probability of disability when considering whether a fetus or infant should live.

An individual rights approach also assumes that any quality of life concerns that disabled people and their families might face are inherent to that individual (in keeping with a medical model of disability), rather than socially constructed. McMahan (2005) used a *reductio ad absurdum* argument to show that it is morally permissible to abort based on disability. He argued that if it is not acceptable to abort, then we may as well conclude that it would be acceptable to disable an otherwise healthy fetus in the womb (because any claim about the wrongness of aborting due to disability must assume that it is just as good, or even better, to be disabled): "So, if being disabled is not harmful to or bad for the disabled person, then causing a fetus to be disabled will violate neither the rights of the fetus (because it does not have any rights) nor the right to bodily integrity of the later person" (p. 98). Singer (1993) made a similar argument, stating that if we really thought that giving birth to "normal" and disabled children was morally equivalent, then we should not take drugs off the market that are known to cause birth defects.

This position rests upon the assumption that if disability leads to a lesser quality of life, it is innate to the individual and it therefore would be acceptable, or even obligatory, to avoid suffering by selectively aborting (or even euthanizing infants, in the case of Kuhse & Singer, 1985; and Giubilini & Minerva, 2012). McMahan did concede that some opponents of selective abortion claim that any suffering one has is caused not by individual impairment, but by society, a view consistent with the social model of disability. With a more pluralistic social constructivist model, such as one informed by pragmatism and social ethics, in which the individual and social are more organic and less distinguishable, McMahan would have a more complicated critique to deal with—one which posits the complexity and diversity of human experience and the standpoint of individual parents and children within social relationships, and which does not necessarily result in a competition of resources. Such a model could be useful in attempting to find the cause of and to alleviate suffering in the way that we relate to each other. If suffering is indeed caused in part by the lack of social support and accessibility, we can do something to improve quality of life (in addition to considering abortion as one solution).

In this case, the question of quality of life requires that we accept the philosophical and logical import of context and individual standpoint, rather than purely objective argument. It may be that ethicists like Singer and McMahan make clear and reasonable logical arguments without making fully ethical ones; that is, their reasoning hangs together well but does not always refer back to the real lives of people. While there may be extreme cases of pain and suffering for which most of us would agree that ending a life may be better than living it, these are not the conditions of the vast majority of decisions potential parents make regarding the possibility of giving birth to a child with a disability. As we saw in Chapter Eight, quality of life is not static and unidimensional—it is multidimensional and largely subjective. This recognition makes ethical decision making complicated, and requires a great deal of creativity and flexibility in our thinking and in our practices to avoid absolute and universal answers to contextual and subjective questions. After all, Harriet Johnson (2003) reminded us that her life as a disabled person was not as terrible as Singer apparently assumed. Eva Kittay (2010) wrote about the joy her severely disabled daughter found in music and in friendship. And Sophia Wong (2002), in writing about her brother with Down syndrome, noted that it was impossible to say whether his life was any less happy than her own.

In reflecting on her own decision to reject prenatal screening, Amy Becker (2010) wrote that though the disabilities associated with Down syndrome lead to health complications and uncertainty, "we also know that a textbook definition of a syndrome can never capture the reality of any particular human life" (para. 5). And in the case of her daughter with Down syndrome, though learning comes a bit more slowly than for many other children, "no list of developmental problems told us that empathy would be easier for her" (para. 6). While Becker conceded that screening can serve to help parents to feel more prepared for and to celebrate the birth of a child with disabilities, she argued that the way the tests were administered and our cultural conception of people with disabilities contributed to her concern that "prenatal testing more often serves to devalue all human life and to offer parents and doctors an illusion of control" (para. 11). In the end, Becker and her husband declined testing because they would welcome another child with Down syndrome.

Genetic testing and social ethics

There are many critiques of selective abortion and genetic testing from disability advocates, and most seem to emerge from a social model. In some cases, the strongest arguments are about much more than the future life (or death) of an individual baby, but are concerned with the perception of disability and the effects of that perception on currently existing members of the disability community, as well as future members. Selective abortion "expresses" discrimination (Parens & Asch, 1999), and resources that ought to be used to alleviate discrimination are used instead to fix or prevent impairment. In a sense, screening for disability, and subsequently aborting fetuses, implies that reasonable parents would not want a child with disabilities. This assumption, advocates claim, sends a resounding message to people with disabilities that they are "frightening or inhuman" (Saxton, 2010, p. 123) or "a form of pollution, evidence of sin" (Hubbard, 2010, p. 108).

Some disability advocates compare screening for disability to screening for gender or skin color, noting that the general public would be troubled if we screened for other attributes. Even in the case of quality of life (such as the argument that women and people of color often struggle more in our culture than white males), most people would find such practices problematic (Hubbard, 2010; Wong, 2002). To some theorists, selective abortion seems just too similar to eugenics (Hubbard, 2010; Saxton, 2010) and women are pressured to believe that "screening out disabled fetuses is the right thing, the healthy thing to do" (Saxton, 2010, p. 125), which reinforces the message that disability, and disabled people, are to be avoided. According to Saxton, "We are the constituency of the potentially aborted" (p. 127). Prospective parents may rarely consider the issue of disability until they are in a genetic counselor's office, and their beliefs about raising a child with disabilities are likely to be influenced by more general discriminatory views (Saxton, 2010).

On the other hand, ethicists such as Singer (1985, 1994) have worried that limited resources are stretched too thin and that prolonging the life of profoundly disabled children would exacerbate this problem. In this case, the individual rights of the fetus are pitted against the rights of other members of society. Although there are genuine reasons to be concerned about limited resources and access to healthcare, it is unlikely that these problems would be solved by fewer people with disabilities. In many cases, providing healthcare and access are less burdensome than we might think, and, as Parens and Asch (1999) noted, resources spent on prenatal testing and selective abortion could be used instead toward eliminating discrimination, providing better access to healthcare for people with disabilities, and improving social structures in order to enhance quality of life. Regardless, the issue of genetic screening is clearly more complex than it may seem.

A social ethics framework also requires that we imagine how the existence of a diversity of people contributes to our collective, as well as individual, well-being. Wong (2002) wrote about the accomplishments of her brother and others with Down syndrome, grappling with her own views regarding genetic testing. She concluded that, at least in the case of Down syndrome, she opposed selective abortion because it is impossible to calculate the ways in which people like her brother have contributed positively to the world. Likewise, Ian Brown (2011) wrote about the ways in which his life and the lives of other caregivers were enhanced by Walker Brown's existence. For many, the way people with disabilities contribute to collective quality of life is not just in love and friendship, but is in their ability, as Brown suggested, to make us better, more ethical, human beings. These contributions should be part of our ethical discussions of issues such as genetic testing and selective abortion. In what kind of world do we wish to live? One that values diversity, humanity, and the unique experiences afforded by difference; or one that is perfectly healthy? While recognizing that social ethics invites families, caregivers, and communities to consider particular contexts as they make decisions about genetic testing and selective abortion, perhaps ethicists should also acknowledge the wider ramifications of our decisions and take the time to consider how we can better inform ourselves about issues such as quality of life and the value of people of diverse intelligences to our communities.

Surrogacy and bioethics

Many people with intellectual disability are more capable than the public might assume to make important life decisions and, as we saw in Chapter Eight, agency in making these decisions contributes substantially to quality of life. However, there are cases in which family members and medical professionals are required to make decisions regarding the interests of individuals with disabilities, especially in cases of severe decisional compromise (Hester, 2010).

In the case of adults, disabilities sometimes make it difficult or impossible for individuals to have full charge of their medical decisions. Though often these conditions, such as dementia or brain injuries, fall outside the technical definition of intellectual disabilities (which emerge prior to the age of 18) it makes sense to discuss such cases briefly in order to get a sense of when surrogacy fits into our view of moral agency. For example, Hilde Lindemann (2010) wrote about criteria for "holding" another in her identity in the case of dementia. As we saw in Chapter Five, Lindemann started from a metaphysical view of the self as socially constructed, primarily through the stories told by families, and then by the individual herself. "Holding" another simply means to help her to maintain her sense of self in an evolving life narrative, with the aim of preserving, rather than constricting, her agency. Helping an elderly person struggling with dementia to maintain her identity and to make sense of her world may also help her to maintain the ability to make decisions about her life.

However, there are times when it is impossible to have a sense of self strong enough to maintain moral agency. Micah Hester (2010) recounted cases in which individuals completely lacked the capacity to make decisions due to brain injury. Also using a framework of the individual self having a social and narrative structure, he suggested that a surrogate's responsibility is to attempt, as well as possible, to "take on the patient's narrative voice" (pp. 119–120) in authoring the final chapter of a loved one's life. Hester noted that this takes a great deal of sensitivity, as well as knowledge of an individual's story. Commitment to empathizing with the story of the other, rather than imposing one's own beliefs and goals, may be the difference between surrogacy and paternalism. This distinction is less clear when the individual's story is not yet written (as in the case of newborns) or her sense of identity does not seem to have enough clarity for others to be confident about her best interests (as in the case of profound disability).

The traditional view regarding end of life and other major medical decisions for infants is to act in their "best interests" (Wilkinson, 2006). Singer (1993, 2007) has been a proponent of this view, and has argued that in cases such as Tay–Sachs disease it is reasonable to assume that life may not be worth living due to the potential for pain and suffering. Hester (2010), however, found some elements of the "best interests" view to be problematic. First, it is difficult to imagine what is in the best interest of someone, an infant, who has not yet developed self-regarding interests. Although one strategy is to act on whatever a reasonable person would agree is in a person's best interest, Hester worried that this approach lacked individual context, including family relationships. From a pragmatic moral perspective, he reminded that self-interests are social, a fact which should be taken into consideration in individual cases. For example, he suggested that in addition to individual interests *for* a particular infant (such as avoiding suffering, having beneficial medical treatment, and having future-oriented goals), we also have possible interests *in* the infant (such as family, state, and cultural beliefs, especially in values like dignity and respect). Hester argued that the more inclusive of interests we can be in our moral deliberations, the better, and that we should avoid automatic deferrals to parents, doctors, or the state. Though some interests, such as the parents', may be stronger, there are no sole authors to our stories, and, of course, even the beliefs of parents are part of a wider cultural narrative.

What is in a child's, or anyone's, best interests, then, is highly complex and requires sensitive deliberation beyond medical prognosis, and even beyond utilitarian principles such as avoiding suffering. There is a burden here, because pluralistic thinking about interests complicates moral decision making exponentially. A case that seems straightforward in Kuhse and Singer (1985) might seem muddled and tragic in Hester (2010). Perhaps that is the burden of surrogacy rather than paternalism. As surrogates, or ethicists, we accept the complexity of moral situations, the fact that we cannot fully comprehend the myriad interests involved, that we might make mistakes, and thus that we must think and act with humility. In cases where Singer and Kuhse might propose euthanasia, an option with no room for error or changes of heart, Hester (2010) would argue that we put our resources into palliative care as an act of humility because we cannot fully know an infant's best interests (or whether or how she suffers) and "palliative care allows for flexibility in decision making" (p. 150). While acknowledging the greater complexity of moral questions, we argue that a theoretical approach in bioethics, such as pragmatism, which recognizes the value of both tragedy and flexibility gives families more moral power as they deliberate about how best to care for loved ones.

Surrogacy and care

There are many other moral decisions that require surrogate or paternalistic roles, most having to do not with end of life issues but with the experience of daily living. As we saw in Chapter Two, there was a time not so long ago when involuntary sterilization was practiced in order to protect people with intellectual disability from themselves and to protect society from the potential that they would have offspring. Though sterilization is largely a thing of the past in most countries, there are current cases that cause us to consider the complexities of surrogacy and paternalism, or treating others as moral patients rather than agents. In 2006, the parents and doctors of Ashley X, a then six-year-old Seattle child with profound physical and intellectual disability, made headlines with the publication of their decision to use hormonal therapy to stunt their daughter's growth, and to otherwise surgically alter her to keep her physically childlike (with a hysterectomy and removal of her breast buds). With the help of endocrinologist Daniel Gunther, who offered what became known as the "Ashley treatment," the stated aim of the parents was to keep Ashley small so that they could continue to care for her at home and to keep her sexually childlike so that she could avoid the discomfort of menstruation and to prevent her from being the victim of sexual abuse in the event that she needed to be cared for outside the home (Gunther & Diekema, 2006). Several other children have since received versions of the Ashley treatment to enhance, their parents insist, their quality of life (Pilkington & McVeigh, 2012).

As with any controversial moral matter, there are both supporters and critics of the Ashley treatment. Singer (2007), in a *New York Times* column, used the best interest principle to argue that Ashley's treatment was morally right, or at least morally acceptable. He rejected claims that the treatment was unnatural or a slippery slope, and argued that if dignity should play a role at all, it was more dignified for Ashley's body growth to be more consistent with her mental age.

Critics of the treatment, such as S. E. Smith (2012), suggested that the family's best interest was being protected at the expense of the girl's, especially in the case of growth attenuation. Keeping Ashley small would help her family care for her, but only, Smith wrote, "because they live in a world where people with disabilities are undervalued and their parents fear their capacity to care for them and move through public spaces with them" (para. 7). Smith argued that the Ashley treatment would not be acceptable for parents to impose on non-disabled children, and to believe otherwise rests on the assumption that disabled people are not human. Other critics took issue with the description of Ashley and similar kids as "pillow angels," stating that the term itself is infantilizing and may be indicative of a heavy-handed paternalism (Berubé, 2010).

Anne McDonald (2007), whose story we encountered in Chapter Two, took an especially critical position of growth attenuation from the perspective of having lived through a similar experience at St. Nicholas Hospital in Melbourne. Sharing common aspects of her own institutionalization with the medically induced attenuation of the Ashley treatment, McDonald argued that children believed to have even profound disabilities should be allowed to achieve their full potential for growth, both physically and intellectually. Experiences such as McDonald's and Ruth Sienkiewicz-Mercer's, of the Belchertown, MA State School, might give us pause in our hurry to categorize and to subsequently make major irreversible decisions for other people. Hester's (2010) analysis of best interests would remind us that we also need to consider what these decisions mean culturally, and that more complex moral situations call for greater flexibility in our decisions. A pragmatist relational moral perspective embraces flexibility and cultural context as alternatives to absolute thinking about people and their circumstances. The consequence for McDonald of a unilaterally applied view of rationality as necessary to moral choice, or even choice about her daily living situation, was neglect and misery. Only when someone took the time to relate to her personally and to understand her context did McDonald learn to communicate, to discover her own moral voice, and to become her own best advocate. McDonald (2007) worried that no one was taking the time to see if Ashley could grow further and become more than a "pillow angel."

Singer (2007) attempted to ward off criticisms that the Ashley treatment was primarily for the emotional or physical benefit of the parents. He wrote, "the line between improving Ashley's life and making it easier for her parents to handle her scarcely exists, because anything that makes it possible for Ashley's parents to involve her in family life is in her interest" (para. 4). A Hastings Center working group (Wilfond et al., 2010) on this issue also highlighted the importance of Ashley's place in family life, but noted that her parents faced a dilemma. On the one hand, critics claimed that Ashley's difficulties were socially constructed, and so she needed social resources rather than medical treatment. On the other hand, these resources were lacking, so attempting to fix her impairment medically may have seemed like the only viable option to her parents. In some sense, it was a dilemma of models. The working group wrote:

> If we as a society believe that it is undignified, as a matter of human rights, for Ashley to undergo these treatments, then we must be prepared to provide her caregivers with enough assistance and support that they would not have to resort to these means. Upholding human dignity comes with a price, and if it is what we should value as a society, then we must be prepared to pay to uphold it.

As may be the case in most important ethical matters, perhaps there are no universal answers to questions such as genetic testing, selective abortion, and growth attenuation. However, there are some general values that may be useful to consider, based on caring relationships in moral communities (Dewey, 1988/1922; Hester, 2001; Noddings, 1984), helping individuals to function well (Nussbaum, 2011), and that point to best practices, rather than universal answers. First, we have to recognize that ethical questions have a context and our current beliefs are socially situated. If prospective parents, and their doctors, have not had the opportunity to adequately explore the possibility of life with a disabled child, then their decision will not have the benefit of a full range of options. This is a problem in Singer's philosophy—he seems to assume that our beliefs about quality of life and suffering are fixed. Second, we have to understand that current social conditions are also malleable. As the Hastings Center working group suggested, if we find the Ashley treatment problematic, then we ought to be prepared to initiate change in the social conditions that made the treatment seem like the only option to her family. Third, though we may prefer clear-cut moral truths, it may be that the social nature of ethics leads us rather to pluralist approaches. In this case, we are humbled by the fact that while logical arguments are important and useful in clarifying beliefs and goals for action (such as pointing out that it is inconsistent to make claims about moral status and mental capacities, such as in the case of infants versus fetuses), any truth that logic helps us to achieve is also social, cultural, and otherwise bound by the contingencies of our particular context. As we noted at the conclusion of Chapter Eight, some pragmatist ethicists emphasize moral "artistry," rather than analytic argumentation (Alexander, 1987), even in bioethics (Hester, 2001, 2010), noting that moral deliberation is more akin to the social imagination required of jazz improvisation than to argument building (Fesmire, 2003).

Technology and ethics: Present and future challenges

Global concerns exist concerning the nature of modern science and technology and their role in the lives of people with intellectual disability (Parmenter, 2007). These concerns reach from the role of safety surveillance technology (e.g., wristband locators for people who might wander away from home; Moonen, Ojasalo, Seppälä, & Suomalainen, 2010) and remote data collection (on daily behaviors such as eating, use of appliances, sleeping; Bowes, Dawson, & Bell, 2012) to such advanced possibilities as genetic manipulation (Stowe, Turnbull, Schrandt, & Rack, 2007), brain communicator systems for "locked in" (i.e., profoundly physically disabled) people (Kennedy et al., 2004), or robotic caretakers (Turkle, 2011).

These areas of technological innovation and a number of others proceeding along similar lines, raise important ethical questions that have not, in some cases (e.g., data monitoring/surveillance) received the discussion they deserve, and technology development has to date outstripped that discussion (Bowes et al., 2012). Moonen et al. (2010) reported preliminary findings of an ongoing study showing that some individuals with intellectual disability say they would find wristband surveillance technology acceptable, but to date it is not clear whether these people would actually wear the wristbands, or what additional unforeseen consequences might accompany the technology. Such technologies as brain–machine interface (BMI) currently exist in laboratories, and have had trials with humans and with nonhuman primates (Patoine, 2009); will it become practical for humans with significant physical disabilities to control such devices as robotic arms using only brain waves? And, given the likely expense and sophistication of such technology, will it be available to people with intellectual disability? Who should decide? And how? These are questions that will inevitably face individuals with disabilities, families and caretakers, and researchers as technological research continues. Assistive technology is now readily available for such activities as communication, environmental control, and mobility in affluent nations; however, just as extremely expensive future brain-based technology may be prohibitively expensive to people with intellectual disability in high-income countries, currently available technology is already beyond the reach of the vast majority of people with disabilities in most places in the world.

This state of affairs led Botelho (2010) to propose ways of bringing free computer technology to poor countries, and harkens back to the prescient words of E. F. Schumacher (1973) in his remarkable book *Small is Beautiful: Economics as if People Mattered*: "In many places in the world today the poor are getting poorer while the rich are getting richer" (p. 171). Schumacher went on to describe the importance of affordable "intermediate" technology—more productive than indigenous technology or no technology, but not so enormous as to destroy traditional workplaces. Such intermediate technology is relevant not only for poor workers in the developing world, but also to workers with intellectual disability who may find themselves increasingly unable to cope with environments that demand sophisticated technological skills. And, ironically, at a time when people widely recognize the value of community for those with intellectual disability, the world of technology, of social networking and electronic communication, may be diminishing the traditional meaning of community, the world of "the coffee shops, the parks, and the barbershops that used to be points of assembly for acquaintances and neighbors, the people who made up the landscape of life" (Turkle, 2011, p. 239). How, in a highly technologized era, will we find ways to create and maintain the Deweyan notion of "cultivating a social climate of moral equality and human connection" (Danforth, 2008, p. 62)?

10

Epilogue
Visions of the Future

We concluded Chapter One with the hope that in the case of intelligence and ethics, the common aspects of our humanity are more relevant and pervasive than those that make us different, and that there will come a time when labels like "intellectually disabled" will be replaced by labels such as citizen, neighbor, friend, and employee. It seems clear from a study of history that we are closer to that time, though we still have some way to go. However, there are people and groups living well and making progress, and perhaps in telling these stories we will contribute to a reconceptualization and reframing of the concept of intellectual disability. Our best practices are only as good as our ideals, and any change we would like to see should start with our beliefs, perceptions, and theories.

Changing Public Perceptions

Chapter Three began with the horrible story of the Hartheim Castle euthanasia site, now a memorial, museum, and research center. While Hartheim will always be a memorial—nothing can erase from history the atrocities committed there—visitors can now consider contemporary images of intellectual disability in a more realistic light (Hartheim Castle, 2002). The "Value of Life" exhibit ends with a section on equality, which contends that justice will never touch all lives until we understand each other. Thus, people with intellectual disability are depicted (as actors, not as exhibits, the museum insists) living their lives: commuting, loving, arguing, enjoying

Intellectual Disability: Ethics, Dehumanization, and a New Moral Community, First Edition.
Heather E. Keith and Kenneth D. Keith.

life, struggling, and working. The last thing a visitor to the castle sees is not the gas chamber or the extensive history of eugenics and injustice, but a room full of pictures involving media depictions of disability, along with criticisms of those depictions by people with intellectual disability. This is perhaps the brightest spot at Hartheim—the equal opportunity to argue and debate among human friends and colleagues.

Living in Community: New Orientations for Services

For more than four decades, the aim of community integration of people with intellectual disability has been a central focus of advocates (Dybwad, 1969), as well as a major theme in quality of life at least since the 1990s (e.g., Keith 1990). In the four decades ending with the year 2008, the number of people identified with intellectual disability living in state institutions in the US declined from a peak of more than 194,000 in 1967 to fewer than 35,000 in 2008 (Larson, Scott, Salmi, & Lakin, 2009). Tens of thousands of people have moved from institutions. Yet in discussion of community life it is important to distinguish between living *in the community* and living *in community*; too many people live in the community, but do not live in community, in the sense that living in community connotes a sense of belonging and interconnectedness with others (Rapley, 2000). Nevertheless, since at least the last quarter of the twentieth century, community integration has been an objective of the normalization movement (Flynn & Lemay, 1999).

Living among family, friends, and colleagues is the goal of many of today's organizations that work to improve quality of life for people with intellectual disability, though some, of course, accomplish this better than others. Even the Glenwood Resource Center, the former Asylum for Feeble-minded Children of the State of Iowa, and longtime home of Mayo Buckner, now has the goal of helping clients to live in the community, and claims that "discharge planning begins at admission" (The Iowa Department of Human Services, n.d., para. 1). And institutions like the State School at Belchertown, MA, are now defunct historical sites (Schulelt, 2008).

Many organizations offer dynamic opportunities for people with disabilities to live in the community in ways that not only enhance their own quality of life, but also engage other community members in important ways. For example, the international L'Arche organization sees its members and residents not as clients or patients, but as "friends, teachers, and companions" with unique talents; and its aim, as much as anything else, is to provide nondisabled people the opportunity for growth in their encounters with disabled citizens (L'Arche USA, 2012). Ian Brown (2009) visited L'Arche communities in Canada and France and was struck by the relationships among residents of all abilities. In responding to Brown's question about how he came to work at L'Arche, one staff member said, "It's living. Being. Working is only part of it. Everyone who comes here is transformed by it. Relationship is our priority" (p. 196). Contrary to the assumptions of most social contract theory (such as we saw in Locke), L'Arche founder Jean Vanier argued that we are at our most human when we cultivate noncompetitive and interdependent relationships (Sider, 2012). The theoretical foundation of L'Arche, in Vanier's noncompetitive theology and anthropology, does not only accept disability as part of being human, but suggests that we learn to be most human via vulnerability and, in this sense, through life modeled on disability (Sider, 2012).

Public Policy and an Improved Quality of Life

> The moral test of government is how that government treats those who are in the dawn of life, the children; those who are in the twilight of life, the elderly; and those who are in the shadows of life—the sick, the needy, and the handicapped.

These were the words of Hubert H. Humphrey in a 1977 speech, not long before his death. By Humphrey's standard, as we saw in Chapter Two, government has not always passed this moral test. Clearly, public policy has a significant influence on people with intellectual disability, an influence occurring at the level of the person (inclusion, empowerment, self-determination, individualized services, family) and at the level of systems and supports (accountability, coordination, antidiscrimination; Shogren, Bradley, Gomez, Yeager, & Schalock, 2009). Policy shaped the lives of people with intellectual disability at least as early as the seventeenth century in England (Rushton, 1988), and in late-nineteenth-century America, when Bicknell (1895) argued that "The feeble-minded must be supported by the public" (p. 88)—a public that sometimes enabled policies that worked to disastrous effect, as when "Planning for the mentally retarded during the last twenty years of the 19th century involved a monstrous warping and twisting of the idealistic programs started by Seguin, Howe, and Wilbur" (White & Wolfensberger, 1969, p. 9), or when zoos spent more per day to maintain animals than institutions spent caring for people with disabilities (Blatt, 1969).

Yet public policy can also work wonders. In 1959 the Danish government enacted a law creating the Mental Retardation Service and a decentralized regional system of services for people with intellectual disability (Bank-Mikkelsen, 1969). In the late 1960s and 1970s a coalition of parents, people with intellectual disability, local professionals, county and state officials, and volunteers and community activists came together in Nebraska to create humane policies and ground-breaking community services that changed the face of communities across the state (Perske, 2002). The result of these policy changes and many others like them was an improved life and life quality for large numbers of people with intellectual disability in ordinary communities across the US and in other countries. At the federal level, the US government, in 1981, authorized the Medicaid Home and Community Based Services (HCBS) program, allowing states to receive cost-sharing funds for noninstitutional services for people with disabilities who might otherwise be consigned to nursing homes or other institutional settings (Lakin, Prouty, Alba, & Scott, 2008). From about 1400 recipients in 1982, this program grew to serve more than 501,000 in 2007, with government expenditures of more than US$20 billion (Lakin et al., 2008)—another example of the power of public policy to effect profound change.

Benefits for Research and Scholarship

We explored the idea in Chapter Seven that the wider academic world can learn from disability studies and from people with intellectual disability. Noting the irony that we are writing *about* people with disabilities, and not *with* them, we hope to continue to see self-advocacy not only in the community, but also in academic work. Nancy Ward (2000) argued that a respectable future would include people in self-advocacy groups banding together to elect political officials so that "issues that affect people with a disability would be heard and taken seriously" (p. 36). Both Ward and Ollie Webb (2002), an early participant in the People First movement, became leaders as advocates for the rights of people with intellectual disability. Researchers have begun to realize that, just as people with disabilities are involved in decisions about their living arrangements, employment, and services, so too should they have a voice in planning, making decisions, and monitoring research that affects them (Freedman, 2001). Because policy tends to reflect our beliefs, it is important that we make space in our houses of theory for people with disabilities to be at home there, as well as in advocacy movements.

Academic work in philosophy will benefit, as well, from more engagement with disability studies and from the involvement of people with disabilities. Such theoretical work should find a willing home in pluralistic perspectives such as pragmatism and feminism, which historically have evolved with the problems and ideals of humanity. About the growing contribution to philosophy of another historically disadvantaged group—women—John Dewey (1988/1918) wrote, "we cannot conceive that it will be the same in viewpoint or tenor as that composed from the standpoint of the different masculine experience of things" (p. 45). We can imagine that Dewey, especially with an interest in progressive education, political equality, and the potential for growth toward ordered richness of each individual person, would welcome the opportunity to learn from people with intellectual disability and their colleagues working in applied philosophy, psychology, and education; and that people writing in the pragmatist tradition in these disciplines today will concur.

Valor and Values for a New Age

Finally, we want to end our study of intellectual disability and ethics with Wolf Wolfensberger's concept of social role valorization. Emerging from the principle of normalization, a perspective first achieving prominence in the work of Nirje (1969), the term *social role valorization* came into the literature of intellectual disability in 1983 when Wolfensberger proposed it as a new term for the principle of normalization. Though he began applying social role theory to intellectual disability in the 1980s, we believe that Wolfensberger's (2000) idea of valuing the roles that people play—citizen, neighbor, friend, colleague, advocate—gets us closer to justice, morality, improved living conditions, and other "good things in life" (p. 105), and is worth our continuing consideration. Wolfensberger argued (1983) that how, or whether, we value individuals depends on our perception of their social roles and relationships, much, perhaps, in the way contemporary linguists (e.g., Lakoff, 2002) discuss the concept of framing, and there is ample evidence (e.g., Johnson, 1993) that language structures our experience and conveys power, status, and values (Devine, 2004). If we view someone as having a positive social role, for example as a coworker or colleague, rather than a welfare recipient (in the domain of economic productivity; Wolfensberger, 2000), then other goods tend to follow. This is true also in social and physical environments: if one is in a "hospital," as was Anne McDonald in St. Nicholas in Melbourne, then others (and oneself) should assume that one is sick or impaired and needing to be healed or fixed. Likewise, Wolfensberger noted that if an institution had cages (as some did) and seemed fit for animals, then its residents must be less than human.

Social roles are important, because "almost all of one's relational behavior is profoundly informed and shaped by the roles one holds" and "it is largely via roles that people define and situate others in the world" (Wolfensberger, 2000, p. 111). How individual roles are perceived by others determines to a large extent, Wolfensberger (1983) argued, whether people are valued or devalued, and in turn how people behave in response to others' expectations. Devalued people, at best, receive few social goods. At worst, they are "at risk of being brutalized and violated, even to the point of being made dead" (2000, p. 109). These roles are malleable, however, which offers us the opportunity to reframe our relationships in more positive terms, and to highlight some roles that will be perceived more positively. Seeing people with disabilities as citizens, colleagues, friends, companions, neighbors, and taxpayers results in more value and better treatment. For this reason, Wolfensberger (1987) termed this idea "valorization," because it implies that we upgrade someone's value, which is useful to assistants, social workers, and other caregivers in helping people with disabilities to grow and live better in community. As we saw in Chapter One, normalization as valorization, far from being an achievement on an intelligence test, means that we see people as ordinary participants in daily life, whether in apartments and houses, using public transportation, shopping, going to school, working, paying taxes, participating in religious activities, enjoying meals together, or working in the community (Perske & Perske, 1980).

The pragmatist philosopher and psychologist William James understood the importance of the ways we conceptualize ourselves and others to the quality and meaning of our lives. In *The Sentiment of Rationality* (1977a/1879), James recounted an example of a person standing at the edge of an abyss, with no other way of escape, wondering whether he could make it across if he jumped. For James, to believe that he could make it made it far more likely that he would because "faith creates its own verification" (p. 337). This faith, however, must have a foundation in real possibility. In *The Will to Believe* (1977b/1896), James noted that "who gains promotions, boons, appointments, but the man in whose life they are seen to play the part of live hypotheses?" (pp. 730–731). James and Wolfensberger might agree today that though we have come a long way since the days of eugenics, T4, and dehumanizing institutions, we must continue working to value, and valorize, all humans. If we see others, as well as ourselves, as moral agents, political citizens, and partners in improving life, then we just might find that we have become those things.

We hope we have shown that issues of intellectual disability, such as moral status, quality of life, intelligence, social norms and roles, and best practices such as inclusive education and valorization, are fluid and evolving, rather than static and rigid. In fact, perhaps it makes sense to think of these topics, and disability itself, as pragmatic, rather than ontological, distinctions—ideas which, unlike Plato's Forms or Goddard's apparent clarity about genetics, are appropriately vague and used only to advance arguments about how we can be more inclusive and make lives better. As we saw in case studies and narrative accounts, moral beliefs and decisions are perhaps as much about art and creativity as they are logic and science, especially when, as Blatt (1987) suggested, even our scientific understanding of the world and its people depends on culture. An expansive moral community relies on a little faith, too; not necessarily religious faith, though certainly for some people religious conviction is part of the process of valuing what it means to be human. The faith we need is in the possibility that opening ourselves up to understanding disability, and people with disabilities, will lead to a stronger, richer, more caring, and more creative moral community. And in opening ourselves to possibilities, we may find, along with Robert and Martha Perske (1980), that

> Some of the best friends I have can neither read or write. But the many things they have been able to do with me and for me have outweighed many times the things they could not do. And my relationships with such people have been so rich that my world-view has changed for the better. Over the years, they have introduced me to a world I had never known before. And as bewildering as it seems, it is a world that society had programmed me to shun and stay away from. But I didn't stay away (p. 77).

If faith creates its own verification, then we have to believe we can make a difference in order to do so. It is a faith founded, as James would have wished, in real possibility.

References

Aaron, R. (1971). *John Locke* (3rd ed.). Oxford, UK: Clarendon Press.

Addams, J. (1902). *Democracy and social ethics.* New York, NY: Macmillan.

Alderson, P. (2001). Down's syndrome: Cost, quality and value of life. *Social Science and Medicine, 53,* 627–639.

Alexander, T. (1987). *John Dewey's theory of art, experience, and nature: The horizons of feeling.* Albany, NY: The State University of New York Press.

Algoe, S. & Haidt, J. (2009). Witnessing excellence in action: The "other-praising" emotions of elevation, gratitude, and admiration. *Journal of Positive Psychology, 4,* 105–127.

Allport, G. W. (1954). *The nature of prejudice.* Cambridge, MA: Addison-Wesley.

Al Thani, H. (2005, October). Welcome address: A Europe for all. An inclusion international conference on poverty and intellectual disability. Bucharest, Romania: United Nations Special Rapporteur on Disability. Retrieved from: http://www.srdisability.org/regions/europe/romania/speech_oct05.html (accessed December 17, 2012).

Amado, A. N., Conklin, F., & Wells, J. (1990). *Friends: A manual for connecting persons with disabilities and community members.* St. Paul, MN: Human Services Research and Development Center.

American Medical Association (1965). *Mental retardation: A handbook for the primary physician.* Chicago, IL: Author.

Ames, R. T. (2011). *Confucian role ethics: A vocabulary.* Hong Kong, China: Chinese University Press.

Anastasi, A., & Urbino, S. (1996). *Psychological testing.* New York, NY: Prentice-Hall.

Anderson, N. B., & Nickerson, K. J. (2005). Genes, race, and psychology in the genome era. *American Psychologist, 60,* 5–8.

Intellectual Disability: Ethics, Dehumanization, and a New Moral Community, First Edition.
Heather E. Keith and Kenneth D. Keith.

Antaki, C., & Rapley, M. (1996). 'Quality of life' talk: The liberal paradox of psychological testing. *Discourse and Society, 7*, 293–316.

ARC of Nebraska (2002). *2002 Nebraska developmental disabilities provider profiles.* Lincoln, NE: ARC of Nebraska.

ARC of Nebraska (2003). *2003 Nebraska developmental disabilities provider profiles.* Lincoln, NE: ARC of Nebraska.

Archibald, O. W. (1877, November). *Report of the superintendent.* Glenwood, IA: Iowa State Asylum for Feeble-minded Children.

Aristotle (1962). *Nicomachean ethics* (M. Ostwald, Trans.). Indianapolis, IN: Bobbs-Merrill (original work c. 325 BCE).

Aristotle (1988). *Politics* (S. Everson, Trans.). Cambridge, UK: Cambridge University Press (original work c. 350 BCE).

Augustine (1993). *Confessions* (F. J. Sheed, Trans.) Indianapolis, IN: Hackett (original work c. 398 CE).

Ayres. L. P. (1909). *Laggards in our schools: A study of retardation and elimination in city school systems.* New York, NY: Charities Publication Committee.

Azuma, H., & Kashiwagi, K. (1987). Descriptions for an intelligent person: A Japanese study. *Japanese Psychological Research, 29*, 17–26.

Baier, A. (1995). The need for more than justice. In V. Held (Ed.), *Justice and care: Essential readings in feminist ethics* (pp. 47–60). Boulder, CO: Westview.

Ball, T. S. (1970). Training generalized imitation: Variations on an historical theme. *American Journal on Mental Deficiency, 75*, 135–141.

Bank-Mikkelsen, N. E. (1969). A metropolitan area in Denmark: Copenhagen. In R. B. Kugel & W. Wolfensberger (Eds), *Changing patterns in residential services for the mentally retarded* (pp. 227–254). Washington, DC: President's Committee on Mental Retardation.

Barr, M. W. (1899). The how, the why, and the wherefore of the training of feeble-minded children. *Journal of Psycho-Asthenics, 4*, 204–212.

Barr, M. W. (1902). The imbecile and epileptic *versus* the tax-payer and the community. *Proceedings of the National Conference of Charities and Correction*, 161–165.

Barr, M. W. (1904). *Mental defectives: Their history, treatment and training.* Philadelphia, PA: P. Blakiston's Son & Co.

Bartlett, F. L. (1964). Institutional peonage: Our exploitation of mental patients. *Atlantic Monthly, 214*(1), 116–119.

Bartlett, F. L. (1967). Present-day requirements for state hospitals joining the community. *New England Journal of Medicine, 276*, 90–94.

Bateman, F. (1897). *The idiot: His place in creation, and his claims on society* (2nd ed.). London, UK: Jarrold & Sons.

Beart, S., Hardy, G., & Buchan, L. (2004). Changing selves: A grounded theory account of belonging to a self-advocacy group for people with intellectual disabilities. *Journal of Applied Research in Intellectual Disabilities, 17*, 91–100.

Beart, S., Hardy, G., & Buchan, L. (2005). How people with intellectual disabilities view their social identity: A review of the literature. *Journal of Applied Research in Intellectual Disabilities, 18*, 47–56.

Becker, A. (2010, September 14). Why prenatal testing harms as much as it hurts. *New York Times.* Retrieved from: http://parenting.blogs.nytimes.com/2010/09/14/deciding-not-to-screen-for-down-syndrome/ (accessed December 17, 2012).

Becker, H. (1963). *Outsiders: Studies in the sociology of deviance.* New York, NY: Free Press.

Beins, B. C. (2009). *Research methods: A tool for life* (2nd ed.). Boston, MA: Pearson.

Beirne-Smith, M., Patton, J. R., Ittenbach, R. (1994). *Mental retardation* (4th ed.). New York, NY: Merrill.

Bell, C. (2010). Is disability studies actually white disability studies? In L. Davis (Ed.), *The disability studies reader* (3rd ed) (pp. 374–382). New York, NY: Routledge.

Bentham, J. (1798). *An Introduction to the principles of morals and legislation.* London, UK: British Library, Historical Print Editions.

Berkson, G. (2006). Mental disabilities in western civilization from ancient Rome to the Prerogativa Regis. *Mental Retardation, 44*, 28–40.

Bérubé, M. (2010). Equality, freedom, and/or justice for all: A response to Martha Nussbaum. In E. F. Kittay & L. Carlson (Eds), *Cognitive disability and its challenge to moral philosophy* (pp. 97–109). Chichester, UK: Wiley-Blackwell.

Bicknell, E. P. (1895). Custodial care of the adult feeble-minded. *The Charities Review, 5*, 76–88.

Biklen, D., Saha, N., & Kliewer, C. (1995). How teachers confirm authorship of facilitated communication. *Journal of the Association for Persons with Severe Handicaps, 20*, 45–56.

Binet, A. (1903). *L'étude expérimentale de l'intelligence* [Experimental studies of intelligence]. Paris, France: Schleichter.

Binet, A., & Henri, V. (1895). La psychologie individuelle. *L'Annee Psychologique, 2*, 411–465.

Blatt, B. (1969). Purgatory. In R. B. Kugel & W. Wolfensberger (Eds), *Changing patterns in residential services for the mentally retarded* (pp. 35–49). Washington, DC: President's Committee on Mental Retardation.

Blatt, B. (1981). How to destroy lives by telling stories. *Journal of Psychiatric Treatment and Evaluation, 3*, 183–191.

Blatt, B. (1985). The implications of the language of mental retardation for LD. *Journal of Learning Disabilities, 18*, 625–626.

Blatt, B. (1987). *The conquest of mental retardation.* Austin, TX: Pro-Ed.

Blatt, B., & Kaplan, F. (1966). *Christmas in purgatory: A photographic essay on mental retardation.* Boston, MA: Allyn and Bacon.

Blatt, B., Ozolins, A., & McNally, J. (1979). *The family papers: A return to purgatory.* New York, NY: Longman.

Bliss, G. (1919). Mental defectives and the war. *Journal of Psycho-Asthenics, 24*, 11–17.

Block, N., & Dworkin, G. (Eds). (1976). *The IQ controversy*. New York, NY: Random House.

Boddington, P., & Podpadec, T. (1991). Who are the mentally handicapped? *Journal of Applied Philosophy, 8*, 177–190.

Bogdan, R. (1986). Exhibiting mentally retarded people for amusement and profit, 1850–1940. *American Journal of Mental Deficiency, 91*, 120–126.

Bogdan, R. (1988). *Freak show: Presenting human oddities for amusement and profit.* Chicago, IL: The University of Chicago Press.

Bogdan, R., & Taylor, S. (1976). The judged, not the judges: An insider's view of mental retardation. *American Psychologist, 31*, 47–52.

Bonham, G. S., Basehart, S., & Marchand, C. B. (2000). *Ask Me! FY 2000.* Annapolis, MD: ARC of Maryland.

Bonham, G. S., Basehart, S., Schalock, R. L., Marchan, C. B., Kirchner, N., & Rumenap, J. M. (2004). Consumer-based quality of life assessment: The Maryland Ask Me! Project. *Mental Retardation, 42*, 338–355.

Botelho, F (2010, February). We need an assistive technology strategy not devices. Educational Technology Debate. Retrieved from: https://edutechdebate.org/assistive-technology/we-need-an-assistive-technology-strategy/ (accessed December 17, 2012).

Bowd, A. D. (1989). Client satisfaction and normalization of residential services for persons with developmental handicaps. *Canadian Journal of Community Mental Health, 8*, 63–73.

Bowes, A., Dawson, A., & Bell, D. (2012). Ethical implications of using lifestyle monitoring data in ageing research. *Information, Communication and Society, 15*, 5–22.

Boxall, K. (2002). Individual and social models of disability and the experiences of people with learning difficulties. In D. G. Race (Ed.), *Learning disability—A social approach* (pp. 209–226). London, UK: Routledge.

Braddock, D. L., & Parish, S. L. (2001). An institutional history of disability. In G. L. Albrecht, K. D. Seelman, & M. Bury (Eds), *Handbook of disability studies* (pp. 11–68). Thousand Oaks, CA: Sage.

Bramston, P., Bruggerman, K., & Petty, G. (2002). Community perspectives and subjective quality of life. *International Journal of Disability, Development and Education, 49*, 385–397.

Brislin, R. (1993). *Understanding culture's influence on behavior.* Fort Worth, TX: Harcourt Brace Jovanovich.

Bronowski, J. (1973). *The ascent of man.* Boston, MA: Little, Brown and Company.

Brown, I. (2009). *The boy in the moon: A father's journey to understand his extraordinary son.* New York, NY: St. Martin's Press.

Brown, R. I. (2000). Quality of life: Challenges and confrontation. In K. D. Keith & R. L. Schalock (Eds), *Cross-cultural perspectives on quality of life* (pp. 347–362). Washington, DC: American Association on Mental Retardation.

Brown, R. I., Brown, P. M., & Bayer, M. B. (1994). A quality of life model: New challenges arising from a six year study. In D. Goode (Ed.), *Quality of life for persons with disabilities: International perspectives and issues* (pp. 39–56). Cambridge, MA: Brookline.

Bruess, B. J. & Pearson, F. C. (2002). The debate continues: Are there gender differences in moral reasoning as defined by Kohlberg? *College Student Affairs Journal, 21*, 38–52.

Bullard, W. N. (1910). The high grade mental defectives. *Journal of Psycho-Asthenics, 14*, 14–15.

Burgdorf, M. P., & Burgdorf, R., Jr (1975). A history of unequal treatment: The qualifications of handicapped persons as a "suspect class" under the equal protection clause. *Santa Clara Lawyer, 15*(4), 855–910.

Burns, J. (2000). Gender identity and women with learning difficulties: the third sex. *Clinical Psychology Forum, 137*, 137–139.

Caballo, C., Crespo, M., Janaro, C., Verdugo, M. A., & Martinez, J. L. (2005). Factor structure of the Schalock and Keith Quality of Life Questionnaire (QOL.Q): Validation on Mexican and Spanish samples. *Journal of Intellectual Disability Research, 49*, 773–776.

Campbell, A., Converse, P. & Rodgers, W. L. (1976). *The quality of American life: Perceptions, evaluations, and satisfactions.* New York, NY: Russell Sage Foundation.

Carlson, L. 2010. *The faces of intellectual disability: Philosophical reflections.* Bloomington, IN: Indiana University Press.

Carraher, T. N., Carraher, D., & Schliemann, A. D. (1985). Mathematics in the streets and in the schools. *British Journal of Developmental Psychology, 3*, 21–29.

Carroll, C. F., & Reppucci, N. D. (1978). Meanings that professionals attach to labels for children. *Journal of Consulting and Clinical Psychology, 46*, 372–374.

Castles, E. E. (1996). *We're people first: The social and emotional lives of individuals with mental retardation.* Westport, CT: Praeger/Greenwood.

Cattell, J. M. (1890). Mental tests and measurements. *Mind, 15*, 373–380.

Center for Disability Rights, Law and Advocacy (2007). *An indictment of difference: A report of the investigation of the Beatrice State Developmental Center.* Lincoln, NE: Nebraska Advocacy Services, Inc.

Chiu, L. H. (1972). A cross-cultural comparison of cognitive styles in Chinese and American children. *International Journal of Psychology, 7*, 235–242.

Choi, I., Dalal, R., Kim-Prieto, C., & Park, H. (2003). Culture and judgment of causal relevance. *Journal of Personality and Social Psychology, 84*, 46–59.

Chowdhury, M., & Benson, B. A. (2011). Deinstitutionalization and quality of life of individuals with intellectual disability: A review of the international literature. *Journal of Policy and Practice in Intellectual Disabilities*, *8*, 256–265.

Chua, H. F., Boland, J. E., & Nisbett, R. E. (2005). Cultural variation in eye movements during scene perception. *Proceedings of the National Academy of Sciences*, *102*, 12629–12633.

Cianciolo, A. T., & Sternberg, R. J. (2004). *Intelligence: A brief history*. Malden, MA: Blackwell.

Clarke, B. (1975). *Mental disorder in earlier Britain*. Cardiff, UK: University of Wales Press.

Coles, R. (1989). *The call of stories: Teaching and the moral imagination*. Boston, MA: Houghton Mifflin.

Confucius (2003). *The Analects* (E. Slingerland, Trans.). Indianapolis, IN: Hackett.

Conyers, L. M. (2003). Disability culture: A cultural model of disability. *Rehabilitation Education*, *17*, 139–154.

Crossley, R., & McDonald, A. (1984). *Annie's coming out*. Harmondsworth, UK: Penguin.

Cummins, R. A. (1991). The Comprehensive Quality of Life Scale—Intellectual Disability: An instrument under development. *Australia and New Zealand Journal of Developmental Disabilities*, *17*, 259–264.

Cummins, R. A. (1995). Assessing quality of life. In R. I. Brown (Ed.), *Quality of life for handicapped people* (pp. 102–120). London, UK: Chapman & Hall.

Cummins, R. A. (1997). *Comprehensive Quality of Life Scale—Intellectual Disability* (5th ed.). Melbourne, Australia: Deakin University School of Psychology.

Cummins, R. A. (1998, Sept.). Measuring subjective life quality by proxy response. Paper presented at the National Conference of the Australian Society for the Study of Intellectual Disability. Adelaide, South Australia.

Cummins, R. A. (2005). Moving from the quality of life concept to a theory. *Journal of Intellectual Disability Research*, *49*, 699–706.

Cummins, R. A., McCabe, M. P., Romeo, Y., Reid, S., & Waters, L. (1997). An initial evaluation of the Comprehensive Quality of Life Scale-Intellectual Disability. *International Journal of Disability, Development and Education*, *44*, 7–19.

Damasio, A. (1994). *Descartes' error: Emotion, reason, and the human brain*. New York, NY: Avon Books.

Danforth, S. (2002). New words for new purposes: A challenge for the AAMR. *Mental Retardation*, *40*, 51–52.

Danforth, S. (2008). John Dewey's contributions to an educational philosophy of intellectual disability. *Educational Theory*, *58*, 45–62.

Darwin, C. (1859). *On the origin of species by means of natural selection, or the preservation of favoured races in the struggle for life*. London, UK: John Murray.

Davies, S. P. (1930). *Social control of the mentally deficient*. New York, NY: Crowell.

Davis, L. (Ed.), *The disability studies reader.* London, UK: Routledge.

D'Eath, M., Walls, M., Hodgins, M., & Cronin, M. (2003). *Quality of life of young people with intellectual disability in Ireland.* Dublin, Ireland: National Disability Authority.

De Clerck, G. A. M. (2010). Deaf epistemologies as a critique and alternative to the practice of science: An anthropological perspective. *American Annals of the Deaf, 154,* 435–446.

Dempsey, J. (2000, July 12). Worcester State Hospital Hillside Cemetery renovation project. *Worcester Telegram & Gazette.* Retrieved from: http://www.rootsweb.ancestry.com/~vtcstjoh/cemetery/hillside.htm (accessed December 17, 2012).

Dennis, R. E., Williams, W., Giangreco, M. F., & Cloninger, C. J. (1993). Quality of life as context for planning and evaluation of services for people with disabilities. *Exceptional Children, 59,* 499–512.

Descartes, R. (1952). *Discourse on method.* L. LaFleur (Trans.). Upper Saddle River, NJ: Prentice Hall (original work published 1637).

Descartes, R. (1952). *Meditations.* L. LaFleur (Trans.). Upper Saddle River, NJ: Prentice Hall (original work published 1641).

Deveau, R., & McGill, P. (2009). Physical interventions for adults with intellectual disabilities: Survey of use, policy, training and monitoring. *Journal of Applied Research in Intellectual Disabilities, 22,* 145–151.

Devine, M. (2004). Being a 'doer' instead of a 'viewer': The role of inclusive leisure contexts in determining social acceptance for people with disabilities. *Journal of Leisure Research, 36,* 137–159.

Devlieger, J. P., Rusch, F., & Pfeiffer, D. (Eds). (2003). *Rethinking disability: The emergence of new definition, concepts, and communities.* Antwerp, Belgium: Garant.

De Waal, C. (2002). *On Mead.* Belmont, CA: Wadsworth.

De Waal, F. (2009). *The age of empathy: Nature's lessons for a kinder society.* New York, NY: Crown.

Dewey, J. (1934). *Art as experience.* New York, NY: Capricorn.

Dewey, J. (1983). *Ethics.* In J. Boydston (Ed.). *The middle works of John Dewey, 1899–1924, vol. 5.* Carbondale, IL: Southern Illinois University Press (original work published 1908).

Dewey, J. (1985). *Democracy and education.* In J. Boydston (Ed.). *The middle works of John Dewey, 1899–1924, vol. 9.* Carbondale, IL: Southern Illinois University Press (original work published 1918).

Dewey, J. (1985). *The need for a recovery of philosophy.* In J. Boydston (Ed.), *The middle works of John Dewey, 1899–1924, vol. 10.* Carbondale,IL: Southern Illinois University Press (original work published 1917).

Dewey, J. (1988). *Experience and Nature.* In J. Boydston (Ed.), *The later works of John Dewey, 1925–1953, vol. 1.* Carbondale, IL: Southern Illinois University Press. (Original work published 1925).

Dewey, J. (1988). *Human nature and conduct.* In J. Boydston (Ed.), *The middle works of John Dewey, 1925–1953, vol. 14.* Carbondale, IL: Southern Illinois University Press (original work published 1922).

Dewey, J. (1988). *Philosophy and democracy.* In J. Boydston (Ed.), *The middle works of John Dewey, 1899–1924, vol. 11.* Carbondale, IL: Southern Illinois University Press (original work published 1918).

Dewey, J. (1988) The public and its problems. In J. Boydston (Ed.), *The later works of John Dewey, 1925–1953, vol. 2.* Carbondale, IL: Southern Illinois University Press (original work published 1927).

Dewey, J. (1988). The quest for certainty. In J. Boydston (Ed.), *The later works of John Dewey, 1925–1953, vol. 4.* Carbondale, IL: Southern Illinois University Press (original work published 1929).

Dewey, J. (1991). Liberalism and social action. In J. Boydston (Ed.), *The later works of John Dewey, 1925–1953, vol. 11.* Carbondale, IL: Southern Illinois University Press (original work published 1935).

Diekema, D. S. (2003). Involuntary sterilization of persons with mental retardation: An ethical analysis. *Mental Retardation and Developmental Disabilities Research Reviews, 9,* 21–26.

Dobbs, D. (2007, July 8). The gregarious brain. *NY Times Magazine.* Retrieved from: http://www.nytimes.com/2007/07/08/magazine/08sociability-t.html?pagewanted=all (accessed December 17, 2012).

Down, J. L. H. (1866). Observations on an ethnic classification of idiots. *Clinical Lecture Reports, London Hospital, 3,* 259–262.

Doyle, O. (2000, January 30). Programme sheds light on grave injustice. *The Sunday Tribune* [Dublin].

Drew, C. J., Hardman, M. L., & Logan, D. R. (1996). *Mental retardation: A life cycle approach* (6th ed.). Englewood Cliffs, NJ: Prentice-Hall.

Dudley, M., & Gale, F. (2002). Psychiatrists as moral community? Psychiatry under the Nazis and its contemporary relevance. *Australian and New Zealand Journal of Psychiatry, 36,* 585–594.

Duggan, J. (2012, July 10). Beatrice Center abuse trial. *Omaha World-Herald,* pp. 1A–2A.

Dunn, L. M. (1969). Small, special-purpose residential facilities for the retarded. In R. B. Kugel & W. Wolfensberger (Eds), *Changing patterns in residential services for the mentally retarded* (pp. 211–226). Washington, DC: President's Committee on Mental Retardation.

Dybwad, G. (1969). Action implications, U.S.A. today. In R. B. Kugel & W. Wolfensberger (Eds), *Changing patterns in residential services for the mentally retarded* (pp. 383–428). Washington, DC: President's Committee on Mental Retardation.

Ebel, R. L. (1974). And still the dryads linger. *American Psychologist, 29,* 485–492.

Eddey, G. E., & Robey, K. L. (2005). Considering the culture of disability in cultural competence education. *Academic Medicine, 80*, 706–712.

Edgerton, R. B. (1990). Quality of life from a longitudinal research perspective. In R. L. Schalock (Ed.), *Quality of life: Perspectives and issues* (pp. 149–160). Washington, DC: American Association on Mental Retardation.

Edgerton, R. B. (1993). *The cloak of competence* (rev. ed.). Berkeley, CA: University of California Press.

Edgerton, R. B. (1996). A longitudinal-ethnographic research perspective on quality of life. In R. L. Schalock (Ed.), *Quality of life: Volume I. Conceptualization and measurement* (pp. 83–90). Washington DC: American Association on Mental Retardation.

Edgerton, R. B., & Gaston, M. A. (Eds). (1991). "*I've seen it all.*" Baltimore, MD: Paul H. Brookes.

Edwards, K. (2011, May/June). Restoring dignity: Genealogists spearhead efforts to identify deaths at a historic state hospital. *Family Tree Magazine.* Retrieved from: http://www.familytreemagazine.com/article/state-hospital-cemetery-preservation (accessed December 17, 2012).

Edwards, M. L. (1996). The cultural context of deformity in the ancient Greek world. *Ancient History Bulletin, 10*, 79–92.

Eldridge, M. (1988). *Transforming experience: John Dewey's cultural instrumentalism.* Nashville, TN: Vanderbilt University Press.

Elks, M. A. (2005). Visual indictment: A contextual analysis of *The Kallikak Family* photographs. *Mental Retardation, 43*, 268–280.

Elliott, J., & Sandberg, L. (2007, July 24). Texas records detail abuse of mentally retarded. *Houston Chronicle.* Retrieved from: http://www.chron.com/news/houston-texas/article/Texas-records-detail-abuse-of-mentally-retarded-1814187.php (accessed December 17, 2012).

Emerson, E. (2007). Poverty and people with intellectual disabilities. *Mental Retardation and Developmental Disabilities Research Review, 13*, 107–113.

Emerson, E. (2010). The quality of life of disabled children. In R. Kober (Ed.), *Enhancing the quality of life of people with intellectual disabilities: From theory to practice* (pp. 223–240). Dordrecht, Netherlands: Springer.

Emerson, E., & Hatton, C. (2007). Poverty, socio-economic position, social capital and the health of children and adolescents with intellectual disabilities in Britain: A replication. *Journal of Intellectual Disability Research, 51*, 866–874.

Emerson, E., Fujiura, G. T., & Hatton, C. (2007). International perspectives. In S. L. Odom, R. H. Horner, M. Snell, & J. Blacher (Eds), *Handbook on developmental disabilities* (pp. 591–613). New York, NY: Guilford.

Emerson, E., Honey, A., Madden, R., Llewellyn, G. (2009). The well-being of Australian adolescents and young adults with self-reported long-term health conditions, impairments, or disabilities: 2001 and 2006. *Australian Journal of Social Issues, 44*(1), 39–53.

Emerson, E., McConkey, R., Walsh, P. N., & Felce, D. (2008). Intellectual disability in a global context. *Journal of Policy and Practice in Intellectual Disabilites, 5*, 79–80.

Eshun, S., & Gurung, R. A. R. (Eds). (2009). *Culture and mental health: Sociocultural influences, theory, and practice*. Malden, MA: Wiley-Blackwell.

Evans, E. C. (1945). Galen the physician as physiognomist. *Transactions and Proceedings of the American Philological Association, 76*, 374–382.

Farina, A. (1982). The stigma of mental disorders. In A. G. Miller (Ed.), *In the eye of the beholder: Contemporary approaches to stereotyping* (pp. 305–363). New York, NY: Praeger.

Felce, D. (1996, July). Defining and applying the concept of quality of life. Paper presented at the World Congress of the International Association for Scientific Study of Intellectual Disabilities, Helsinki, Finland.

Felce, D. (2000). Engagement in activity as an indicator of quality of life in British research. In K. D. Keith & R. L. Schalock (Eds), *Cross-cultural perspectives on quality of life* (pp. 173–190). Washington, DC: American Association on Mental Retardation.

Felce, D., Lowe, K., & de Paiva, S. (1994). Ordinary housing for people with severe learning disabilities and challenging behaviours. In E. Emerson, P. McGill, & J. Mansell (Eds), *Severe learning disabilities and challenging behaviours* (pp. 97–118). London: UK: Chapman & Hall.

Felce, D., Perry, J., & Kerr, M. (2011). A comparison of activity levels among adults with intellectual disabilities living in family homes and out-of-family placements. *Journal of Applied Research in Intellectual Disabilities, 24*, 421–426.

Ferguson, P. M. (1994). *Abandoned to their fate: Social policy and practice toward severely retarded people in America, 1820–1920*. Philadelphia, PA: Temple University Press.

Fernald, W. E. (1893). The history of the treatment of the feeble-minded. *Proceedings of the National Conference of Charities and Correction*, 203–221.

Fernald, W. E. (1902). The Massachusetts Farm Colony for the Feeble-Minded. In I. C. Barrows (Ed.), *Proceedings of the National Conference of Charities and Correction, Twenty-Ninth Annual Session* (pp. 487–490). Boston, MA: Geo. H. Ellis Co.

Fernald, W. E. (1904). Care of the feeble-minded. *Proceedings of the National Conference of Charities and Correction*, 380–390.

Fernald, W. E. (1912). The burden of feeble-mindedness. *Journal of Psycho-Asthenics, 17*, 87–111.

Fernald, W. E. (1915). What is practical in the way of prevention of mental defect? *Proceedings of the National Conference of Charities and Correction*, 289–297.

Ferri, B. A., & Connor, D. (2005). In the Shadow of *Brown*: Special education and overrepresentation of students of color. *Remedial and Special Education, 26*(2), 93–100.

Fesmire, S. (2003). *John Dewey and moral imagination: Pragmatism in ethics.* Bloomington, IN: Indiana University Press.

Fesmire, S. (2010). Ecological imagination. *Environmental Ethics, 32,* 183–203.

Finerman, R., & Bennett, L. A. (1995). Guilt blame and shame: Responsibility in health and sickness. *Social Science and Medicine, 40,* 1–3.

Finlay, N. (2000). Outside of life: Traditions of infant burial in Ireland from *cillín* to cist. *World Archaeology, 31,* 407–422.

Flynn, R. J., & Lemay, R. A. (Eds). (1999). *A quarter-century of normalization and social role valorization: Evolution and impact.* Ottawa, Canada: University of Ottawa Press.

Flynn, R. J., & Nitsch, K. E. (Eds). (1980). *Normalization, social integration, and community services.* Baltimore, MD: University Park Press.

Forrest, D. W. (1974). *Francis Galton: The life and work of a Victorian genius.* London, UK: Paul Elek.

Foucault, M. (2006). *History of madness.* New York, NY: Routledge (original work published 1961).

Frankl, V. E. (1959). *Man's search for meaning: An introduction to logotherapy* (4th ed.). Boston, MA: Beacon Press.

Freedman, R. I. (2001). Ethical challenges in the conduct of research involving persons with mental retardation. *Mental Retardation, 39,* 130–141.

Friedman, P. R. (1977). Human and legal rights of mentally retarded persons. *International Journal of Mental Health, 6,* 50–72.

Fundamental Rights Agency (2012). Fundamental rights of persons with intellectual disabilities and persons with mental health problems. Vienna, Austria: Author. Retrieved from: http://fra.europa.eu/fraWebsite/about_fra/about_fra_en.htm (accessed December 17, 2012).

Galton, F. (1869). *Hereditary genius: An inquiry into its laws and consequences.* London, UK: Macmillan.

Galton, F. (1883). *Inquiry into human faculty and its development.* London, UK: Macmillan.

Gardner, H. (1983). *Frames of mind: The theory of multiple intelligences.* New York, NY: Basic Books.

Gardner, H. (1999). *Intelligence reframed: Multiple intelligences for the 21st century.* New York, NY: Basic Books.

Gardner, H. (2011). The theory of multiple intelligences. In M. A. Gernsbacher, R. W. Pew, L. M. Hough, & J. R. Pomerantz (Eds), *Psychology and the real world* (pp. 122–130). New York, NY: Worth.

Gardner, J., Carran, D. T., & Nudler, S. (2001). Measuring quality of life and quality of services through personal outcome measures: Implications for public policy. *International Review of Research in Mental Retardation, 24,* 75–100.

Garland-Thomson, R. (2011a). Misfits: A feminist materialist disability concept. *Hypatia, 26*(3), 591–609.

Garland-Thomson, R. (2011b). Integrating disability, transforming feminist theory. In K. Q. Hall (Ed.), *Feminist disability studies* (pp. 13–47). Bloomington, IN: Indiana University Press.

Garrett, H. E. (1951). *Great experiments in psychology* (3rd ed.). New York, NY: Appleton-Century-Crofts.

Gelhaar, P. E. (1981). Institutionalized patient workers and their right to compensation in the aftermath of National League of Cities v. Usery. *Boston College Law Review, 22*(3), 510–543.

Gelb, S. A. (1995). The beast in man: Degenerationism and mental retardation, 1900–1920. *Mental Retardation, 33*, 1–9.

Gelb, S. A. (1997). The problem of typological thinking in mental retardation. *Mental Retardation, 35*, 448–457.

Gerber, D. A. (1992). Volition and valorization in the analysis of the 'careers' of people exhibited in freak shows. *Disability, Handicap & Society, 7*, 53–69.

Gerdes, K. E., & Segal, E. A. (2011). Importance of empathy for social work practice: Integrating new science. *Social Work, 56*, 141–148.

Gerdes, K. E., Lietz, C. A., & Segal, E. A. (2011). Measuring empathy in the 21st century: Development of an empathy index rooted in social cognitive neuroscience and social justice. *Social Work Research, 35*, 83–93.

Gert, B. & Culver, C. (1979) The justification of paternalism. *Ethics, 89*(2), 199–210.

Gilbert, D. T., & Malone, P. S. (1995). The correspondence bias. *Psychological Bulletin, 117*, 21–38.

Gilligan, C. (1982). *In a different voice: Psychological theory and women's development.* Cambridge, MA: Harvard University Press.

Giordano, P. J. (2011). Culture and theories of personality: Western, Confucian, and Buddhist perspectives. In K. D. Keith (Ed.), *Cross-cultural psychology: Contemporary themes and perspectives* (pp. 423–444). Malden, MA: Wiley-Blackwell.

Giubilini, A., & Minerva, F. (2012, February 23). After-birth abortion: Why should the baby live? *Journal of Medical Ethics.* Retrieved from: www.jme.bmj.com

Goddard, H. H. (1912). *The Kallikak family: A study in the heredity of feeble-mindedness.* New York, NY: Macmillan.

Goddard, H. H. (1913). The Binet tests in relation to immigration. *Journal of Psycho-Asthenics, 18*(2), 105–110.

Goddard, H. H. (1914). *Feeble-mindedness: Its causes and consequences.* New York, NY: Macmillan.

Goddard, H. H. (1915). The possibilities of research as applied to the prevention of feeble-mindedness. *Proceedings of the National Conference of Charities and Correction*, 307–312.

Goddard, H. H. (1917). Mental tests and the immigrant. *Journal of Delinquency, 2*, 243–277.

Goddard, H. H. (1927). Who is a moron? *Scientific Monthly, 24*, 41–46.

Goddard, H. H. (1928). Feeblemindedness: A question of definition. *Journal of Psycho-Asthenics, 33,* 219–227.

Goffman, I. (1963). *Stigma.* Englewood Cliffs, NJ: Prentice-Hall.

Goode, D. (1997). Quality of life as international disability policy: Implications for international research. In R. L. Schalock (Ed.), *Quality of life. Volume II. Application to persons with disabilities* (pp. 211–221). Washington, DC: American Association on Mental Retardation.

Goode, D., & Hogg, J. (1994). Towards an understanding of holistic quality of life in people with profound intellectual and multiple disabilities. In D. Goode (Ed.), *Quality of life for persons with disabilities: International perspectives and issues* (pp. 197–207). Cambridge, MA: Brookline.

Goodey, C. F. (2011). *A history of intelligence and "intellectual disability": The shaping of psychology in early modern Europe.* Farnham, UK: Ashgate.

Goodwin, C. J. (2008). *A history of modern psychology* (3rd ed.). New York, NY: John Wiley & Sons.

Gould, S. J. (1981). *The mismeasure of man.* New York, NY: Norton.

Greenwood, J. D. (2009). *A conceptual history of psychology.* New York, NY: McGraw-Hill.

Groce, N. E. (1985). *Everyone here spoke sign language: Hereditary deafness on Martha's Vineyard.* Cambridge, MA: Harvard University Press.

Gross, R. H., Cox, A., Tatyrek, R., Pollay, M., & Barnes, W. A. (1983). Early management and decision-making for the treatment of myelomeningocele. *Pediatrics, 72,* 450–458.

Grossman, H. J. (Ed.). (1973). *Manual on terminology and classification in mental retardation.* Washington, DC: American Association on Mental Deficiency.

Groulx, R., Doré, R., & Doré, L. (2000). My quality of life as I see it. In K. D. Keith & R. L. Schalock (Eds), *Cross-cultural perspectives on quality of life* (pp. 23–27). Washington, DC: American Association on Mental Retardation.

Gunther, D., & Diekema, D. (2006). Attenuating growth in children with profound developmental disability: A new approach to an old dilemma. *Archives of Pediatrics and Adolescent Medicine, 160,* 1013–1017.

Gurung, R. A. R. (2011). Cultural influences on health. In K. D. Keith (Ed.), *Cross-cultural psychology*: Contemporary themes and perspectives (pp. 259–273). Malden, MA: Wiley-Blackwell.

Habermas, J. (1991). The paradigm shift in Mead. In M. Aboulafia (Ed.), *Philosophy, social theory, and the thought of George Herbert Mead* (pp. 137–168). Albany, NY: State University of New York Press.

Haidt, J. (2000). The positive emotion of elevation. *Prevention and Treatment, 3,* 1–5.

Haidt, J. (2003). Elevation and the positive psychology of morality. In C. L. M. Keyes & J. Haidt (Eds), *Flourishing: Positive psychology and the life well-lived.* Washington, D.C.: American Psychological Association.

Hall, D. & Ames, R. (1998). *Thinking from the Han: Self, truth, and transcendence in Chinese and Western culture* Albany, NY: State University of New York Press.

Hall, E. T. (1976). *Beyond culture.* New York, NY: Anchor Books.

Halpern, S. (2008). *Can't remember what I forgot: The good news from the front lines of memory research.* New York, NY: Harmony Books.

Harding, S. (1991). *Whose science? Whose knowledge? Thinking from women's lives.* Ithaca, NY: Cornell University Press.

Hare, R. M. (1976). Survival of the weakest. In S. Gorovitz (Ed.), *Moral problems in medicine* (pp. 364–369). Englewood Cliffs, NH: Prentice Hall.

Harner, C. J., & Heal, L. W. (1993). The Multifaceted Lifestyle Satisfaction Scale (MLSS): Psychometric properties of an interview schedule for assessing personal satisfaction of adults with limited intelligence. *Research in Developmental Disabilities, 14,* 221–236.

Harris, J. (2010). Developmental perspective on the emergence of moral personhood. In E. F. Kittay & L. Carlson (Eds), *Cognitive disability and its challenge to moral philosophy* (pp. 55–74). Chichester, UK: Wiley-Blackwell.

Harris, P. (1995). Who am I? Concepts of disability and their implications for people with learning difficulties. *Disability and Society, 10,* 341–351.

Hartheim Castle: Place of learning and remembrance (2002). Retrieved from: www.schloss-hartheim.at (accessed December 17, 2012).

Hartsock, N. C. M. (1998). *The feminist standpoint revisited and other essays.* Boulder, CO: Westview Press.

Harvey, P. (2000). *An introduction to Buddhist ethics: Foundations, values and issues.* Cambridge, UK: Cambridge University Press.

Hatton, C. (1998). Whose quality of life is it anyway? Some problems with the emerging quality of life consensus. *Mental Retardation, 33,* 295–303.

Hawkins, B. A., Kim, K., & Eklund, S. J. (1995). Validity and reliability of a five dimensional life satisfaction index. *Mental Retardation, 33,* 295–303.

Heal, L. W., & Chadsey-Rusch, J. (1985). The Lifestyle Satisfaction Scale (LSS): Assessing individuals' satisfaction with residence, community setting, and associated services. *Applied Research in Mental Retardation, 6,* 475–490.

Heal, L. W., & Sigelman, C. K. (1995). Response biases in interviews of individuals with limited mental ability. *Journal of Intellectual Disability Research, 39,* 331–340.

Heal, L. W., & Sigelman, C. K. (1996). Methodological issues in quality of life measurement. In R. L. Schalock (Ed.), *Quality of life:Volume I. Conceptualization and measurement* (pp. 91–104). Washington, DC: American Association on Mental Retardation.

Heal, L. W., Borthwick-Duffy, S. A., & Saunders, R. R. (1996). Assessment of quality of life. In J. W. Jacobson & J. A. Mulik (Eds), *Manual of diagnosis and professional practices in mental retardation* (pp. 199–209). Washington, DC: American Psychological Association.

Heal, L. W., Rubin, S. S., & Park, W. (1995). *Lifestyle Satisfaction Scale.* Champaign-Urbana, IL: Transition Research Institute, University of Illinois.

Heine, S. J. (2012). *Cultural psychology* (2nd ed.). New York, NY: W. W. Norton.

Held, V. (2006). *The Ethics of care: Personal, political, and global.* Oxford, UK: Oxford University Press.

Helle, S. (2000). Quality of life: A personal perspective from Finland. In K. D. Keith & R. L. Schalock (Eds), *Cross-cultural perspectives on quality of life* (pp. 29–31). Washington, DC: American Association on Mental Retardation.

Hensel, E. (2001). Is satisfaction a valid concept in the assessment of quality of life of people with intellectual disabilities? A review of the literature. *Journal of Applied Research in Intellectual Disabilities, 14,* 311–326.

Hensel, E., Rose, J., Stenfert Kroese, B., & Banks-Smith, J. (2002). Subjective judgements of quality of life: A comparison study between people with intellectual disability and those without disability. *Journal of Intellectual Disability Research, 46,* 95–107.

Herndon, J. (1971). *How to survive in your native land.* New York, NY: Simon and Schuster.

Hester, M. (2001). *Community as healing.* New York, NY: Roman and Littlefield.

Hester, M. (2010). *End of life care and pragmatic decision making: A bioethical perspective.* Cambridge, UK: Cambridge University Press.

Heward, W. L., & Cavanaugh, R.A. (2001). Educational equality for students with disabilities. In J. A. Banks & C. A. M. Banks (Eds), *Multicultural education: Issues and perspectives* (4th ed.) (pp. 295–326). New York, NY: John Wiley & Sons.

Higgins, L., & Mansell, J. (2009). Quality of life in group homes and older persons' homes. *British Journal of Learning Disabilities, 37,* 207–212.

Higgins, L. T., Lian, C. D., & Zheng, R. C. (2003). Psychological testing in China today. *Testing International, 13*(2), 3–8.

Hobbes, T. (1973). *Leviathan.* London, UK: Everyman's Library (original work published 1660).

Hoffman, M. L. (1979). Development of moral thought, feeling, and behavior. *American Psychologist, 34,* 958–966.

Hoffman, M. L. (2000). *Empathy and moral development: Implications for caring and justice.* Cambridge, UK: Cambridge University Press.

Holland, T., Clare, I. C. H., & Mukhopadhyay, T. (2002). Prevalence of "criminal offending" by men and women with intellectual disability and the characteristics of "offenders": Implications for research and service development. *Journal of Intellectual Disability Research, 46,* Supplement 1, 6–20.

Hollingworth, L. S. (1914). *Functional periodicity: An experimental study of the mental and motor abilities of women during menstruation.* New York, NY: Teachers College, Columbia University.

Holtgraves, T. (1997). Styles of language use: Individual and cultural variability in conversational indirectness. *Journal of Personality and Social Psychology, 73,* 624–637.

Hopper, K., Harrison, G., Janca, A., & Sartorius, N. (Eds). (2007). *Recovery from schizophrenia: A report from the WHO Collaborative Project, the international study of schizophrenia.* Oxford, UK: University of Oxford Press.

Horner-Johnson, W. & Drum, C. E. (2006). Prevalence of maltreatment of people with intellectual disabilities: A review of recently published research. *Mental Retardation and Developmental Disabilities Research Reviews, 12,* 57–69.

Hothersall, D. (1984). *History of psychology.* Philadelphia, PA: Temple University Press.

Howe, S. G. (1848). *Report made to the legislature of Massachusetts, upon idiocy.* Boston, MA: Coolidge & Wiley.

Howe, S. G. (1851). On training and educating idiots: The second annual report made to the legislature of Massachusetts. *American Journal of Insanity, VIII,* 97–118.

Hubbard, (2010). Abortion and disability: Who should and should not inhabit the world? In L. Davis (Ed.), *The disability studies reader* (pp. 107–119). London, UK: Routledge.

Hughes, C., & Hwang, B. (1996). Attempts to conceptualize and measure quality of life. In R. L. Schalock (Ed.), *Quality of life: Volume I. Conceptualization and measurement* (pp. 51–61). Washington, DC: American Association on Mental Retardation.

Hughes, C., Hwang, B., Kim, J., Eisenman, L. T., & Killian, D. J. (1995). Quality of life in applied research: A review and analysis of empirical measures. *American Journal on Mental Retardation, 99,* 623–641.

Hunt, M. (1994). *The story of psychology.* New York, NY: Anchor Books.

Hutchison, P. (1990). A qualitative study of the friendships of people with disabilities. In B. J. A. Smale (Ed.), *Leisure challenges: Bringing people, resources and policy into play* (n.p.). Waterloo, Canada: Ontario Research Council on Leisure.

Inclusion International (2012). Priorities for people with intellectual disabilities in implementing the United Nations Convention on the Rights of People with Disabilities. London, UK: Author. Retrieved from: http://ii.gmalik.com/pdfs/UN_brochure_screen.pdf (accessed December 17, 2012).

The Iowa Department of Human Services, (n.d.). Glenwood Resource Center. Retrieved from: www.dhs.iowa.gov.

Itard, J. M. G. (1962/1801). *The wild boy of Aveyron* (trans. G. Humphrey & M. Humphrey). New York, NY: Appleton–Century-Crofts.

Ivanhoe, P. (2002). *Ethics in the Confucian tradition.* Indianapolis, IN: Hackett (original work published 1990).

Iwakuma, M. (2002). The body as embodiment: An investigation of the body by Merleau-Ponty. In M. Corker & T. Shakespeare (Eds), *Disability/postmodernity: Embodying disability theory* (pp. 76–87). New York, NY: Continuum.

James, W. (1950). *The principles of psychology.* New York, NY: Dover (original work published 1890).

James, W. (1977/1879). The sentiment of rationality. In J. J. McDermott (Ed.), *The writings of William James: A comprehensive edition* (pp. 317–345). Chicago, IL: The University of Chicago Press.

James, W. (1977/1896). The will to believe. In J. J. McDermott (Ed.), *The writings of William James: A comprehensive edition* (pp. 717–735). Chicago, IL: The University of Chicago Press.

Jaworska, A. (2010). Caring and full moral standing redux. In E. F. Kittay & L. Carlson (Eds), *Cognitive disability and its challenge to moral philosophy* (pp. 369–392). Chichester, UK: Wiley-Blackwell.

Jennings, B. (2010). Agency and moral relationship in dementia. In E. Kittay & L. Carlson (Eds), *Cognitive disability and its challenge to moral philosophy* (pp. 171–182). Malden, MA: Wiley-Blackwell.

Jensen, A. R. (1968). Social class, race and genetics: Implications for education. *American Educational Research Journal, 5*, 1–42.

Ji, L-H., Nisbett, R. E., & Zhang, Z. (2004). Is it culture or is it language? Examination of language effects in cross-cultural research on categorization. *Journal of Personality and Social Psychology, 87*, 57–65.

Johnson, A. (1899). Concerning a form of degeneracy. II. The education and care of the feeble-minded. *American Journal of Sociology, 4*, 463–473.

Johnson, H. (2003, February 16). Unspeakable conversations. *New York Times.* Retrieved from http://www.nytimes.com/2003/02/16/magazine/unspeakable-conversations.html?pagewanted=all&src=pm (accessed December 17, 2012).

Johnson, M. (1987). *The body in the mind.* Chicago, IL: The University of Chicago Press.

Johnson, M. (1993). *Moral Imagination.* Chicago, IL: The University of Chicago Press.

Jones, E., Perry, J., Lowe, K., Felce, D., Toogood, S., Dunstan, F., Allen, D., & Pagler, J. (1997). *Opportunity and the promotion of activity among adults with severe learning disabilities living in community housing: The impact of training staff in active support.* Cardiff, UK: University of Wales College of Medicine.

Jones, E. E. & Harris, V.A. (1967). The attribution of attitudes. *Journal of Experimental Social Psychology, 3*, 1–24.

Kant, I. (1983) *Grounding for the metaphysics of morals*, in J. W. Ellington (Ed.), *Immanuel Kant: Ethical philosophy.* Indianapolis, IN: Hackett Publishing Company (original work published 1785).

Keith, H. E. (1999). Feminism and pragmatism: George Herbert Mead's ethics of care. *Transactions of the Charles S. Peirce Society, 36*, 328–344.

Keith, H. E. (2008). The ethics of care. In J. Lachs & R. Talisse (Eds), *American philosophy: An encyclopedia* (pp. 252–254). New York, NY: Routledge.

Keith, H. E. (2009). Transforming ren: The de of George Herbert Mead's social self. *Journal of Chinese Philosophy, 36*, 69–84.

Keith, H. E. (2012). *Natural caring: A pragmatist feminist approach to ethics in the more-than-human world.* In Hammington, M. & Bardwell-Jones, C. (Eds), Contemporary Feminist Pragmatism (pp. 255–268). New York, NY: Routledge.

Keith, K. D. (1990). Quality of life: Issues in community integration. In R. L. Schalock (Ed.), *Quality of life: Perspectives and issues* (pp. 93–100). Washington, DC: American Association on Mental Retardation.

Keith, K. D. (1996). Measuring quality of life across cultures: Issues and challenges. In R. L. Schalock (Ed.), *Quality of life: Volume I. Conceptualization and measurement* (pp. 73–82). Washington DC: American Association on Mental Retardation.

Keith, K. D. (2001). International quality of life: Current conceptual, measurement, and implementation issues. *International Review of Research in Mental Retardation, 24*, 49–74.

Keith, K. D. (2002). Promises to keep. In R. L. Schalock (Ed.), *Out of the darkness and into the light: Nebraska's experience with mental retardation* (pp. 229–234). Washington, DC: American Association on Mental Retardation.

Keith, K. D. (2007). Quality of life. In A. Carr, G. O'Reilly, P. N. Walsh, & J. McEvoy (Eds), *The handbook of intellectual disability and clinical psychology practice* (pp. 143–168). London, UK: Routledge.

Keith, K. D., & Bonham, G. S. (2005). The use of quality of life data at the organization and systems level. *Journal of Intellectual Disability Research, 49*, 799–805.

Keith, K. D., & Ferdinand, L. R. (1984). Changes in levels of mental retardation: A comparison of institutional and community populations. *Journal of the Association for Persons with Severe Handicaps, 9*, 26–30.

Keith, K. D., & Ferdinand, L. R. (2000). *Project to compare quality of life of Nebraskans with developmental disabilities and citizens without disabilities.* Lincoln, NE: Governor's Planning Council on Developmental Disabilities.

Keith, K. D., & Schalock, R. L. (1994). The measurement of quality of life in adolescence: The Quality of Student Life Questionnaire. *The American Journal of Family Therapy, 22*(1), 83–87.

Keith, K. D., & Schalock, R. L. (1995). *Quality of Student Life Questionnaire.* Worthington, OH: IDS.

Keith, K. D., Heal, L. W., & Schalock, R. L. (1996). Cross-cultural measurement of critical quality of life concepts. *Journal of Intellectual and Developmental Disability, 21*, 273–293.

Keith, K. D., Schalock, R. L., & Hoffman, K. (1986). *Quality of life: Measurement and programmatic implications.* Lincoln, NE: Region V Mental Retardation Services.

Kennedy, P., Andreasen, D., Ehirim, P., King, B. Kirby, T., Mao, H., & Moore, M. (2004). Using human extra-cortical local field potentials to control a switch. *Journal of Neural Engineering, 1*, 72–77.

Kerlin, I. N. (1877). The organization of establishments for the idiotic and imbecile classes. *Organization of Institutions for Idiots*, No. *22*, 25–31.

Kerlin, I. N. (1885). Report of standing committee. *Proceedings of the National Conference of Charities and Correction*, 158–178.

Kerlin, I. N. (1886). Report of the committee on provision for idiotic and feeble-minded persons. *Proceedings of the National Conference of Charities and Correction*, 288–297.

Kerlin, I. N. (1891). *The manual of Elwyn: 1864–1891*. Philadelphia, PA: J. B. Lippincott Co.

Kim, D., Pan, Y., & Park, H. S. (1998). High- versus low-context culture: A comparison of Chinese, Korean, and American cultures. *Psychology and Marketing, 15*, 507–521.

Kishi, G., Teelucksingh, B., Zollers, N., Park-Lee, S., & Meyer, L. (1988). Daily decision-making in community residences: A social comparison of adults with and without mental retardation. *American Journal on Mental Retardation, 92*, 430–435.

Kitayama, S., Duffy, S., Kawamura, T., & Larsen, J. T. (2003). Perceiving an object and its context in different cultures: A cultural look at new look. *Psychological Science, 14*, 201–206.

Kittay, E. (2008). At the margins of moral personhood. *Bioethical Inquiry, 5*, 137–156.

Kittay, E. (2010). The personal is philosophical is political: A philosopher and mother of a cognitively disabled person sends notes from the battlefield. In E. F. Kittay & L. Carlson (Eds), *Cognitive disability and its challenge to moral philosophy* (pp. 331–334). Chichester, UK: Wiley-Blackwell.

Kittay, E. F., Schriempf, A., Silvers, A., & Wendell, S. (2001). Introduction. *Hypatia, 16*(4), vii–xii.

Kixmiller, J. S., Keith, K. D., & Schalock, R. L. (1991). Views on town and neighborhood: Adults with mental retardation and their neighbors. *Nebraska Journal of Psychology, 1*, 18–22.

Kloefkorn, W. (1974). *Alvin Turner as farmer.* Lincoln, NE: Windflower Press.

Klotz, M. B. (2010, December). *IDEA in practice. Communiqué Online, 39*(4), 1. Retrieved from: http://www.nasponline.org/publications/cq/mocq394IDEA.aspx (accessed December 17, 2012).

Knight, G. H. (1879). Status of the work. *Proceedings of the Association of Medical Officers of American Institutions for Idiotic and Feeble Minded Persons, 4*, 96.

Knight, G. H. (1891). Colony care for adult idiots. *Proceedings of the National Conference of Charities and Correction*, 107–108.

Knox, M., & Hickson, F. (2001). The meanings of close friendship: The views of four people with intellectual disabilities. *Journal of Applied Research in Intellectual Disabilities, 14*, 276–291.

Kober, R., & Eggleton, I. R. C. (2002). Factor stability of the Schalock and Keith (1993) Quality of Life Questionnaire. *Mental Retardation, 40*, 157–165.

Kohlberg, L. (1981). *The meaning and measurement of moral development.* Cambridge, UK: Oelgeschlager, Gunn and Haine.

Kozleski, E. B, & Sands, D. J. (1992). The yardstick of social validity: Evaluating quality of life as perceived by adults without disabilities. *Education and Training in Mental Retardation, 27*(2), 119–131.

Kreiner, D. S. (2011). Language and culture: Commonality, variation, and mistaken assumptions. In K. D. Keith (Ed.), *Cross-cultural psychology: Contemporary themes and perspectives* (pp. 383–399). Malden, MA: Wiley-Blackwell.

Kuhlman, F. (1916). Part played by the state institutions in the care of the feeble-minded. *Journal of Psycho-Asthenics, 21*, 3–24.

Kuhse, H., & Singer, P. (1985). *Should the baby live?* Oxford, UK: Oxford University Press.

Kupfer, J. H. (1983). *Experience as art: Aesthetics in everyday life.* Albany, NY: State University of New York Press.

Lachappelle, Y., Wehmeyer, M. L., Haelewyck, M.-C., Courbois, Y., Keith, K. D., Schalock, R. L., Verdugo, M. A., & Walsh, P. N. (2005). The relationship between quality of life and self-determination: An international study. *Journal of Intellectual Disability Research, 49*, 740–744.

Lakin, K. C., Prouty, R., Alba, K., & Scott, N. (2008). Twenty-five years of Medicaid Home and Community Based Services (HCBS): Significant milestones reached in 2007. *Intellectual and Developmental Disabilities, 46*, 325–328.

Lakeoff, G. (2002). *Moral politics* (2nd ed.). Chicago, IL: The University of Chicago Press.

Lakoff, G., & Johnson, M. (1980). *Metaphors we live by.* Chicago, IL: The University of Chicago Press.

Landesman, S. (1986). Quality of life and personal life satisfaction: Definition and measurement issues. *Mental Retardation, 24*, 141–143.

L'Arche USA (2012). The L'Arche difference. Retrieved from www.larcheusa.org (accessed December 17, 2012).

Larson, S. A., Scott, N., Salmi, P., & Lakin, K. C. (2009). Changes in number and characteristics of people living in state institutions, 1977–2008. *Intellectual and developmental disabilities, 47*, 329–333.

Lazarus, M., & Lazarus, A. (1888). *The poems of Emma Lazarus.* Boston, MA: Houghton Mifflin.

Lea, S. J. (1988). Mental retardation: Social construction or clinical reality? *Disability, Handicap, & Society, 3*, 63–69.

Lekan, T. (2009). Disabilities and educational opportunity: A Deweyan approach. *Transactions of the Charles S. Peirce Society*, *45*, 213–230.

Lesjak, D. (2007, January/February). Mass grave uncovered. *WWII Today*, 9–10.

Lewiston, H., & Holtman, J. (1968). *Freak show man: The autobiography of Harry Lewiston as told to Jerry Holtman.* Los Angeles, CA: Holloway House.

Light, A. (1996). *Environmental pragmatism.* Abingdon, UK: Taylor & Francis.

Lindemann, H. (2010) Holding one another (well, wrongly, clumsily) in a time of dementia. In E. F. Kittay & L. Carlson (Eds), *Cognitive disability and its challenge to moral philosophy* (pp. 163–169). Chichester, UK: Wiley-Blackwell.

Lippmann, W. (1922a, October 25). The mental age of Americans. *New Republic*, *32*(412), 213–215.

Lippmann, W. (1922b, November 1). The mental age of Americans. *New Republic*, *32*(413), 246–248.

Lippmann, W. (1922c, November 8). The mental age of Americans. *New Republic*, *32*(414), 275–277.

Lippmann, W. (1922d, November 15). The mental age of Americans, *New Republic*, *32*(415), 297–298.

Lippmann, W. (1922e, November 22). The mental age of Americans, *New Republic*, *32*(416), 328–330.

Lippmann, W. (1922f, November 29). The mental age of Americans, *New Republic*, *32*(417), 9–11.

Locke, J. (1952). *The second treatise of government.* T. Peardon (Ed.). New York, NY: The Library of Liberal Arts/Macmillan (original work published 1690).

Locke, J. (1959). *An essay concerning human understanding.* Mineola, NY: Dover (original work published 1690).

Lovern, L. (2008). Native American worldview and the discourse on disability. *Essays in Philosophy*, *9*(1), article 14, 1–8.

Luckasson, R. (1990). A lawyer's perspective on quality of life. In R. L. Schalock (Ed.), *Quality of life: Perspectives and issues* (pp. 211–214). Washington, DC: American Association on Mental Retardation.

MacCorquodale, K., & Meehl, P. (1948). On a distinction between hypothetical constructs and intervening variables. *Psychological Review*, *55*, 95–107.

MacKay, R. (1974). Standardized tests: Objective/objectivized measures of "competence." In A. Cicourel, K. Jennings, S. Jennings, K. Leiter, R. MacKay, H. Mehan, & D. Roth (Eds). *Language use and school performance* (pp. 218–247). New York, NY: Academic Press.

MacMillan, N. A. (1987). Beyond the categorical/continuous distinction: A psychophysical approach to processing modes. In S. Harnad (Ed.), *Categorical perception: The groundwork of cognition* (pp. 53–85). Cambridge, UK: Cambridge University Press.

McDonald, A. (2007, June 16). The other story from a "Pillow Angel." *Seattle Pi.* Retrieved from: http://www.seattlepi.com/local/opinion/article/The-other-story-from-a-Pillow-Angel-1240555.php (accessed December 17, 2012).

McDonnell, J. J., Hardman, M. L., McDonnell, A. P., & Kiefer-O'Donnell, R. (1995). *An introduction to persons with severe disabilities: Educational and social issues.* Needham Heights, MA: Allyn & Bacon.

McGill, P., Emerson, E., & Mansell, J. (1994). Individually designed residential provision for people with seriously challenging behaviours. In E. Emerson, P. McGill, & J. Mansell (Eds), *Severe learning disabilities and challenging behaviours* (pp. 119–156). London, UK: Chapman Hall.

McMahan, J. (2002). *The ethics of killing: Problems at the margins of life.* Oxford, UK: Oxford University Press.

McMahan, J. (2005). Causing disabled people to exist and causing people to be disabled. *Ethics, 116*, 77–99.

McMahan, J. (2010). Cognitive disability and cognitive enhancement. In E. F. Kittay & L. Carlson (Eds), *Cognitive disability and its challenge to moral philosophy* (pp. 345–367). Chichester, UK: Wiley-Blackwell.

McMillan, I. (2006). Inspection finds 'institutional abuse' at Cornwall NHS trust. *Learning Disability Practice, 9*(6), 4.

McPherson, T. (1984). The moral patient. *Philosophy, 59*(228), 171–183.

Mahowald, M. (1998). Is feminism compatible with advocacy for the disabled? *Social Philosophy Today, 14*, 271–283.

Manion, M., & Bersani, H. (1987). Mental retardation as a western sociological construct: a cross cultural analysis. *Disability, Handicap and Society, 2*, 231–244.

Mann, D. (2010, April 19). State abuse: Despite reforms, abuse in state institutions remains high. *Observer.* Retrieved from: http://www.texasobserver.org/cover-story/state-abuse (accessed December 17, 2012).

Markman, E., & Hutchinson, J. (1984). Children's sensitivity to constraints on word meaning: Taxonomic versus thematic relations. *Cognitive Psychology, 16*, 1–27.

Markus, H., & Kitayama, S. (1991). Culture and the self: Implications for cognition, emotion, and motivation. *Psychological Review, 98*, 224–253.

Mastin, J. T. (1916). The new colony plan for the feeble-minded. *Journal of Psycho-Asthenics, 21*, 25–35.

Masuda, T., & Nisbett, R. E. (2001). Attending holistically vs. analytically: Comparing the context sensitivity of Japanese and Americans. *Journal of Personality and Social Psychology, 81*, 922–934.

Masuda, T., Gonzalez, R., Kwan, I., & Nisbett, R. E. (2008). Culture and aesthetic preference: Comparing the attention to context of East Asians and Americans. *Personality and Social Psychology Bulletin, 34*, 1260–1275.

Mateen, F. J., & Boes, C. J. (2010). "Pinheads": The exhibition of neurologic disorders at "The Greatest Show on Earth." *Neurology, 75*, 2028–2032.

Matsumoto, D. (2000). Foreword. In K. D. Keith & R. L. Schalock (Eds), *Cross-cultural perspectives on quality of life* (pp. xxi–xxiv). Washington, DC: American Association on Mental Retardation.

Matsumoto, D., & Juang, L. (2008). *Culture and psychology* (4th ed.). Belmont, CA: Wadsworth.

Matsumoto, D., & Juang, L. (2013). *Culture & psychology* (5th ed.). Belmont, CA: Wadsworth.

Maulik, P. K., Mascarenhas, M. N., Mathers, C. D., Dua, T., & Saxena, S. (2011). Prevalence of intellectual disability: A meta-analysis of population-based studies. *Research in Developmental Disabilities, 32*, 419–436.

Mayer, J. D., & Salovey, P. (1993). The intelligence of emotional intelligence. *Intelligence, 17*, 433–442.

Mayer, J. D., & Salovey, P. (1997). What is emotional intelligence? In P. Salovey & D. Sluyter (Eds), *Emotional development and emotional intelligence: Implications for educators* (pp. 3–31). New York, NY: Basic Books.

Mead, G. (1934). *Mind, self and society: From the standpoint of a social behaviorist.* C. Morris (Ed.). Chicago, IL: The University of Chicago Press.

Mead, G. (1964a). The mechanism of social consciousness. In A. Reck (Ed.), *Selected Writings of George Herbert Mead.* Chicago, IL: The University of Chicago Press.

Mead, G. (1964b). The psychology of social consciousness implied in instruction. In A. Reck (Ed.), *Selected writings of George Herbert Mead.* Chicago, IL: The University of Chicago Press.

Mead, G. (1964c). Social consciousness and the consciousness of meaning. In A. Reck (Ed.), *Selected writings of George Herbert Mead.* Chicago, IL: The University of Chicago Press.

Mead, G. (1964d). Social psychology as counterpart to physiological psychology. In A. Reck (Ed.), *Selected writings of George Herbert Mead.* Chicago, IL: The University of Chicago Press.

Memert, E. M. (1951). *Social pathology: A systematic approach to the theory of sociopathic behavior.* New York, NY: McGraw-Hill.

Menolascino, F. J. (1977). *Challenges in mental retardation: Progressive ideology and services.* New York, NY: Human Sciences Press.

Menolascino, F. J., & Egger, M. L. (1978). *Medical dimensions of mental retardation.* Lincoln, NE: University of Nebraska Press.

Mercier, C., Saxena, S., Lecomte, J., Cumbrera, M. G., & Harnois, G. (2008). WHO ATLAS in global resources for persons with intellectual disabilities 2007: Key findings relevant to low- and middle-income countries. *Journal of Policy and Practices for Persons with Intellectual Disabilities, 5*, 81–88.

Merriam, G. (2010). Rehabilitating Aristotle: A virtue ethics approach to disability and human flourishing. In D. C. Ralston & J. Ho (Eds), *Philosophical Reflections on Disability* (pp. 133–151). New York, NY: Springer.

Meuleners, L. B., & Lee, A. H. (2005). Quality of Life Profile—Adolescent Version: Assessing the relationship of covariates to scale scores using structural equation modeling. *Quality of Life Research, 14,* 1057–1063.

Milgram, S. (1974). *Obedience to authority.* New York, NY: Harper & Row.

Mill, J. S. (2002) *Utilitarianism* (2nd ed.). Indianapolis, IN: Hackett Publishing Company (original work published 1861).

Miller, J. G. (1984). Culture and the development of everyday social explanation. *Journal of Personality and Social Psychology, 46,* 961–978.

Millington, M. J., Szymanski, E. M., & Hanley-Maxwell, C. (1994). Effect of the label of mental retardation on employer concerns and selection. *Rehabilitation Counseling Bulletin, 38,* 27–43.

Mistry, J., & Rogoff, B. (1994). Remembering in cultural context. In W. Lonner & R. Malpass (Eds), *Psychology and culture* (pp. 139–144). New York, NY: Allyn and Bacon.

Mitchell, S. (2000). *The Bhagavad Gita: A new translation.* New York, NY: Three Rivers Press.

Miyamoto, Y., Nisbett, R. E., & Masuda, T. (2006). Culture and the physical environment: Holistic versus analytic perceptual affordances. *Psychological Science, 2,* 113–119.

Moonen, R., Ojasalo, J., Seppälä, H., & Suomalainen, N. (2010). Designing safety services for intellectually disabled people at home: Preliminary findings from an ongoing empirical study. In *User modeling and adaptation for daily routines* (pp. 25–30; Proceedings of the International Conference on User Modeling, Adaptation and Personalization). Kona, HI: UMAP.

Moore, J. (2010). Philosophy of science, with special consideration given to behaviorism as the philosophy of the science of behavior. *The Psychological Record, 60,* 137–150.

Morey, L. C. (1991). Classification of mental disorder as a collection of hypothetical constructs. *Journal of Abnormal Psychology, 100,* 289–293.

Morisaki, S., & Gudykunst, W. B. (1994). Face in Japan and the United States. In S. Ting-Toomey (Ed.), *The challenge of facework: Cross-cultural and interpersonal issues* (pp. 47–94). Albany, NY: State University of New York Press.

Morris, J. (1993). *Independent lives: Community care and disabled people.* Basingstoke, UK: Macmillan.

Murphy, E. (2011). Children's burial grounds in Ireland (cillíní) and parental emotions toward infant death. *International Journal of Historical Archaeology, 15,* 409–428.

Murrell, S. A., & Norris, F. H. (1983). Quality of life as the criterion for need assessment and community psychology. *Journal of Community Psychology, 11,* 88–97.

Murtaugh, M. (1985). The practice of arithmetic by American grocery shoppers. *Anthropology and Education Quarterly, 16*(3), 186–192.

Myers, D. G. (2010). *Psychology* (9th ed.). New York, NY: Worth Publishers.

National Center for Education Statistics (2012). *The condition of education.* Washington, DC: Author.

National Education Association (2012, July 11). Letter to the Senate on UN Convention on the Rights of Persons with Disabilities. Retrieved from: http://www.nea.org/home/52549.htm (accessed December 17, 2012).

Neugebauer, R. (1996). Mental handicap in medieval and early modern England. In D. Wright & Digby (Eds), *From idiocy to mental deficiency* (pp. 22–43). London, UK: Routledge.

Nirje, B. (1969). The normalization principle and its human management implications. In R. B. Kugel & W. Wolfensberger (Eds), *Changing patterns in residential services for the mentally retarded* (pp. 179–195). Washington, DC: President's Committee on Mental Retardation.

Noack, T., & Fangeroa, H. (2007). Eugenics, euthanasia, and aftermath. *International Journal of Mental Health, 36,* 112–124.

Noddings, N. (1984). *Caring: A feminine approach to ethics and moral education.* Berkeley, CA: University of California Press.

Nord, E. (1999). *Cost-value analysis in health care.* Cambridge, UK: Cambridge University Press.

Norenzayan, A., Smith, E. E., Kim, B. J., & Nisbett, R. E. (2002). Cultural preferences for formal versus intuitive reasoning. *Cognitive Science: A Multidisciplinary Journal, 26,* 653–684.

Nussbaum, M. C. (2006). *Frontiers of justice: Disability, nationality, species membership.* Cambridge, MA: Harvard University Press, Belknap Press.

Nussbaum, M. C. (2011). *Creating capabilities: The human development approach.* Cambridge, MA: Harvard University Press.

Ochs, E., & Capps, L. (1996). Narrating the self, *Annual Review of Anthropology, 25,* 19–43.

O'Donovan, M. (2010). Cognitive diversity in the global academy: Why the voices of persons with cognitive disabilities are vital to intellectual diversity. *Journal of Academic Ethics, 8*(3), 171–185.

Otrębski, W. (2000). Quality of life of people with mental retardation living in two environments in Poland. In K. D. Keith & R. L. Schalock (Eds), *Cross-cultural perspectives on quality of life* (pp. 83–92). Washington DC: American Association on Mental Retardation.

Ouellette-Kuntz, H. & McCreary, B. (1996). Quality of life assessment for persons with severe developmental disabilities. In R. Renwick, I. Brown, & M. Nagler (Eds), *Quality of life in health promotion and rehabilitation: Conceptual approaches, issues, and applications* (pp. 268–278). Thousand Oaks, CA: Sage.

Page, S. (1977). Effects of the mental illness label in attempts to obtain accommodation. *Canadian Journal of Behavioral Science, 9,* 84–90.

Palmer, D. J. (1979). Regular-classroom teachers' attributions and instructional prescriptions for handicapped and nonhandicapped pupils. *The Journal of Special Education, 13*, 325–337.

Pan American Health Organization (2004, October 6). *The Montreal Declaration on Intellectual Disabilities.* Montreal, Canada: Author.

Pappas, G. (2008). Dewey's ethics. In J. Lachs & R. Talisse (Eds) *American philosophy: An encyclopedia* (pp. 181–183). New York, NY: Routledge.

Parens, E. & Asch, A. (1999). *A special supplement: The disability rights critique of prenatal genetic testing reflections and recommendations.* In *The Hastings Center Report, 29*(5), S1–S22.

Parmenter, T. R. (1992). Quality of life of people with developmental disabilities. *International Review of Research in Mental Retardation, 18*, 247–287.

Parmenter, T. R. (2007). Should science strive to correct human imperfections? A moral, ethical, or scientific question. *Journal on Developmental Disabilities, 13*, 93–96.

Parmenter, T. R. (2011). What is intellectual disability? How is it assessed and classified? *International Journal of Disability, Development and Education, 58*, 303–319.

Patoine, B. (2009). Brain-machine interfaces: Sci-fi concepts make clinical inroads. In B. Mauk (Ed.), *2009 Progress report on brain reseach* (pp. 43–52). New York, NY: The Dana Alliance for Brain Initiatives.

Peirce, C. S. (1958). The fixation of belief. In J. Weiner (Ed.), *Charles S. Peirce: Selected* Writings. New York, NY: Dover (original work published 1877).

Pengra, L. M. (2000). Lakota quality of life: Mitakuye oyasin. In K. D. Keith & R. L. Schalock (Eds), *Cross-cultural perspectives on quality of life* (pp. 191–204). Washington, DC: American Association on Mental Retardation.

Pepper, F. C. (1976). Teaching the American Indian child in mainstream settings. In R. L. Jones (Ed.), *Mainstreaming and the minority child* (pp. 135–136). Reston, VA: Council for Exceptional Children.

Perry, J., & Felce, D. (2002). Subjective and objective quality of life assessment: Responsiveness, response bias, and resident: proxy concordance. *Mental Retardation, 40*, 445–456.

Perry, J., Felce, D., Allen, D., & Meek, A. (2011). Resettlement outcomes for people with severe challenging behaviour moving from institutional to community living. *Journal of Applied Research in Intellectual Disabilities, 24*, 1–17.

Perry, J., Shervington, T., Mungur, N., Marston, G., Martin, D., & Brown, G. (2007). Why are people with intellectual disability moved "out of area"? *Journal of Policy and Practice in Intellectual Disabilities, 4*, 203–209.

Perske, R. (1972). Dignity of risk and the mentally retarded. *Mental Retardation, 10*, 24–27.

Perske, R. (2002). Foreword. In R. L. Schalock (Ed.), *Out of the darkness and into the light: Nebraska's experience with mental retardation* (pp. xi–xv). Washington, DC: American Association on Mental Retardation.

Perske, R., & Perske, M. (1980). *New life in the neighborhood: How persons with retardation or other disabilities can help make a good community better.* Nashville, TN: Abingdon.

Philo, C. (2012). Troubled proximities: Asylums and cemeteries in nineteenth-century England. *History of Psychiatry, 23*, 91–103.

Phinney, J. S. (1996). When we talk about American ethnic groups, what do we mean? *American Psychologist, 51*, 1167–1180.

Pilkington, E., & McVeigh, K. (2012, March 15). Ashley treatment on the rise amid concerns from disability groups. *The Guardian.* Retrieved from: http://www.guardian.co.uk/society/2012/mar/15/ashley-treatment-rise-amid-concerns (accessed December 17, 2012).

Plato (1950). *Republic.* A. D. Lindsay (Trans.). London, UK: Everyman's Library (original work c. 380 BCE).

Plato (1981). *Apology.* In G. M. A. Grube (Trans.), *Five Dialogues* (pp. 23–44). Indianapolis, IN: Hackett (original work c. 399 BCE).

Plato (1995). *Phaedrus.* A. Nehamas & P. Woodruff (Trans.). Indianapolis, IN: Hackett (original work c. 360 BCE).

Plucker, J. A. (Ed.). (2003). Human intelligence: Historical influences, current controversies, teaching resources. Retrieved from: http://www.indiana.edu/~intell (accessed December 17, 2012).

Powell, F. M. (1887). The care and training of feeble-minded children. *Proceedings of the National Conference of Charities and Correction*, 250–260.

Rabin, R. (2007, January 9). Screen all pregnancies for Down syndrome, doctors say. *New York Times.* Retrieved from: http://www.nytimes.com/2007/01/09/health/09preg.html (accessed December 2012).

Race, D. (2002). The historical context. In D. G. Race (Ed.), *Learning disability—A social approach* (pp. 23–52). London, UK: Routledge.

Rahula, W. (1974). *What the Buddha taught.* New York, NY: Grove Weidenfeld (original work published 1959).

Randall, J. (1976). *The making of the modern mind.* New York, NY: Columbia University Press (original work published 1926).

Raphael, D. (1996). Defining quality of life: Eleven debates concerning its measurement. In R. Renwick, I. Brown, & M. Nagler (Eds), *Quality of life in health promotion and rehabilitation: Conceptual approaches, issues and applications* (pp. 146–165). Thousand Oaks, CA: Sage.

Raphael, D., Rukholm, E., Brown, I., Hill-Bailey, P., & Donato, E. (1996). The quality of life profile—adolescent version: Background, description, and initial validation. *Journal of Adolescent Health, 19*, 366–375.

Rapley, M. (2000). The social construction of "quality of life": The interpersonal production of well-being revisited. In K. D. Keith & R. L. Schalock (Eds), *Cross-cultural perspectives on quality of life* (pp. 155–172). Washington, DC: American Association on Mental Retardation.

Rapley, M. (2003). *Quality of life research: A critical introduction.* London, UK: Sage.

Rapley, M. (2004). *The social construction of intellectual disability.* New York, NY: Cambridge University Press.

Rapley, M., & Hopgood, L. (1997). Quality of life in a community-based service in rural Australia. *Journal of Intellectual & Developmental Disability, 22,* 125–141.

Rapley, M., Kiernan, P., & Antaki, C. (1998). Invisible to themselves or negotiating identity? The interactional management of "being intellectually disabled." *Disability and Society, 13,* 807–827.

Rapley, M., & Lobley, J. (1995). Factor analysis of the Schalock and Keith (1993) Quality of Life Questionnaire: A replication. *Mental Handicap Research, 8,* 194–202.

Rapley, M., Ridgway, J., & Beyer, S. (1998). Staff:staff and staff:client reliability of the Schalock & Keith (1993) Quality of Life Questionnaire. *Journal of Intellectual Disability Research, 42,* 37–42.

Rawlings, S. (1985). Behaviour and skills of severely retarded adults in hospitals and small residential homes. *British Journal of Psychiatry, 146,* 358–366.

Rawls, J. (1999). *A theory of justice.* Cambridge, MA: Belknap Press of Harvard University Press (original work published 1971).

Raynes, N. V., Sumpton, R. C., & Pettipher, C. (1989). *The index of community involvement.* Manchester, UK: The University Department of Social Policy and Social Work.

Reed, A. C. (1913). Going through Ellis Island. *The Popular Science Monthly, 82,* 5–18.

Reeves, H. T. (1938). The later years of a mental defective. *Journal of Psycho-Asthenics, 43,* 194–200.

Renwick, R., & Brown, I. (1996). The Centre for Health Promotion's conceptual approach to quality of life: Being, belonging, and becoming. In R. Renwick, I. Brown, & M. Nagler (Eds), *Quality of life in health promotion and rehabilitation: Conceptual approaches, issues, and applications* (pp. 75–86). Thousand Oaks, CA: Sage.

Renwick, R., Brown, I., & Raphael, D. (2000). Person-centred quality of life: Contributions from Canada to an international understanding. In K. D. Keith & R. L. Schalock (Eds), *Cross-cultural perspectives on quality of life* (pp. 5–21). Washington, DC: American Association on Mental Retardation.

Rimmerman, A., & Crossman, R. (2004). The quality of life of single adults with severe disabilities participating in extended employment programs in Northern Israel. *Journal of Rehabilitation, 70*(2), 47–52.

Robertson, W. S., Cattell, J. W., Russell, A. J., & Archibald, O. W. (1877). *First biennial report of the Board of Trustees of the Asylum for Feeble Minded Children of the State of Iowa at Glenwood.* Des Moines, IA: R. P. Clarkson.

Rosch, E. (1978). Principles of categorization. In E. Rosch & B. B. Lloyd (Eds), *Cognition and categorization* (pp. 27–48). Hillsdale, NJ: Lawrence Erlbaum.

Rose, N. (1999). *Governing the soul: The shaping of the private self* (2nd ed.). London, UK: Free Association Books.

Rosenhan, D. L. (1973). On being sane in insane places. *Science, 179,* 250–258.

Ross, L. D. (1977). The intuitive psychologist and his shortcomings. In L. Berkowitz (Ed.), *Advances in experimental social psychology* (Vol. 10, pp. 174–220). New York, NY: Academic Press.

Rugg, A. V. (1983). *Children of misfortune: One hundred years of public care for people with mental retardation in Wisconsin, 1871–1971.* Madison, WI: The Wisconsin Council on Developmental Disabilities.

Rushton, P. (1988). Lunatics and idiots: Mental disability, the community, and the poor law in North-East England, 1600–1800. *Medical History, 32,* 34–50.

Ruzgis, P., & Grigoenko, E. L. (1994). Cultural meaning systems, intelligence, and personality. In R. J. Sternberg & P. Ruzgis (Eds), *Personality and intelligence* (pp. 248–270). New York, NY: Cambridge University Press.

Sacks, H. (1984). On doing "being ordinary." In J. M. Atkinson & J. Heritage (Eds), *Structures of social action: Studies in conversation analysis* (pp. 413–429). Cambridge, UK: Cambridge University Press.

Sacks, O. (2007). Musicophilia: Tales of music and the brain. New York, NY: Alfred A. Knopf.

Sanders, K. (2009). The effects of an action plan, staff training, management support and monitoring on restraint use and costs of work-related injuries. *Journal of Applied Research in Intellectual Disabilities, 22,* 216–220.

Sands, D. J., & Kozleski, E. B. (1994). Quality of life differences between adults with and without disabilities. *Education and Training in Mental Retardation and Developmental Disabilities, 29,* 90–101.

Saxton, M. (2010). Disability rights and selective abortion. In L. Davis (Ed.), *The disability studies reader* (pp. 120–132). London, UK: Routledge.

Schalock, R. L. (1990). Preface. In R. L. Schalock (Ed.), *Quality of life: Perspectives and issues* (pp. ix–xii). Washington, DC: American Association on Mental Retardation.

Schalock, R. L. (1994). The concept of quality of lie and its current applications in the field of mental retardation/developmental disabilities. In D. Goode (Ed.), *Quality of life for persons with disabilities: International perspectives and issues* (pp. 266–284). Cambridge, MA: Brookline.

Schalock, R. L. (1996). Reconsidering the conceptualization and measurement of quality of life. In R. L. Schalock (Ed.), *Quality of life: Volume I. Conceptualization and measurement* (pp. 123–139). Washington, DC: American Association on Mental Retardation.

Schalock, R. L. (2010). The measurement and use of quality of life-related personal outcomes. In R. Kober (Ed.), *Enhancing the quality of life of people with intellectual disabilities: From theory to practice* (pp. 3–16). Dordrecht, Netherlands: Springer.

Schalock, R. L. (2011). International perspectives on intellectual disability. In K. D. Keith (Ed.), *Cross-cultural psychology: Contemporary themes and perspectives* (pp. 312–328). Malden, MA: Wiley-Blackwell.

Schalock, R. L., & Keith, K. D. (1993). *Quality of life questionnaire.* Worthington, OH: IDS.

Schalock, R. L., & Verdugo, M. A. (2002). *Handbook on quality of life for human service practitioners.* Washington, DC: American Association on Mental Retardation.

Schalock, R. L., Borthwick-Duffy, S. A., Bradley, V. J., Buntinx, W. H. E., Coulter, D. L., Craig, E. M. et al. (2010). *Intellectual disability: Definition, classification, and systems of support* (11th ed.). Washington, DC: American Association on Intellectual and Developmental Disabilities.

Schalock, R. L. Brown, I., Brown, R., Cummins, R. A. Felce, D., Matikka, L., Keith, K. D., & Parmenter, T. (2002). Conceptualization, measurement, and application of quality of life for persons with intellectual disabilities: Report of an international panel of experts. *Mental Retardation, 40,* 457–470.

Schalock, R. L., Keith, K. D., & Hoffman, K. (1990). *1990 Quality of Life Questionnaire: Standardization Manual.* Hastings, NE: Mid-Nebraska Mental Retardation Services.

Schalock, R. L, Keith, K. D., Hoffman, K., & Karan, O. C. (1989). Quality of life: Its measurement and use. *Mental Retardation, 27,* 25–31.

Schalock, R. L., Luckasson, R. A., Shogren, K. A., Borthwick-Duffy, S., Bradley, V., Buntinx, W. H. E. et al. (2007). The renaming of *mental retardation*: Understanding the change to the term *intellectual disability. Intellectual and Developmental Disabilities, 45,* 116–124.

Schlereth, T. J. (1991). *Victorian America: Transformations in everyday life.* New York, NY: HarperCollins.

Schneider, M. (2009). The difference a word makes: Responding to questions on "disability" and "difficulty" in South Africa. *Disability and Rehabilitation, 31*(1), 42–50.

Schönfeld, M. (1992). Who or what has moral standing? *American Philosophical Quarterly, 29,* 353–362.

Schulelt, A. (2008). State hospitals of Massachusetts: Belchertown State School. Retrieved from: http://www.1856.org/belchertown/belchertown.html (accessed December 17, 2012).

Schumacher, E. F. (1973). *Small is beautiful: Economics as if people mattered.* New York, NY: Harper & Row.

Schumm, D. Y. (2010). Reimaging disability. *Journal of Feminist Studies in Religion, 26*(2), 132–137.

Séguin, E. (1866). *Idiocy: And its treatment by the physiological method.* New York, NY: William Wood.

Seligman, M. (2011). *Flourish: A visionary new understanding of happiness and well being.* New York, NY: Free Press.

Sen, A. (1975). Mental retardation in India: A short description. *Mental Retardation, 13*(4), 11–13.

Sen, A. (1985). *Commodities and capabilities.* Amsterdam, Netherlands: North-Holland Press.

Senoo, T. (1985). Introduction to welfare services for mentally retarded persons. In *Services for people with mental retardation—1985 revision* (pp. 1–16). Tokyo, Japan: Japan League for the Mentally Retarded.

Serpell, R. (1974). Aspects of intelligence in a developing country. *African Social Research, 17*, 578–596.

Shakepeare, T. (2010). The social model of disability. In L. J. Davis (Ed.), *The disabilities studies reader* (3rd ed.) (pp. 266–273). New York, NY: Routledge.

Shakespeare, T. & Watson, N. (2001). The social model of disability: An outdated ideology? In S. Barnartt & B. Altman (Eds), *Exploring theories and expanding methodologies: Where are we and where do we need to go?* (pp. 9–28). New York, NY: JAI.

Shaver, K. G. (1970). Defensive attribution: Effects of severity and relevance on the responsibility assigned for an accident. *Journal of Personality and Social Psychology, 14*, 101–113.

Sheldon, T. (2000). Dutch GP cleared after helping to end man's "hopeless existence." *British Medical Journal, 321*, 117.

Shogren, K. A., Bradley, V. J., Gomez, S. C., Yeager, M. H., & Schalock, R. L. (2009). Public policy and the enhancement of desired outcomes for persons with intellectual disability. *Intellectual and Developmental Disabilities, 47*, 307–319.

Shogren, K. A., & Turnbull, H. R. (2010). Public policy and outcomes for persons with intellectual disability: Extending and expanding the public policy framework of AAIDD's 11th edition of *Intellectual Disability: Definition, Classification, and Systems of Support. Intellectual and Developmental Disabilities, 48*, 375–386.

Sider, J. (2012). On becoming human: Jean Vanier, Carl Rogers, and James Allison on disability, acceptance, and a noncompetitive theological anthropology. *Journal of Religion, Disability, and Health, 16*, 16–32.

Siebers, T. (2010). Disability and the theory of complex embodiment – for identity politics in a new register. In L. J. Davis (Ed.), *The disability studies reader* (3rd ed.) (pp. 316–335). New York, NY: Routledge.

Sienkiewicz-Mercer, R., & Kaplan, S. B. (1989). *I raise my eyes to say yes.* Boston, MA: Houghton-Mifflin.

Silvers, A., Waserman, D. T., & Mahowald, M. B. (1998). *Disability, difference, discrimination: Perspectives on justice in bioethics and public policy.* New York, NY: Lanham, Rowman & Littlefield.

Simpson, M. K. (1999). The moral government of idiots: Moral treatment in the work of Seguin. *History of Psychiatry, 10,* 227–243.

Singer, P. (1975). *Animal liberation: A new ethics for our treatment of animals.* New York, NY: Random House.

Singer, P. (1993). *Practical Ethics* (2nd ed.). Cambridge, UK: Cambridge University Press.

Singer, P. (1994). *Rethinking life and death: The collapse of our traditional ethics.* New York, NY: St. Martin's Griffin.

Singer, P. (2007, January 26). A convenient truth about disability. *New York Times.* Retrieved from: http://www.nytimes.com/2007/01/26/opinion/26singer.html (accessed December 17, 2012).

Singer, P. (2009). *Animal liberation: The definitive classic of the animal movement.* New York, NY: Harper Perennial Modern Classics (original work published 1975).

Singer, P. (2010). Speciesism and moral status. In E. F. Kittay & L. Carlson (Eds), *Cognitive disability and its challenge to moral philosophy* (pp. 331–344). Chichester, UK: Wiley-Blackwell.

Skeels, H. M. (1966). Adult status of children with contrasting early life experiences. *Monographs of the Society for Research in Child Development, 31,* 1–65.

Skeels, H. M., & Dye, H. B. (1939). A study of the effects of differential stimulation of mentally retarded children. *Proceedings of the American Association on Mental Deficiency, 44,* 114–136.

Skoe, E. E. A. (2010). The relationship between empathy-related constructs and care-based moral development in young adulthood. *Journal of Moral Education, 39,* 191–211.

Smith, J. D. (1989). *The sterilization of Carrie Buck.* New York, NY: New Horizons.

Smith, J. D. (1995). *Pieces of purgatory: Mental retardation in and out of institutions.* Pacific Grove, CA: Brooks/Cole.

Smith, J. D., & Lazaroff, K. (2006). "Uncle Sam Needs You" or does he? Intellectual disabilities and lessons from the "Great Wars." *Mental Retardation, 44,* 433–437.

Smith, J. D., & Smallwood, G. (2007). From whence came mental retardation? Asking why while saying goodbye. *Intellectual and Developmental Disabilities, 45,* 132–135.

Smith, S. E. (2012, March 16). Is the Ashley treatment right? Ask yourself if disabled people are human. *The Guardian.* Retrieved from: http://www.guardian.co.uk/commentisfree/2012/mar/16/ashley-treatment-disabled-people (accessed December 17, 2012).

Snyder, M. (1994). The development of social intelligence in psychotherapy: Empathic and dialogic processes. *Journal of Humanistic Psychology, 34,* 84–108.

Sofair, A., & Kaldjian, L. (2000). Eugenic sterilization and qualified Nazi analogy: The United States and Germany, 1930–1945. *Annals of Internal Medicine, 132*, 312–319.

Sonnander, K., & Claesson, M. (1997). Classification, prevalence, prevention and rehabilitation of intellectual disability: An overview of research in the People's Republic of China. *Journal of Intellectual Disability Research, 41*, 180–192.

Special Olympics (2005). Changing attitudes, changing the world: Media's portrayal of people with intellectual disabilities. Retrieved from: http://www.specialolympics.org/uploadedFiles/LandingPage/WhatWeDo/Research_Studies_Desciption_Pages/Policy_paper_media_portrayal.pdf (accessed December 17, 2012).

Stainton, T. (2001a). Medieval charitable institutions and intellectual impairment c. 1066–1600. *Journal of Developmental Disabilities, 8*, 34–44.

Stainton, T. (2001b) Reason and value: The thought of Plato and Aristotle and the construction of intellectual disability. *Mental Retardation, 39*, 452–460.

Stancliffe, R. J. (1999). Proxy respondents and the reliability of the Quality of Life Questionnaire Empowerment factor. *Journal of Intellectual Disability Research, 43*, 185–193.

Stern, W. (1914). *The psychological methods of testing intelligence.* Baltimore, MD: Warwick & York.

Sternberg, R. J. (1986). *Intelligence applied: Understanding and increasing your intellectual skills.* San Diego, CA: Harcourt Brace Jovanovich.

Sternberg, R. J. (1996). *Successful intelligence: How practical and creative intelligence determine success in life.* New York, NY: Simon & Schuster.

Sternberg, R. J., & Kaufman, J. C. (1998). Human abilities. *Annual Review of Psychology*, 49, 479–502.

Stevens-Roseman, E. S. (2007). Aging workers: Achieving 'goodness-of-fit' for worker-workplace advantage. *Journal of Workplace Behavioral Health, 22*(4), 81–96.

Stowe, M. J., Turnbull, H. R., III, Schrandt, S., & Rack, J. (2007). Looking to the future: Intellectual and developmental disabilities in the genetics era. *Journal on Developmental Disabilities, 13*, 1–64.

Street, W. R. (1994). *A chronology of noteworthy events in American psychology.* Washington, DC: American Psychological Association.

Strnadova, I., & Evans, D. (2012). Subjective quality of life of women with intellectual disabilities: The role of perceived control over their own life in self-determined behaviour. *Journal of Applied Research in Intellectual Disabilities, 25*, 71–79.

Strous, R. (2006) Nazi euthanasia of the mentally ill at Hadamar. *The American Journal of Psychiatry, 163*, 27.

Stubblefield, A. (2010). The entanglement of race and cognitive dis/ability. In E. F. Kittay & L. Carlson (Eds), *Cognitive disability and its challenge to moral philosophy* (pp. 293–313). Chichester, UK: Wiley-Blackwell.

Sumner, W. G. (1906). *Folkways: A study of the sociological importance of usages, manners, customs, mores, and morals.* Boston, MA: Ginn and Co.

Super, C. M., & Harkness, S. (1982). The infants' niche in rural Kenya and metropolitan America. In L. L. Adler (Ed.), *Cross-cultural research at issue* (pp. 47–55). New York, NY: Academic Press.

Switzky, H. N., & Greenspan, S. (2006). Summary and conclusion: Can so many diverse ideas be integrated? Multiparadigmatic models of understanding MR in the 21st century. In H. N. Switzky & S. Greenspan (Eds), *What is mental retardation? Ideas for an evolving disability* (pp. 337–354). Washington, DC: American Association on Mental Retardation.

Taylor, S. J. (1994). In support of research on quality of life, but against QOL. In D. Goode (Ed.), *Quality of life for persons with disabilities: International perspectives and issues* (pp. 260–265). Cambridge, MA: Brookline.

Taylor, S. J., & Bogdan, R. (1984). *Introduction to qualitative research methods* (2nd ed.). New York, NY: Wiley.

Taylor, S. J., & Bogdan, R. (1996). Quality of life and the individual's perspective. In R. L. Schalock (Ed.), *Quality of life: Volume I. Conceptualization and measurement* (pp. 11–22). Washington DC: American Association on Mental Retardation.

tenBroek, J. (1966). The right to live in the world: The disabled in the law of torts. *California Law Review, 54*(2), 841–919.

Terman, L. M. (1913a). Psychological principles underlying the Binet-Simon scale and some practical considerations for its correct use. *Journal of Psycho-Asthenics, 18*(2), 93–104.

Terman, L. M. (1913b). Suggestions for revising, extending and supplementing the Binet intelligence tests. *Journal of Psycho-Asthenics, 18*(1), 20–33.

Terman, L. M. (1916). *The measurement of intelligence.* Boston, MA: Houghton Mifflin.

Throne, J. M. (1972). The assessment of intelligence: Towards what end? *Mental Retardation, 10*(5), 9–11.

Townsend-White, C., Pham, A. N. T., & Vassos, M. V. (2011). A systematic review of quality of life measures for people with intellectual disabilities and challenging behaviours. *Journal of Intellectual Disability Research, 56*, 270–284.

Tredgold, A. F. (1914). *Mental deficiency (amentia)* (2nd ed.). London, UK: Baillière, Tindall and Cox.

Trent, J. W. (1994). *Inventing the feeble mind: A history of mental retardation in the United States.* Berkeley, CA: University of California Press.

Tronto, J. C. (1989). Women and caring: what can feminists learn about morality from caring? In A. Jaggar & S. Bordo (Eds), *Gender/body/knowledge reconstructions of being and knowing* (pp. 172–187). New Brunswick, NJ: Rutgers University Press.

Tuan, Y.-F. (1984). *Dominance and affection: The making of pets.* New Haven, CT: Yale University Press.

Turkle, S. (2011). *Alone together: Why we expect more from technology and less from each other.* New York, NY: Basic Books.

Tynan, H., & Allen, D. (2002). The impact of service user cognitive level on carer attributions for aggressive behaviour. *Journal of Applied Research in Intellectual Disabilities, 15*, 213–223.

United Nations (2006, August). *International Convention on the Rights of Persons with Disabilities: Some facts about persons with disabilities.* New York, NY: Author.

United Nations General Assembly (1948). *The universal declaration of human rights.* New York, NY: Author.

United Nations General Assembly (1971). *Declaration on the rights of mentally retarded persons.* New York, NY: Author.

United Nations General Assembly (1975). *Declaration on the rights of disabled persons.* New York, NY: Author.

United Nations General Assembly (2006). *Convention on the rights of persons with disabilities and optional protocol.* New York, NY: Author.

United States Department of Labor (2012). Equal employment opportunity. Retrieved from: http://www.dol.gov/dol/topic/discrimination/disabilitydisc.htm (accessed December 17, 2012).

US Department of Justice (2012). ADA home page: Information and technical assistance on the Americans with Disabilities Act. Retrieved from: http://www.ada.gov/ (accessed December 17, 2012).

US Equal Employment Opportunity Commission (2011). Questions & answers about persons with intellectual disabilities in the workplace and the Americans with Disabilities Act. Washington, DC: Author. Retrieved from: http://www.eeoc.gov/facts/intellectual_disabilities.html (accessed December 17, 2012).

Vail, D. J. (1967). *Dehumanization and the institutional career.* Springfield, IL: Charles C. Thomas.

Van Wagenen, B. (1914). Surgical sterilization as a eugenic measure. *Journal of Psycho-Asthenics, 18*(4), 185–196.

Védie, C., & Breathnach, C. S. (2005). The cemetery associated with Leyme Mental Hospital. *History of Psychiatry, 16*, 111–115.

Veenhoven, R. (1996). Happy Life-expectancy: A comprehensive measure of quality-of-life in nations. *Social Indicators Research, 39*, 1–58.

Verdonschot, M. M., deWitte, L. P., Reichrath, E., Buntinx, W. H., & Curfs, L. M. (2009). Community participation of people with an intellectual disability: A review of empirical findings. *Journal of Intellectual Disability Research, 53*, 303–318.

Wallace, R. (1958, March 24). Mental homes wrongly hold thousands like Mayo Buckner. *Life, 44*(12), 120–136.

Walsh, P. N. (2000). Quality of life and social inclusion. In K. D. Keith & R. L. Schalock (Eds), *Cross-cultural perspectives on quality of life* (pp. 315–326). Washington, DC: American Association on Mental Retardation.

Wanless, L. K., & Jahoda, A. (2002). Responses of staff towards people with mild to moderate intellectual disability who behave aggressively: A cognitive emotional analysis. *Journal of Intellectual Disability Research, 46*, 507–516.

Ward, N. (2000). The universal power of speaking for oneself. In K. D. Keith & R. L. Schalock (Eds), *Cross-cultural perspectives on quality of life* (pp. 33–36). Washington, DC: American Association on Mental Retardation.

Ward, N. A., & Keith, K. D. (1996). Self-advocacy: Foundation for quality of life. In R. L. Schalock (Ed.), *Quality of life: Volume I. Conceptualization and measurement* (pp. 5–10). Washington, DC: American Association on Mental Retardation.

Warren, J. M. (1851, April). An account of two remarkable Indian dwarfs exhibited in Boston under the name of Aztec children. *American Journal of the Medical Sciences*, No. *42*, 285–293.

Warren, K. (2000). *Ecofeminist philosophy: A western perspective on what it is and why it matters.* Lanham, MD: Rowman & Littlefield.

Waters. E. (2010). *Crazy like us: The globalization of the American psyche.* New York, NY: Free Press.

Watson, S. M. R., & Keith, K. D. (2002). Comparing the quality of life of school-age children with and without disabilities. *Mental Retardation, 40*, 304–312.

Webb, O. M. (2002). Call me by my name. In R. L. Schalock (Ed.), *Out of the darkness and into the light: Nebraska's experience with mental retardation* (pp. 55–61). Washington, DC: American Association on Mental Retardation.

Wechsler, D. (1939). *The measurement of adult intelligence.* Baltimore, MD: Williams & Wilkins.

Wechsler, D. (1955). *The range of human capacities* (2nd ed.). Baltimore, MD: Williams & Wilkins.

Wehmeyer, M. L. (2003). Eugenics and sterilization in the heartland. *Mental Retardation, 41*, 57–60.

Wehmeyer, M., & Schwartz, M. (1998). The relationship between self-determination and quality of life for adults with mental retardation. *Education and Training in Mental Retardation and Developmental Disabilities, 33*, 3–12.

Wehmeyer, M. L., Buntinx, H. E., Lachapelle, Y., Luckasson, R. A., Schalock, R. L., Verdugo, M. A. et al. (2008). The intellectual disability construct and its relation to human functioning. *Intellectual and Developmental Disabilities, 46*, 311–318.

Weisz, J. R. (1981). Effects of the "mentally retarded" label on adult judgments about child failure. *Journal of Abnormal Psychology, 90*, 371–374.

Wendell, S. (2008). Toward a feminist theory of disability. In A. Bailey & C. Cuomo (Eds), *The feminist philosophy reader* (pp. 826–841). Boston, MA: McGraw-Hill.

Wheeler, D. L., Jacobson, J. W., Paglieri, R. A., & Schwartz, A. A. (1993). An experimental assessment of facilitated communication. *Mental Retardation, 31*, 49–60.

White, W. D., & Wolfensberger, W. (1969). The evolution of dehumanization in our institutions. *Mental Retardation, 7*(3), 5–9.

Whitney, E. A. (1949). The historical approach to the subject of mental retardation. *American Journal of Mental Deficiency, 53*, 419–424.

Wickham, P. (2001). Images of idiocy in Puritan New England. *Mental Retardation, 39*, 147–151.

Wigdor, A. K., & Garner, W. R. (Eds). (1982). *Ability testing: Uses, consequences, and controversies.* Washington, DC: National Academy Press.

Wilfond, B., Miller, P., Korfiatis, C., Diekema, D. Dudzinski, D., Goreing, S., and the Seattle Growth Attenuation and Ethics Working Group (2010, November–December). Navigating growth attenuation in children with profound disabilities: children's interests, family decision-making, and community concerns. *The Hastings Center Report.* Retrieved from: www.thehastingscenter.org (accessed December 17, 2012).

Wilkinson, D. (2006). Is it in the best interests of an intellectually disabled infant to die? *Journal of Medical Ethics, 32*, 454–459.

Williams, P., & Shoultz, B. (1982). *We can speak for ourselves: Self-advocacy by mentally handicapped people.* London, UK: Souvenir Press.

Wolfensberger, W. (1969). The origin and nature of our institutional models. In R. B. Kugel & W. Wolfensberger (Eds), *Changing patterns in residential services for the mentally retarded* (pp. 59–171). Washington, DC: President's Committee on Mental Retardation.

Wolfensberger, W. (1975). *The origin and nature of our institutional models.* Syracuse, NY: Human Policy Press.

Wolfensberger, W. (1983). Social role valorization: A proposed new term for the principle of normalization. *Mental Retardation, 21*, 234–239.

Wolfensberger, W. (2000). A brief overview of social role valorization. *Mental Retardation, 38*, 105–123.

Wolfensberger, W. (2002). Needed or at least wanted: Sanity in the language wars. *Mental Retardation, 40*, 75–80.

Wong. S. (2002). At home with Down Syndrome and gender. *Hypatia, 17*(3), 89–117.

Wood, E. J. (1868). *Giants and dwarfs.* London, UK: Richard Bentley.

World Bank (2012). *World development report 2012: Gender equality and development.* Washington, DC: Author.

World Health Organization (2001). *International classification of functioning, disability, and health: ICF.* Geneva, Switzerland: Author.

World Health Organization (2004). *The role of international human rights in national mental health legislation.* Geneva, Switzerland: Author.

World Health Organization (2007). *Atlas: Global resources for persons with intellectual disabilities 2007.* Geneva, Switzerland: Author.

Yoakum, C. S., & Yerkes, R. M. (1920). *Army mental tests.* New York, NY: Holt.

Young, D. A., & Quibell, R. (2000). Why rights are never enough: Rights, intellectual disability and understanding. *Disability and Society, 15,* 747–764.

Yount, L. (2000). *Physician-assisted suicide and euthanasia.* New York, NY: Facts on File.

Zekovic, B., & Renwick, R (2003). Quality of life for children and adolescents with developmental disabilities: Review of conceptual and methodological issues relevant to public policy. *Disability and Society, 18,* 19–34.

Zoech, I. (2003, October 12). Named: The baby boy who was Nazis' first euthanasia victim. *The Telegraph* (London, UK). Retrieved from: http://www.telegraph.co.uk/news/worldnews/europe/germany/1443967/Named-the-baby-boy-who-was-Nazis-first-euthanasia-victim.html (accessed December 17, 2012).

Zuckerman, M. (1990). Some dubious premises in research and theory on racial differences: Scientific, social, and ethical issues. *American Psychologist, 45,* 1297–1303.

Name Index

Intellectual Disability: Ethics, Dehumanization, and a New Moral Community, First Edition.
Heather E. Keith and Kenneth D. Keith.

Subject Index

Intellectual Disability: Ethics, Dehumanization, and a New Moral Community, First Edition.
Heather E. Keith and Kenneth D. Keith.